Studies on Entrepreneurship, Structural Change and Industrial Dynamics

The ‘Studies on Entrepreneurship, Structural Change and Industrial Dynamics’ series showcases exceptional scholarly work being developed on the still unexplored complex relationship between entrepreneurship, structural change and industrial dynamics, by addressing structural and technological determinants of the evolutionary pathway of innovative and entrepreneurial activity.

The series invites proposals based on sound research methodologies and approaches to the above topics. Volumes in the series may include research monographs and edited/contributed works.

This is a SCOPUS-indexed series.

More information about this series at https://link.springer.com/bookseries/15330

Andrei Rudskoi • Askar Akaev •
Tessaleno Devezas
Editors

Digital Transformation and the World Economy

Critical Factors and Sector-Focused Mathematical Models

Springer

Editors
Andrei Rudskoi
Peter the Great St. Petersburg Polytechnic University
St. Petersburg, Russia

Askar Akaev
Lomonosov Moscow State University
Moscow, Russia

Tessaleno Devezas
Atlântica - Instituto Universitário
Lisbon, Portugal

ISSN 2511-2023 ISSN 2511-2031 (electronic)
Studies on Entrepreneurship, Structural Change and Industrial Dynamics
ISBN 978-3-030-89831-1 ISBN 978-3-030-89832-8 (eBook)
https://doi.org/10.1007/978-3-030-89832-8

This Springer imprint is published by the registered company Springer Nature Switzerland AG.
The registered company address is: Gewerbestrasse 11, 6330 Cham, Switzerland

Preface

Since the last quarter of the twentieth century, human society has witnessed the burgeoning of a completely new technosphere, which was fully entrenched at the onset of the new century/millennium, and is defining our way of life on Earth. The leading sector of this radical new technosphere is an interwoven set of new digital technologies mostly known by the acronym IT (information technologies), which encompasses a bundle of revolutionary innovations appeared in the last 30 years.

The huge impact of digital technologies is profoundly transforming all human activities, with an unpredictable reach that in turn brings us insecurities and uncertainties regarding our future. This highly uncertain type of socioeconomic environment deserves to expand our knowledge on the inevitable changes caused by this digital transformation, which has been the subject of two previous volumes of the Springer series "*Studies on Entrepreneurship, Structural Change, and Industrial Change*," namely *Industry 4.0* (Devezas et al. 2017) and *The Economics of Digital Transformation* (Devezas et al. 2021). This volume titled "*Digital Transformation and the World Economy*" intends to continue the amplification of this necessary knowledge, in order to allow us to surf safely the current turbulent wave of transformation of our socioeconomic realm.

This book consists of 12 chapters that thoroughly examine the immense impact of digitization on the world economy, focusing mainly on mathematical modeling and predictive estimates of the technological progress and economic dynamics parameters of this new digital era. The following lines exhibit a short overview on the content of the whole collection of chapters:

Chapter 1: Akaev, Rudskoy, Devezas—*Rethinking Theory on the Role of Technological Innovation in Economic Development*

The authors argue that analysis of publications on the role of innovation in the technological development indicates that the basic statements of the theory of innovative development, dating back to the works of J. Schumpeter, have not undergone any significant changes. In this chapter, the well-known approaches are reconsidered, and new interpretations are proposed that can significantly expand the tools to study innovative processes in the economy and assess the evolution of technology and machinery.

Chapter 2: Akaev, Rudskoy, Khusainov, Zeman—*Information Model for Calculating the Rate of Technical Progress*

Classical models of economic growth have been modified due to new global economic trends that emerged under the influence of the large-scale digitization and robotization of today's capitalist economy. In this chapter, aiming to calculate prognostic dynamics of the technical progress, the authors provide an information model based on the use of different modes for producing technological information. The proposed model relies on the principle of forming and changing an amount of technological knowledge, Kurzweil's law of accelerating returns (LARR) for ICT, and also particular provisions of the Isenson–Hartman model for describing informational dynamics.

Chapter 3: Akaev, Devezas, Tick—*K-Waves and the Innovation-Technological Paradigm of Schumpeter–Mensch–Freeman–Hirooka*

Kondratiev long economic cycle has been dubbed one of the most debatable macroeconomic phenomena for over half a century. This paper considers an intrinsic link between Kondratiev long waves and the Schumpeterian growth paradigm. In this chapter, the authors recognize the significant contribution of some economists such as G. Mensch, Ch. Freeman, and M. Hirooka in evolution of the Kondratiev–Schumpeter's theory of innovative cyclical economic development. Furthermore, the authors thoroughly examine the diffusion of innovations (DOI) theory, together with the Hirooka's innovative paradigm, and reveal the important role of S. Dubovsky in designing a mathematical procedure used for assessment of technological capacity. Overall, the underlying idea of this chapter is that governments should draw on Kondratiev–Schumpeter's theory while strategizing their long-term economic and financial policies.

Chapter 4: Khusainov, Kaimoldina, Nussupov, Shirov—*Assessment of the Quality of Growth of National Economies in the Context of Digital Transformation*

The purpose of the authors in this chapter is to assess and analyze the impact of digitalization indicators on the quality of growth of developed and developing countries. As a novelty it presents an assessment of the impact of digitalization indicators on nontraditional measures of the pace and quality of economic growth for national economies. The methodology used is the econometric modeling of the impact of ICT sector indicators on the dynamics and determinants of the quality of growth of national economies based on panel data.

Chapter 5: Akaev, Ziadullaev, Sarygulov, Petryakov—*Digital Transformation and Growth Models*

In this chapter, the authors argue that the economic development of vanguard countries during last forty years contributed to a large disturbance of the two key empirical regularities that underlie neoclassical economic theory: the effect of the

"Bowley law" and one of the "stylized facts" of Kaldor. There is more and more empirical evidence that the famous Kuznets curve is no longer valid. Income inequality is growing in all developed countries, particularly in the USA, Great Britain, and Canada. Hence, it should be expected that a new stage of technological development, in the form of digital technologies, will contribute to the reinforcement of these trends. The authors propose a modified neoclassical model of income growth and distribution, which considers the new empirical regularities.

Chapter 6: Akaev, Rudskoy, Ungvari—*The Dualistic Nature of Technological Convergence and Human Resources*

The convergence of technologies significantly changes both the patterns of production and the very nature of socioeconomic systems. The need for constant knowledge updating and the continuity of the education process are becoming one of the key factors in achieving social harmony in society. However, uneven economic and technological development poses certain threats to both employment and production systems that create economic benefits in the form of goods or services. In this chapter, the authors analyze the dualistic nature of the advance of technology and formation of human capital, considering that constantly and rapidly updating technologies may contribute to the ousting of mainly middle-skilled employees from the labor market. A means of overcoming this situation is the extensive training of engineering personnel and qualified specialists capable of working in the environment of man--machine intelligent systems.

Chapter 7: Akaev, Petryakov, Jorg, Ungyari—*Education System and Labor Market in the Context of Digital Transformation*

Modern economic systems are characterized by great flexibility and ever-changing demands in relation to labor skill level. The need for constant knowledge renewal and continuity of the education process are becoming key factors in ensuring sustainability in the labor market. In this chapter, the authors analyze current trends in professional training found in different OECD countries and Russia and evaluate the adjustment level of higher education systems to new technological challenges. It is shown that despite dynamic changes in the education sector, it remains largely geared toward training professionals to staff the "Third Industrial Revolution." A structural shift from training medium-skilled professionals to training high-skilled professionals, including those in STEM (science, technologies, engineering, and mathematics) fields, will become a pivotal moment in education development.

Chapter 8: Petryakov, Sarygulov, Zeman, Khusainov—*Structural Change in Developed Economies in the Digital Age*

The economic development of OECD countries in the past 50 years has been marked by a decline in the share of manufacturing and an increase in the share of the service sector in their national economies. Empirical data analysis for the leading OECD countries shows that the decline in the share of people employed in manufacturing has practically stabilized by 2020, while production volumes continue to grow. Based on the new role of ICT, the authors in this chapter propose a five-sector model of the economy, as it best reflects the technological trends of modern development. In particular, it is proposed to single out a separate sector related to human resources, which includes education, health care, social services, and science as a single group. Another sector should be manufacturing, construction, transport, and mining, the development of which will largely depend on the use of ICT.

Chapter 9: Ablyazov, Baizakov—*Theory and Practice of Territories Spatial Development Based on the Smart City Concept*

Spatial development of territories in digital economy is a relevant area of research since the introduction of digital technologies has become an integral trend of urban development which happened from the beginning of the twenty-first century in order to ensure a comfortable and safe living environment. In this chapter, the authors analyze the theoretical approaches to spatial development of territories and definition of Smart City, as well as justify the relevance of Smart City strategy development and implementation as the most important stage in territory spatial development. The existing programs for spatial development of territories are described; digital technologies, which are tools for implementing Smart City strategies, are examined, and projects planning and implementing approaches on spatial development of territories based on the Smart City concept are analyzed in the work as well.

Chapter 10: Antonov, Kaliaev, Zaborovskij—*Exo-intelligent Data-driven Reconfigurable Computing Platform*

The key concept of the digital age is based on the Turing machine abstraction, which defines computational processes as the evolution of the states of a machine that performs a basic set of computational operations (BSCO) step by step. Based on Ludwig Boltzmann's statement that "available energy is the main object at stake in the struggle for the evolution of the world," the authors in this chapter discuss the possibility of creating a heterogeneous computing platform using specialized hardware to perform a basic set of operations that reduce costs energy for algorithm implementation. The platform presented has a certain entropy potential in relation to possible options for hardware and software configurations of the computational structure and composition of the BSCO, which is formed using so-called basic computational equivalent (BCE) which can build on standard universal multi-core processors (CPU), GPU accelerators, or FPGA-based reconfigurable coprocessors.

Chapter 11: Ilin, Iliashenko, Dubgorn, Esser—*Critical Factors and Challenges of Healthcare Digital Transformation*

Healthcare organizations are seriously considering how to evaluate the effectiveness of the introduction of new technologies and how to correctly correlate it with the cost treatment and optimize costs within the healthcare system. This chapter analyzes modern trends in the field of health care, such as value-based, personalized, and value-oriented medicine. Within this framework, the authors make an overview of the current state of digitalization of health care not only in the Russian Federation, but also in the world arena. The key factors in the development of digital health care are discussed, as well as the risks in the implementation of digital solutions.

Chapter 12: Ilin, Borremans, Levina, Esser—*Digital Transformation Maturity Model*

Currently, digitalization has become a key engine for the development of all industries. More and more enterprises are focusing on the digitalization of their processes and the introduction of digital services. However, the transition from business to digital is quite complex and requires a gradual transition. The authors in this chapter raise questions of the maturity of various enterprises and their processes, as well as criteria and attributes for assessing maturity. The authors perform a comparative analysis of some of the existing maturity models and a five-level model for assessing the maturity of digital enterprises is presented, which was developed on the basis of modern maturity models, such as CMMI, OPM3, and others.

St. Petersburg, Russia — Andrei Rudskoi
Moscow, Russia — Askar Akaev
Lisbon, Portugal — Tessaleno Devezas
August 2021

References

Devezas, T., Leitão, J., & Sarygulov, A. (2017, February). *Industry 4.0 – Entrepreneurship and structural change in the new digital landscape*. Springer.

Devezas, T., Leitão, J., & Sarygulov, A. (2021, February). *The economics of digital transformation: Approaching non-stable and uncertain digitalized production systems*. Springer.

Contents

Rethinking Theory on the Role of Technological Innovation in Economic Development

Askar Akaev, Andrey Rudskoy, and Tessaleno Devezas

Abstract Analysis of recent publications on the role of innovation in technological development indicates that the basic statements of the theory of innovative development, dating back to the works of J. Schumpeter, have not undergone any significant changes. However, the rapid development of information and communication technologies, especially digital ones, the emergence of a shared economy, and new turbulent processes like the COVID-19 pandemic, encouraged researchers to revise these works in order to find answers to the new challenges of our time. In this work, the well-known approaches are reconsidered, and new interpretations are proposed that can significantly expand the tools to study innovative processes in the economy and assess the evolution of technology and machinery.

Keywords Technological innovation · Economic development · Evolution of technology and machinery

1 Introduction

Technology is constantly changing the world. According to the theoretical views of Karl Marx, changes in production technologies are the main factor influencing human and social relations, as well as organizational structure of the society. However, the idea becomes increasingly popular that technologies are not

A. Akaev
Institute for Mathematical Research of Complex Systems, Lomonosov Moscow State University, Moscow, Russia

A. Rudskoy
Peter the Great Saint Petersburg Polytechnic University, Saint Petersburg, Russia
e-mail: rector@spstu.ru

T. Devezas (✉)
Atlântica Instituto Universitário, Lisbon, Portugal
e-mail: tdevezas@uatlantica.pt

A. Rudskoi et al. (eds.), *Digital Transformation and the World Economy*, Studies on Entrepreneurship, Structural Change and Industrial Dynamics,
https://doi.org/10.1007/978-3-030-89832-8_1

autonomous and they are amenable to democratic control (Marx & Smith, 1995). According to some researchers, it is the autonomous and social trends in technology development that are key to understanding the nature of technological development (Dafoe, 2015). According to others, the link between the technology and the human factor allows for a deeper understanding of the mechanism of interaction between technology and institutions. This understanding allows us to foresee the limits and possibilities of human development and the use of technology (Orlikowski, 1992). Some researchers consider the process of the technological revolution strictly within the framework of neo-Schumpeterian theoretical positions, where the central place is given to innovations, their emergence and the continuity of the innovation process (Perez, 2009). A number of recent studies deal with certain applied issues of technology development such as information, communication and digital technologies, and assess their impact on the development of small and medium-sized enterprises or the social changes (Kondowe & Chigona, 2019; Morgan-Thomas, 2015). The issues of evolutionary development of technologies and their impact on socioeconomic systems are discussed in the works of Devezas, Leitão, and Sarygulov (2017, 2021).

It is obvious that technological innovation generates and sustains continuous technological progress (TP), which plays a critical role in increasing the growth factors of the real economy. It is responsible for high rates and sustainable economic growth in long-term development, which predetermines the theory of innovation as an important component of the theory of economic growth. J. Schumpeter (1934) considered innovation to be the main function of entrepreneurship and the basis of cyclical fluctuations in the economy. He linked Kondratiev's long waves (Kondratiev, 1935) and the Juglar cycles with the waves of innovation in technology and economics.

Technological innovation is the main engine of economic growth and varies in terms of novelty, duration, and impact. The concept of "epoch-making innovations" was introduced into science by S. Kuznets. He used this term to refer to scientific and technological revolutions that occur once a century and radically change the society: "The main breakthroughs in the development of human knowledge, those that were the main sources of long-term economic growth and were widely spread in the world, can be called epoch-making innovations" (Kuznets, 1971). It is the epoch-making innovations and the waves of basic innovations that realize their potential that underlie the revolutionary acceleration of socioeconomic development. *Basic innovations* result in radical changes in the technological order and in the methods of organizing production. Waves of basic innovations occur approximately once every 40 years, in the process of transition to the next Kondratiev wave. *Improving innovations* are aimed at the development and modification of basic innovations, their distribution in different areas, taking into account their specifics. Streams of improving innovations follow the waves of basic ones, they are orders of magnitude more numerous, but are characterized with much less novelty and a shorter life cycle. *Pseudo-innovation* is a category introduced by Gerhard Mensch (1979). Pseudo-innovations are widespread in the final phase of the life cycle of an outgoing system, when it has basically exhausted its potential, but seeks to preserve its niche in the modern world. Further, we will note a number of important statements discussed in various theoretical works that are vital for a deeper understanding of cause-and-effect relationships in the development of technology, machinery, and economics.

2 The Principle of Turning Points in the Development of Technology

Technological innovation depends on gradual modifications introduced to the design of a machine or product, which remains essentially unchanged over long periods. These time-invariant essential design features of a product determine the *turning points* that are important for the entire course of innovation. The turning point in technology is often associated with the adaptation of the technology to the conditions of its application. All subsequent advances in technology occur through minor modifications to the underlying design that remains essentially unchanged. The turning point of technology is often the culmination of previous technological advances. The evolutionary nature of technological shifts in high-tech branches of technology can be seen everywhere.

The importance of the concept of turning points in the development of technology is confirmed by the history of technology, when earlier models were far superior to the subsequent ones. The design of such a model became the basis for numerous subsequent innovations in the process of the gradual evolution of technology. The launch of microprocessor is a prime example of this process. In 1971, Intel Corp, based in the US Silicon Valley, produced a microchip called the Intel 4004. It was the first commercially available microprocessor—a microcomputer in a single miniature package. It was a miracle of its time and contained 2300 transistors, each about 10 microns in size. Today, Intel is producing nanoprocessors with transistor sizes of about 10 nm, with the distance between them of about 7 nm, which contain more than 20 billion transistors. The number of transistors in Intel microprocessors, in full accordance with Moore's Law, doubled every one and a half years, but their architecture remains the same to this day.

3 The Evolutionary Nature of Innovation

Progress often takes the form of a series of small innovations with cumulative effects, with each innovation being insignificant. D. Sakhal argues *that technological progress by its nature is an evolutionary process* (Sakhal, 1985). This does not mean that fundamental changes and shifts cannot take place in technology. The above statement is to be understood in the sense that fundamental technological innovations are made possible due to numerous minor innovations. The cumulative effect of a large number of seemingly insignificant technological shifts is often quite significant. Thus, Sakhal comes to the interpretation of innovation as a learning-by-doing process.

The essence of the principle of turning points in technology is that the process of technological development invariably leads to a certain basic structure (model), which for many years is to become the basis for further improvements. Furthermore, this design (model) has a decisive impact on the nature of further development.

Any product or production factor has an inherent life cycle. The duration of the life cycle is determined by the time needed not only to make up for the full cost, but also to increase the return at a given rate. The return on technology or the capital invested in it is uneven. The general rule is that returns gradually increase, reaching a maximum close to the middle of the life cycle, and then decrease, so that its dynamics resembles a normal distribution graph.

In a particular case, when the demand for an innovative product $F(t)$ grows according to the logistic law

$$F(t) = \frac{F_m}{1 + \exp(-rt)} \tag{1}$$

where F_m is the maximum demand; is the rate of adaptation to the optimal conditions for the interaction of supply and demand, the return or the rate of replacement of the capital resource is described by the function that has the above form of the normal distribution function:

$$E(t) = \dot{F}(t) = \frac{F_m r \exp(-rt)}{[1 + \exp(-rt)]^2} \tag{2}$$

$E(t)$ is the return per unit of time. Moreover, the total return obtained by integrating expression (2) equals the cost of capital replacement plus a part of the profit going to accumulation.

The life cycle of a product, describing a certain feature, product technology, or market over time, begins with a "loop of mutual reinforcement." At some point, the constantly increasing rate of change begins to slow down, after having reached a certain peak. This peak consists of two interconnected nonlinear processes, namely, the growth process resulting from the "mutual reinforcement loop" and the process of deceleration resulting from the limiting factor. Constraints or limits that determine the level of the change can be physical, economic, social, etc. To the extent that it relates to innovation, they are often associated with the removal of physical or economic constraints.

The evolution of technology is characterized by two factors. First, the development of technology tends to slow down at some point, after which there is a short-term movement toward an equilibrium state. Second, periods of decline in innovation rarely last long.

The main characteristic of the innovation process is nonlinearity, which distinguishes it from many other processes, such as manufacturing and logistics. This leads to the fact that small changes can have significant consequences. For example, small investments can lead to large profits. However, this factor can bring unpredictability and risk to innovation. Another important feature of the innovation process is self-organization at different stages of its life cycle.

4 Nonlinearity and Self-organization of Innovations

The process of launching innovative products into the markets was studied by E. Mansfield (USA) and other researchers (Mansfield, 1968). They found that this process is best described by a logistic function, the graph of which is an S-shaped nonlinear curve. This testifies to the nonlinear nature of the innovation process. Initially, the diffusion of innovations proceeds at an ever-increasing rate, due to the positive feedback. When the diffusion rate reaches a certain critical value, negative feedback is automatically activated, which causes slowdown in the diffusion rate and leads to the saturation of the innovation process. The nonlinear nature of the innovation process means that each diffusion trajectory reaches a saturation level within a finite period of time representing the innovation life cycle. The Japanese researcher Masaaki Hirooka found (2006) that the life cycle of innovations was gradually decreasing since the first industrial revolution (seventeenth century) from 90 to 25 years now. The period of diffusion of innovations in our time lasts about 25–30 years until the market reaches a state of maturity. Experts believe that there is a lower limit here and it is unlikely that it will be possible to reduce this time below 20 years in the near future.

It is important to note that the diffusion of innovations occurs along a logistic trajectory only under favorable economic conditions. If the economy gets into a zone of turbulence and comes to a state of stagnation, then diffusion deviates from the original logistic trajectory. When the economy returns to a boom, the diffusion again comes back into the original trajectory and makes the rest of the way, so there is no need to start from scratch. Another remarkable feature of the innovation process is self-organization, which stems from the nonlinear nature of innovation. Thanks to self-organization, innovations tend to form so-called "clusters." Innovations within one cluster mutually reinforce one another, causing a synergistic effect. Due to the synergistic effect of the interaction of innovations within the cluster they cause a powerful cumulative growth of the economy, providing a breakthrough nature of its development. Clusters of basic technologies lead to the emergence of new industries and start long economic cycles, forming the upward stage of the Kondratiev long wave, which reaches its peak at the time of innovations' development. The aggregate of clusters of basic innovations forms a technological order (TO) (Glaziev, 1993).

In self-organization, an important role is given to nonlinear mechanisms that are responsible for the unpredictable dynamics of the innovation process. The main nonlinear mechanisms of innovation diffusion are the following:

1. Mutual reinforcement loops
2. Constraint loops
3. Locking mechanisms
4. Time lags
5. Selection mechanisms
6. Mechanisms for creating innovations and making adjustments to them

The actions of all these mechanisms are described in detail in two works (Janszen, 2000; Mneyan, 2006), which can serve as a practical guide for large and medium-sized businesses on innovations and innovation management, and on the technological strategy and development.

Mutual reinforcement loops can be either beneficial or unfavorable. One of the examples of a beneficial cross-reinforcement loop is the coevolution of Intel microprocessors and Microsoft's MS-DOS and Windows operating systems (Janszen, 2000). The development of faster microprocessors provided the opportunity for more powerful and user-friendly operating systems, which in turn required the development of even faster microprocessors. Thus, the Mutual reinforcement loops worked in such a way, that even small improvements in each of the technologies led to increased productivity and higher efficiency of computer technology. On the other hand, the Windows operating system formed a cross-reinforcement loop by producing software for its applications and increasing the number of its users. Users were becoming dependent on MS-DOS and Windows as well as a large number of applications compatible with this software. Consequently, it became too costly for them to switch to another company's software. This is how the "locking effect" for Microsoft users emerged, which created a stable competitive position for the corporation (Janszen, 2000).

Every process of growth comes to an end sooner or later. There are limiting loops, or limits to growth, that determine the extent of the future change (Janszen, 2000). Innovation often involves removing physical or economic constraints. The most striking example of innovation designed to overcome the loop of limitations is the jet engine in aviation, which replaced piston engines to overcome the speed limitations. Jet engines made it possible to raise the aircraft speed by 3–5 times and significantly lowered the restrictions.

Locking mechanism is a consequence of the coevolution of technology, products, markets, organizational structures, and so on. Interdependencies can become so close that changes in one of the factors must lead to adaptation of all other factors. But the changes in all factors increase costs to such an extent that they are perceived as too high relative to future benefits. An example of this is the failed transition in the 1980s to high-temperature ceramic internal combustion engines capable of reducing emissions of harmful substances that pollute the atmosphere. The costs of designing and testing new engines were so high that production was suspended. Thus, it became clear that it was possible to achieve this goal by improving the previous engine with other innovative solutions (Janszen, 2000).

Counterproductive results are often caused by time lags in feedback loops. One of the most common examples is delays in the human resource management system in the context of the development of innovative products, when the decision to hire new employees and the time delay caused by their training can lead to a decrease in the overall productivity of the team, and a delay in the release of products. This phenomenon can occur cyclically if the recruitment of new employees lags behind (Janszen, 2000).

Selection mechanisms for innovations are critical factors for economic systems. In particular, markets are selection mechanisms in which consumers make decisions about purchasing certain goods and services based on their preferences for product characteristics. Therefore, it is extremely important to have accurate forecast of consumer preferences in the development of new products and new types of business, since this choice determines the success of the company in the implementation of innovation (Janszen, 2000).

Sources of innovation are localized elements in the system that can form a loop of cross-reinforcement and thus lead to a complete change in all positions.

These mechanisms determine the system's behavior that is especially interesting in terms of innovation, since sometimes small investments can produce significant results. Such situations are due to various mechanisms such as removed barriers, lifted restrictions on growth, loops of cross-reinforcement, and others. However, there are mechanisms that impede innovation and change, such as locking mechanisms or risks associated with undesirable loops of mutual reinforcement.

Evolution in engineering and technology is the result of three main mechanisms: selection; locking, creating innovations and making adjustments to them. In terms of self-organization, some nonlinear mechanisms also play an important role, such as Mutual reinforcement loops, limiting loops, locking mechanisms, and time delays. Mutual reinforcement loops cause small events to have significant results.

The diffusion process of technological innovation is quite obvious. In most studies, the assumption is made about two completely different types of activity: the primary act of creating a fundamentally new technology, and the subsequent process associated with the spread of a new technology, which is routine but reproduces some creative features of the primary act. The distinction between innovation and its subsequent diffusion was first drawn by J. Schumpeter (1934).

Schumpeter's ideas on the diffusion of innovations were later developed, as mentioned above, by E. Mansfield, whose work on the theory of the diffusion process of a new technology had a great influence on other researchers. The main characteristic of the diffusion process is the effect of "taking the winning side." In accordance with it, the decision to install new machinery made by an individual firm depends on the firms that already use this machinery. It can be shown that under some very simple assumptions, this hypothesis implies an S-shaped curve describing the dependence of diffusion on time. In the simplest case, it is a logistic curve, which belongs to the number of symmetric S-curves. Indeed, if the market share captured by the new technology (F) replacing the old one ($1-F$) is a few percent bigger, then further replacement will follow the logistic law established by Fisher and Pry for the first time in 1971 (Fisher & Pry, 1971):

$$\frac{F}{1 - F} = \exp(\lambda t + \beta) \tag{3}$$

or

$$F = \frac{1}{1 + \exp[-(\lambda t + \beta)]} \tag{4}$$

However, data on the diffusion of technological innovations often includes an element of asymmetry. In such cases, the logistic function is not suitable for describing the time dependence of diffusion, and it is necessary to refer to other, asymmetric S-curves, such as the Gompertz function or the lognormal distribution function. Empirically observed diffusion curves include a number of different S-shaped growth time relationships such as the logistic function, the Gompertz function, and the normal and lognormal distribution functions (Luderer et al., 2010).

Until now, the focus of most researchers has been on the factors which determine the rate of diffusion processes. Although the rate of the diffusion process has been studied quite well, there is still no theory that would provide a reliable prediction of the level of innovation diffusion.

The alternative point of view put forward by D. Sakhal in his remarkable book (Sakhal, 1985) is that the diffusion process is closely related to the process of technology development. Therefore, the diffusion of technology can be interpreted in terms of the actual replacement of the old technology with the new one. This means *that diffusion is a nonequilibrium process implying the transition from one equilibrium level, corresponding to the acceptance of the existing technology, to another equilibrium level, corresponding to the adoption of a new technology*. Thus, the diffusion of any innovation is a process of joint evolution of old and new technological innovations, accompanied by numerous changes in their functional characteristics.

D. Sakhal also concludes that the technological progress is characterized by stable cyclical fluctuations. He found a striking coincidence of the cycles of technological activity based on the empirical data with the well-known Kondratiev waves, Kuznets and Juglar (Schumpeter, 1939) that are characteristic of economics. In this regard, he admits that business cycles are most likely to arise in the field of technological activity.

One of the distinctive features of evolutionary processes is that they go along with irreversible changes. Evolution involves overhaul of the structure and changes in the functions of an object. Evolutionary changes accumulate and inevitably transform an entire system, assigning new properties to it. There is an important feature of evolution: the very processes that make possible the evolution of a system at its initial stages, at later stages determine the limits of evolution. There are limits to growth for every system. Often, the evolution of a system slows down long before the system reaches the limits of growth. The reasons for this premature deceleration are clearly economic, but they evolve from the physical processes described above.

Thus, evolution is a process of approaching equilibrium controlled by the internal dynamics of the system.

5 The Principle of Creative Symbiosis

The principle of creative symbiosis implies that the fusion of two technologies in one system removes or pushes back the limits to its evolution. A striking example of the creative symbiosis of technologies is the combination of machine learning and computer technologies, which led to the creation of artificial intelligence (AI). At first, scientists believed that the human brain was similar to a digital computer. Soon it became clear that the architecture of the computer was completely different from the architecture of the brain. Human brain is a self-learning biological machine made up of billions of neurons, the connections between which vary each time it solves a new problem.

In the 1950s, scientists created the first brain models based on neural networks and developed algorithms for their training based on the already existing large amounts of data. After training, the model became capable of solving a problem using current data or achieving a given goal. Machine learning developed on this basis. However, machine learning required huge amounts of computation, which has become possible in real time only now with the advent of modern ultrafast computers, as well as methods for storing and transferring large amounts of data at high speed. Thus, today the creative symbiosis of machine learning technology and the computer has led to another breakthrough—the creation of intelligent machines.

In the conclusions to Chap. 4 of the above-mentioned book by D. Sakhal, it is stated that:

1. Short-term evolution is an equilibrium process determined by the dynamics of the system itself.
2. Long-term evolution is a nonequilibrium process determined by the dynamics of a broader system.

This has two important consequences:

1. Until now, the view has prevailed on the socioeconomic system as an *exogenously controlled homeostatic system* returning to a stationary state after a temporary disturbance, i.e., the processes of socioeconomic changes have been interpreted as the ones inevitably reaching a state of equilibrium. D. Sakhal proposes to consider *socioeconomic systems as endogenously controlled homeodynamic systems* capable of finding new ways of evolution through the hierarchy of instabilities. Thus, the processes of socioeconomic changes are interpreted as nonequilibrium ones. In other words, the traditional approach takes into account only the mechanism of change, while the focus of our attention is on the changing system.

2. A new feature of the modern approach to modeling socioeconomic processes is the desire to explain the course of these processes by the current or expected values of the corresponding variables. D. Sakhal believes that *socioeconomic changes should be considered in terms of cumulative changes in the system.*

These consequences are the result of the combined operation of the principles of turning points and creative symbiosis.

6 Self-organization and Fractal Structure of Innovation

Self-organization occurs at different stages of the development of the innovation process. The formation of clusters of innovations in the stage of depression and in the course of diffusion of innovative products into markets, as well as the development of technological clusters—all this happens due to the mechanism of self-organization.

Hirooka thoroughly studied the self-organization of innovation systems (Hirooka, 2006). He showed that coincidences in the diffusion of innovation and economic recovery meant that Kondratiev's economic waves were driven by clustered innovations. At least one of the reasons for innovation clustering is the creation of innovative products that face obstacles to their distribution in the market during an economic downturn. At this time, innovations also go through a period of stagnation, but with the recovery of the economy, they are launched into the market thus contributing to economic recovery. This is a simple self-organization phenomenon. Thus, the uneven clustering of technical innovations is due to self-organization. Studying discrete systems of innovations, Hirooka established the existence of fractals and the mechanisms of their self-organization.

7 Fractal Structure of Innovation

Despite the fact that the logistic curve is intended to describe a continuous process, the real innovation system is discrete and dissipative. Open systems with an increase in entropy are referred to as dissipative. In such systems, the energy of ordered motion is converted into the energy of chaotic motion, into heat. Dissipative structures in instability states can turn out to be very sensitive to the slightest random deviations in the medium. Thanks to this, they can move into a new ordered state with high rates. Self-organization is an important mechanism in complex systems with a dissipative structure. One of the most important characteristics of the innovation process is that it acts as a discrete system. The trajectory of the innovation paradigm is determined by the amalgamation of separate, discrete elements. A number of new products in innovation are interconnected and thus form the trajectory of its development. Each product with a small logistic structure is isolated, and all elements of the system share a common innovation algorithm. This is the origin of the fractal, and each innovative trajectory consists of a series of fractals.

Hirooka discovered several types of fractals, as well as many self-organizing mechanisms of innovation systems. He investigated the fractal structure of an integrated microcircuit in the electronic paradigm, fractals in the information technology paradigm, fractals of merging trajectories of various industries, fractals of technological systems in various sectors of the economy. This is the first extensive empirical study undertaken to show that innovation is a complex system. It shows that innovative paradigms include various fractals, and these fractals are very important elements, since each trajectory develops through the accumulation of discrete elements that represent a small element of the structure.

Innovations grouped by the ascending stage of Kondratiev's long waves also have a fractal structure. During the innovation, there are three types of fractals: sequential, connecting, and systemic. A number of innovative products line up sequential fractals along a development path. Existing industries are introducing emerging innovative technologies to form connecting fractals along the trajectory of the innovation. Various software systems form system fractals along the trajectory of the innovation development as well. Infra-trajectories induce subsequent innovations to form a fractal cluster.

Hirooka identified two types of fractals: chain and group fractals. In the process of development of an innovative trajectory, the first type develops into chain structures. The second type develops similar to a bundle, and together with the development of the structure, it forms its own group structure. In addition, another, intangible, type of fractals develops into the form of concentric circles around software and systems of innovative paradigms.

8 Chain Fractals of IS Devices

Each innovative product is unique and has its own development history, which, in turn, has a shorter development trajectory. This is the origin of fractals. According to Moore's Law, machinery systems in the electronic paradigm evolve gradually. This means that once every 3–4 years, the degree of integration of the machinery quadruples and attains a higher level. Development is not continuous, but a discrete process. Each of these processes has its own trajectory, which is an element of the fractal. Accumulated fractals constitute the main trajectory of development. The final products form a propagation trajectory with a chain structure of fractals.

9 Scope of Group Fractals

Group fractal structure can be observed in various areas. The trajectory of its development includes various products and areas of their subsequent use. The history of the development of innovative products consists of the trajectory of its development and the distribution of products in various fields, thus forming the trajectory of mergers (Freeman, 1987; Hirooka, 2006). Freeman and Hirooka defined innovation in existing industries as technology fusion. The technology fusion trajectory is called the fusion trajectory. This means that the scope of innovation goes beyond its own products to wider application. For example, microelectronic products (microprocessors, various electronic chips, etc.) have been installed into engines, machine tools, automobiles and have significantly improved their performance. The increased use of innovative technologies enriches the development trajectory and expands the market, thus contributing to institutional change in the economy.

Thus, innovative systems (clusters) consist of various fractals and develop due to the mechanism of self-organization. It has been found that innovative paradigms include various fractals, and these fractals are its important elements, since each trajectory is formed through the accumulation of discrete elements that represent a small element of the structure. Knowledge transfer plays a key role in self-organization according to Hirooka. The knowledge transfer in the innovation paradigm is an actual discrete system, since knowledge transfer occurs from one subject to another. In this innovation system, not only the subjects involved in the transfer of knowledge are discrete, but also the products of the innovation process, which gradually improve in the course of such a discrete process. This leads to the formation of fractals on the trajectory.

Various fractal formations contribute to the diffusion of innovation across increasingly vast markets, which leads to changes in both the techno-economic paradigm and the organizational sphere. As a result, an innovative paradigm with a hierarchical structure develops. This structural ramification is caused by the self-organization mechanism, which, as a driving force, leads to the formation of an integrated system during the development of the innovation process.

10 Synergetic Paradigm

Processes in complex systems are characterized by ambiguity and, generally speaking, do not lead to predictable results. Innovations are especially striking examples of this—the use of multiple technological opportunities leads to the increased complexity of the system, and the wider variety of ideas about the world.

The synergetic paradigm evaluates the role of nonequilibrium and irreversible processes and their relationship with equilibrium and reversible processes in a fundamentally different way. The interaction of many elements within a single system is always a relevant subject for discussion, and nonequilibrium processes are considered as a way to generate stable structures. According to the figurative expression of Ilya Prigogine, nonequilibrium gives rise to "order from chaos" (Prigogine & Stengers, 1984). There is a remarkable regularity: the stability of the system arises not in spite of, but due to nonequilibrium states.

The formation of self-organizing systems can be considered as a certain stage of a system development. Evolution itself can be represented as a transition from one type of self-organizing system to another. As a result, the analysis of evolutionary characteristics turns out to be inextricably linked with the phenomenon of self-organization—the order parameter. Within the framework of this interpretation, the role of order parameters in a complex innovation system is assigned to innovations, and subordinate elements can be changes (technological, economical, and structural) occurring in the innovation space. In this case, we are talking about the processes caused by internal reasons. As for the external causes, they can turn out to be an impulse that contributes to the transition of the system to a new state.

The innovation system, in its essence, is open to all sorts of new ideas, technologies, and information. Critical fluctuations may arise here, manifesting themselves in the form of some instructions to the elements of the system, which are generated in the process of their interaction or in the course of collective behavior. In a synergistic sense, such "instructions—signals" are order parameters.

Self-organization is simply the selection of order parameters during the development of a system. There are certain relationships established between the order parameters. On the one hand, they subjugate the elements of the system, and on the other, they interact with one another, which leads to the emergence of new order parameters.

11 The Triad of Technological Progress: Inventions, Innovations, and Investments

The mechanism of the innovation-technological process includes three interconnected links: inventions, innovations, and investments. However, everything starts with technological and scientific knowledge, and fundamental science is the primary source of innovation.

Following the scientific revolution, there comes the explosion of scientific creativity, and the structure of scientific knowledge is changing, together with the composition of the leading scientific branches and schools. The scientific revolution generates epoch-making innovations, which, in turn, generate a powerful stream of basic innovations. Science is not homogeneous, as it has waves of development. One single breakthrough (such as the invention of the steam engine, light bulb, or transistor) often entails a cascade of secondary inventions (as the chain reaction proceeds), which in turn cause an avalanche of innovation and acceleration of technological progress.

In technology, development often proceeds at an exponential rate, especially when it comes to increasing the efficiency of technological processes. However, when it comes to fundamental research, which requires skills, insights, and expertise we can observe discontinuous equilibrium, when almost nothing changes for a long time, and then suddenly a breakthrough occurs that radically changes the entire scientific world. If you look at the history of fundamental research from Newton to Einstein to the present day, it becomes clear that discontinuous equilibrium more accurately describes the way fundamental science developed.

Knowledge is the most important component of the innovation process, and it is transferred from one subject to another, during which an innovative product is created. An innovative product provides economic growth if it penetrates into many branches and provides high quality. Thus, the innovation process develops through the transfer of knowledge from one subject to another, which creates innovative products, thereby moving the economy forward. The transfer of knowledge can occur both within the framework of one innovation and technological trajectory, and between trajectories. The idea of a "field" for transferring knowledge is especially important, since without transfer of knowledge there will be no innovation process.

Scientific knowledge, embodied in innovation, accelerates technological progress, which is the main source of economic and industrial growth. Nathan Rosenberg thoroughly studied the contribution of science and technology to the process of economic development (Rosenberg, 1974, 2000). Jacob Schmookler pointed out the importance of demand as the primary cause of innovation (Schmookler, 1972). This complements Schumpeter's concept of the contribution of innovation to economic development. Schumpeter believed that innovation is generated by the supply, and gave minor role to the "demand challenge" in his research. The empirical core of Schmukler's work is an attempt to demonstrate that accounting for the influence of forces generated by the demand is the main factor determining the possible variation in the inventive potential. Rosenberg criticized this position of Schmukler: "Many important categories of human needs remained either unmet or badly served for a long time, despite clearly formed demand" (Rosenberg, 1974, p.97).

The innovation process covers the entire cycle of transforming scientific knowledge, scientific ideas and discoveries into innovation. Renewal processes driven by innovation are usually market-oriented, customer-specific, or need-oriented. The cyclical nature of the innovation process—the life cycle of innovations—presupposes the feedback between the consumer of innovations and the scientific and innovative sphere. In the twentieth century, there was a trend toward a rapid reduction in the time interval between the acquisition of new scientific knowledge and its transformation into innovative products.

However, in recent decades, there has been a slowdown in this trend. P. Drucker's gave his opinion on this phenomenon: "Recently it has been widely accepted that today knowledge is being transformed into technology much faster than before. However, reality proves the opposite. One gets the impression that the time of transition of knowledge into technology is increasing. Today, the period of transition of new knowledge into new technology is about thirty to forty years. In addition, the time for the development of new technology and its implementation in new products and processes also seems to increase" (Drucker, 1992).

For innovation, it is extremely important whether it is feasible for production and commercial use. A major drawback of patent statistics is the lack of information on the commercial use of the technology. The patented inventions and the history of major technological innovations reflect mainly the emergence rather than the development of new technology. For the state, for firms and companies, only innovative technologies matter, and P. Drucker states: "In the long term, the only way to pay for other technologies will be producing their own technologies" (Drucker, 1992).

As for the problems of transition to a new technology, it is important to understand that technologies (and products) are characterized not by individual parameters, but by their combination. Moreover, the potential capabilities of any technology can be described in two aspects. One of them is economic parameters, knowledge of which allows us to calculate the economic advantages of the technology, for example, unit production costs or market price and the other is the actual technological parameters.

One of the most common views on technical innovation goes back to the work of Schumpeter. While the concept of technological innovation is central to Schumpeter's views on economic development, the creation of new technology remains largely exogenous in his work. According to Schumpeter's followers, technological innovation by its very nature follows an independent path, i.e., they tend to view technological change as an autonomous phenomenon. In particular, Sakhal also argues that the results of his research lead to a similar conclusion: science and technology evolve largely autonomously. Sakhal believes that technical innovations have primarily technical and only secondarily socioeconomic reasons. Therefore, he believes that technological innovation is a partially regulated process, leading to profound consequences of the socioeconomic nature (Sakhal, 1985).

The general view is that technological change is rarely a direct consequence of scientific discovery. Most often, technological innovations result from the gradual modification of the existing technology in the process of its adaptation to the practical requirements, i.e., in the process of learning by doing. In other words, technical progress is due not to theoretical knowledge but to the development of empirical knowledge. The role of science in technological change is relative rather than absolute.

The main condition for the practical implementation of innovations is the turnaround of investments, both private and public. Without the investments into innovations, it is impossible to ensure the much-desired high rates of economic growth and higher living standards of the country's population.

When imitators seize the initiative from innovators, there is a phenomenon of investment boom: investment growth outstrips a wide renewal of fixed capital that became obsolete during the crisis and depression. Investment projects during this period are clearly innovative in nature. Basic innovation requires a larger and more risky investment. Therefore, initial investments in the development of such innovations require state support and the state should pursue an active innovation and investment policy aimed at implementing the strategy of scientific and technological breakthrough.

12 Selection and Implementation of Innovations

The selection of innovations for practical implementation always takes place in the confrontation of social systems. In this sense, the selection and implementation of innovation are, according to Charles Darwin's classification, *artificial selection* carried out by people.

Who are the subjects of innovative selection? Here is the answer of Yakovets to this question (Yakovets, 2004, p.60–64): These are the authors of the idea—scientists, inventors, entrepreneurs, political and public figures. They are the first to realize the need for change and propose ways to implement innovations in a particular field of society. The second group of subjects is the innovators who implement the selected innovative ideas, allocate the necessary resources, take on the innovative risk and achieve the resulting effect (for example, innovative super-profit—quasi rent). The state is an important player in the field of innovation. It creates a favorable innovation climate, ensures compliance with the established norms and rules of innovation. When the crisis is over, it is time for innovation. Leadership in their selection belongs to entrepreneurs.

E. Hargadon in his book "Innovation Management. The experience of leading companies" explains how to manage innovations and achieve the goals associated with them (Hargadon, 2003). The well-known book by B. Twiss "Management of scientific and technical innovations" (Twiss, 1992) has not lost its relevance either.

What should the entrepreneur of the twenty-first century be like? P. Drucker wrote in his book (Drucker, 1992): "First of all, the entrepreneur will have to learn to understand the dynamics of technology and predict the direction and speed of technological change. If new technologies are created by a lone inventor, there is no need for such an understanding. If we say that a developed economy must quickly respond to innovations and changes, then entrepreneurs must be able to anticipate scientific and technological progress and not miss the opportunities that it opens up."

P. Drucker gives great importance to studying the needs of the market: "Understanding the dynamics of the market is becoming an increasingly important condition for the successful work of an entrepreneur. The market is the most powerful source of new ideas. Over the past few years, the US Department of Commerce has conducted research that has shown that at the heart of most patented products and processes—i.e. products and processes with high technological content—there are market needs, not pure technologies" (Drucker, 1992).

13 State and Innovation

Y. Yakovets formulated the following integral concept of the distribution of roles in the innovation field: "The main initiators of improving innovations carried out at their own expense are innovators—individuals and organizations. However, the state develops a proper innovation strategy, chooses priorities and provides support to basic innovations that determine the technological level and competitiveness of the economy and its place in the global technological and economic space. The state also takes on the responsibility of implementing innovations in the non-market sector of the economy" (Yakovets, 2004, p.388–389). This model is implemented today in the leading countries.

The most important task of the state is the organization of long-term innovative forecasting and the selection of strategic priorities by the leading experts and scientific institutions. It should be noted that a very effective system of long-term forecasting of scientific and technological progress (STP) and choosing priorities was introduced in the USSR. Every 5 years, a comprehensive program of scientific and technological progress and its socioeconomic achievements for 20 years was developed, which served as the starting point for scientific, technical, and innovative progress. Unfortunately, in the early 1990s, this system was destroyed and never revived. The time has come for the revival of this system on a new level.

The long-term forecasts serve as the basis for future innovative and technological development. With regard to the conditions of Russia at the present stage, this is a strategy of an innovative and technological breakthrough, focused on the widespread implementation of the most effective innovations of the fifth order (1980–2020) and the timely development of key technologies of the sixth technological order (2020–2050).

A modern state must have a scientifically grounded long-term technological strategy. Japan was the first to show an example of the successful implementation of a technological strategy. The Japanese quickly learned where to look for new technologies and how to turn the imported ideas into a commodity. P. Drucker states: "In the era of rapid change, a technological strategy is needed not only for prosperity, but also for the very survival of an enterprise and, possibly, even an entire industrialized nation. We must know in advance where to forward our technological resources. Should we focus on modification and improvement, like most industries do in the framework of research and development? Or focus our efforts on the creation of new technologies?" (Drucker, 1992). The selection of technologies for the main sectors of the economy should form the basis of the national strategy. The strategy should contain a technology selection mechanism. Lack of responsibility and thoroughness in the selection of technologies is fraught with dire consequences.

The pace of changes in the prevailing generations of technology in the avant-garde industries in the modern era is approximately 8–10 years, i.e., they determine the rate of the alternation of Juglar's medium-term cycles. The technological order is based on general technological principles, has an internal logic of development, and usually includes 4–5 successive generations of technology. The change in the prevailing technological paradigms is the material and technical basis for the transition to the next Kondratiev long wave (Glaziev, 2010).

Improvement in existing industries is rarely the main driver of productivity gains. When new high-performance industries develop faster than traditional low-productivity industries, the change in the sectoral structure of the economy can trigger its growth. In the next Kondratiev wave, these industries can also develop for a long time. They can even expect a noticeable leap in development. However, in terms of their ability to stimulate further growth of the economy as a whole, these industries are already weak. Despite their own growth and prosperity, these industries will make less contribution to the increase in national income and employment growth. Their ability to stimulate dynamic growth in advanced economies will diminish over time.

Traditional analog photography with its entire industry producing films and specialty papers, chemicals for developing and fixing images, and unique optical lenses for equipping cameras is an example of a large and successful industry that has practically disappeared under the pressure of digital technology. The transition from analog to digital technologies has given the humanity digital photography, which provides the extreme convenience and simplicity of the photographic process, as well as its low cost, almost accessible to anyone.

The earliest indication of the need for major innovation is the decline in the efficiency of capital investments in a large industry. If a large industry requires additional capital investment to produce the same volume of output, especially if the increased capital requirements are nothing more than compensation for job cuts, then it is in the state in the crisis. Whatever prosperous and profitable the industry may seem if business owners fail to correct the negative trend, it will quickly decline.

It is widely believed that the new technology creates new industries, new jobs, and new markets. P. Drucker states: "New technology is only potential. It is marketing, especially innovative marketing, that is able to realize this potential." Drucker was convinced that marketing, i.e., the ability to turn technological innovation into profitable manufacturing is especially important. There is a balance between the technological component and the demand factor. The "trigger" of the technological factor seems to be decisive at the beginning of the development of production, and the "thrust" of the market is even more important in the subsequent development.

The era of innovation and economic change puts serious demands on the government. In times of rapid changes, when new industries become new driving forces, public policy should not constrain the mobility of productive resources. Labor and capital, two mobile resources of any economy, must have the capacity to move from yesterday's low-productivity to modern highly efficient industries. Capital must have the capacity to move towards efficient investments. The more developed the economy is, the more important is the optimal allocation of capital. The economy can be referred to as developed if the capital is steadily increasing its productivity, constantly moving from less productive industries to more productive. This is the only way to ensure a high or growing standard of living and full employment.

In a time of rapid technological changes that lead to the emergence of new industries, the strengthening of the past weakens the future. The alternative to technological changes and economic growth, especially during the period of rapid development of science and technology, is not holding on to the previous positions, but recession.

Any technological revolution brings with it not only a complete restructuring of the production structure, but also changes in government and society. Therefore, we can talk about cyclical patterns of innovative society development.

14 Technological Progress and Economic Growth

Growth is the main goal of the economy. The solution to the problems facing nations is to ensure continued economic growth and increased productivity. The most common indicator of production efficiency is labor productivity. New knowledge, new technological innovations ensure productivity growth. Kuznets states in his works that it is new knowledge, but not capital (and not even labor) that provides productivity growth (Kuznets, 1971). Therefore, Kuznets associated the increase in the rate of economic growth in the industrial era with the accelerated development of science: "The wide-spread use of technological innovations, which is largely the core of modern economic growth, is closely linked with the further progress of science, which, in turn, forms the basis of further technological progress" (Kuznets, 1971).

It is also necessary to highlight the general pattern that characterizes the growth of the efficiency of the productive forces at successive stages of the progress of society. This is reflected in expanded range and improved quality of produced values, their ability to satisfy the ever-increasing and more complex final and intermediate human needs; in reduced costs of social labor; in the relative savings of resources per unit of the final product.

In modern conditions, most technological innovations are based on in-house research and development (R&D). Innovative ideas are born in academic and university laboratories, but they find commercial application in R&D. Therefore, *technological progress* can be viewed as the *result of activities related to the implementation of R&D*. At the same time, R&D expenditures include the acquisition of a certain resource (knowledge), which increases the productivity of other resources. The result of R&D can be a technological innovation that is ready for sale in the market. Successful innovation brings super-profits. Lack of competition and limited implementation of innovation, generating high rates of income, serve as a kind of protection for innovative firms.

Many books have been written about technological progress, its laws and its key role in modern economic growth, among which there is the already mentioned monograph by D. Sakhal, which is called "Technological progress" (Sakhal, 1985). This book examines the laws governing the emergence, diffusion, and development of new technology. Although this book was published thirty years ago, it has not lost its relevance today, since it was written in the era of unprecedented growth of technological progress. The monograph contains general provisions of the theory of the technological innovation evolution. The development of a specific technology is characterized by two main factors. The first factor is training during production and operation, and the second is changing the scale of technology. These two factors play a critical role in shaping and sustaining technological change.

The first factor is based on the well-known concept of the progress function, also called the learning curve. The essence of this concept lies in the fact that the productivity of an enterprise is gradually increasing as experience is accumulated, which makes it possible to eliminate various "bottlenecks" in the technological process and in the organization of labor. This phenomenon was first observed in the aviation industry, where it was found that direct labor costs per unit of output decreased at a constant rate as total output increased (Arrow, 1962). The range of applicability of this concept turned out to be unexpectedly wide—from the manufacturing industry to the office work. Thus, the experience accumulated in the process of production and operation activity is vitally important for the growth of labor productivity over time.

The function of progress can be considered as a model for increasing labor productivity of any system using this technology, since the learning process plays an important role in the use of existing technology. The thesis proposed by Sakhal is that learning processes also underlie the development of a new technology. New technology is usually the result of practical improvements that expand the range of capabilities of the existing machinery.

The above considerations allowed Sakhal to formulate another hypothesis about technological innovation, which it would be appropriate to call the "learning by doing" hypothesis. The expression "learning by doing" was first introduced by K. Arrow (1962). The link between technological progress and the level of production experience is a long-term factor.

One of the most significant characteristics of the system, in terms of its influence on the innovation process, is its scale. First, the very first act of introducing a technology depends on a certain minimum (maximum) effective scale, with deviations from which the use of this technology is less justified. The introduction of technology becomes feasible only at a certain scale. The relationship between technology and the scale of operations, both direct and inverse, can be causal, within certain limits. However, technology depends on scale more than scale depends on technology. There are solid grounds why this relationship can be viewed as predominantly direct one.

Learning and rescaling are two closely related processes that together become the driving force behind innovative change in technology. The factor of learning in its role in technological progress is similar to the factor of time, and the scale is similar to the factor of space. Until now, most socioeconomic studies have focused on the role of time in technological progress and overlooked the role of space. However, space plays the same important role in the development of technology as time. When we consider them simultaneously, we take into account that technical progress occurs both in time and in space. The learning process primarily stimulates the development of the technology itself (Sakhal, 1985). This kind of learning occurs both in design and in production, i.e., learning is essential for increasing the productivity of labor.

15 Conclusion

The ever-growing variety of technological processes and technologies themselves significantly complicates the composition and structure of modern technological systems. In this regard, the study and concept of cause-and-effect relationships in such systems require the use of a broader conceptual apparatus and new research tools. The most significant studies of the recent past have considered these issues. First, they highlighted the existence of turning points that direct the entire course of innovation and are mainly associated with the adaptation of technologies to the conditions of their application. Secondly, they stated that technological progress, by its nature, is an evolutionary process. The evolution of technology has two characteristics. First, the development of technology slows down at some point, after which there is a short-term movement toward an equilibrium state. Second, periods of decline in innovation rarely last long. An important characteristic is the self-organization of innovations and their fractal structure. Nonlinear mechanisms such as: "Mutual reinforcement loops"; "Constraint loops"; "Time delays"; "Locking mechanisms"; "Selection mechanisms"; "Mechanisms for creating innovations and making adjustments to them"—play an important role in the self-organization of innovations. Furthermore, the diffusion of technologies should be viewed as a nonequilibrium process, and socioeconomic changes are best viewed in terms of cumulative changes within the system. Also important is the necessity to use the synergetic paradigm more widely, which evaluates the role of nonequilibrium and irreversible processes and their relationship with equilibrium and reversible processes in a different way. This paradigm considers the interaction of many elements within a single system when nonequilibrium processes are considered as a way to generate stable structures. It should be kept in mind that the experience accumulated in the process of production activity is vitally important for the growth of labor productivity over time. Learning and rescaling are two closely related processes that together become the driving force behind innovative change in technology. The factor of learning in its role in technological progress is similar to the factor of time, and the factor of scale is similar to the factor of space.

References

Arrow, K. (1962). The economic implications of learning-by-doing. *Review of Economic Studies, 29*(80), 155–173.

Dafoe, A. (2015). On technological determinism: A typology, scope conditions, and a mechanism. *Science, Technology, & Human Values, 40*(6), 1047–1076.
Devezas, T., Leitão, J., & Sarygulov, A. (2017). *Industry 4.0—Entrepreneurship and structural change in the new digital landscape*. Springer Verlag.
Devezas, T., Leitão, J., & Sarygulov, A. (2021). *The economics of digital transformation. Approaching non-stable and uncertain digitalized production systems*. Springer Nature.
Drucker, P. (1992). *The age of discontinuity*. Routledge.
Fisher, J. C., & Pry, R. H. (1971). A simple substitution model of technological change. *Technological Forecasting and Social Change, 3*, 75–88.
Freeman, C. (1987). *Technical innovation, diffusion and long cycles of economic development*. The Long-Wave Debate.
Glaziev, S. Y. (1993). *The theory of long-term technical and economic development*. VlaDar.
Glaziev, S. Y. (2010). *Strategy of the outstripping development of Russia in the context of the global crisis*. Economics.
Hargadon, A. (2003). *How breakthroughs happen: The surprising truth about how companies innovate* (1st ed.). Harvard Business Review Press.
Hirooka, M. (2006). *Innovation dynamism and economic growth. A nonlinear perspective*. Edward Elgar.
Janszen, F. (2000). *The age of innovation*. Financial Times Prentice Hall.
Kondowe, C., & Chigona, W. (2019). *Rethinking theory and practice of ICT4D. An analysis of the discourse embedded in the 2016 World Bank Report*. In molecular logic and computational synthetic biology.
Kondratiev, N. D. (1935). The long waves in economic life. *Review of Economics and Statistics, 17* (7), 105–115.
Kuznets, S. (1971). *Modern economic growth: Findings and reflections*. The Sveriges Riksbank Prize in Economic Sciences in Memory of Alfred Nobel. Prize Lecture.
Luderer, B., Nollau, V., & Vetters, K. (2010). *Mathematical formulas for economists*. Springer-Verlag.
Mansfield, E. (1968). *The economics of technological change*. W. W. Norton & Company, Inc.
Marx, L., & Smith, M. R. (1995). *Does technology drive history? The dilemma of technological determinism*. MIT Press.
Mensch, G. (1979). *Stalemate in technology*. Cambridge University Press.
Mneyan, M. G. (2006). *The dynamic image of innovation: Algorithms for innovative development*. M. Vitus-K.
Morgan-Thomas, A. (2015). Rethinking technology in the SME context: Affordances, practices and ICTs. *International Small Business Journal: Researching Entrepreneurship, 34*(8), 1122–1136.
Orlikowski, W. J. (1992). The duality of technology: Rethinking the concept of technology in organizations. *Organization Science, 3*(3), 398–427.
Perez, C. (2009). *Technological revolutions and techno-economic paradigms*. Working Papers in Technology Governance and Economic Dynamics, Working Paper No. 20.
Prigogine, I., & Stengers, I. (1984). *Order out of chaos*. Bantam Book.
Rosenberg, N. (1974). Science, invention and economic growth. *Economic Journal, 84*, 90–108.
Rosenberg, N. (2000). *Schumpeter and the endogeneity of technology*. The Graz Schumpeter Lectures. London: Routledge.
Sakhal, D. (1985). *Technical progress: Concepts, models, estimates*. FinansyiStatistika.
Schmookler, J. (1972). *Patents, invention and economic change*. Harvard University Press.
Schumpeter, J. (1934). *Theory of economic development: An inquiry into profits, capital, credit, interest, and the business cycle*. Harvard University Press.
Schumpeter, J. A. (1939). *Business cycles. A theoretical, historical and statistical analysis of the capitalist process*. McGraw-Hill Book Company, Inc.
Twiss, B. C. (1992). *Managing technological innovation* (4th ed.). Trans-Atlantic Publications.
Yakovets, Y. V. (2004). *Epic innovation of the 21st century*. Economy.

Information Model for Calculating the Rate of Technical Progress

Askar Akaev, Andrei Rudskoy, Bulat Khusainov, and Zoltan Zeman

Abstract Classical models of economic growth have been modified due to new global economic trends that emerged under the influence of the large-scale digitization and robotization of today's capitalist economy. In order to calculate prognostic dynamics of the technical progress (total factor productivity), we have provided the information model based on the use of different modes for producing technological information. The proposed model relies on the principle of forming and changing an amount of technological knowledge, Kurzweil's law of accelerating returns (LARR) for ICT, and also particular provisions of the Isenson-Hartman model for describing informational dynamics. In addition, we have come up with the model for forecast calculations of ICT contribution into the technical progress under conditions of scarce resources. It is stated that the economic impact of digitization across economies will not occur immediately, but with a certain time lag.

Keywords Digital technologies · Digital economy · Information model of the technical progress

A. Akaev (✉)
Institute for Mathematical Research of Complex Systems, Lomonosov Moscow State University, Moscow, Russia

A. Rudskoy
Peter the Great Saint Petersburg Polytechnic University, Saint Petersburg, Russia
e-mail: rector@spstu.ru

B. Khusainov
Economic Research Institute JSC, Nur-Sultan, Kazakhstan

Z. Zeman
Szent Istvan University, Godollo, Hungary
e-mail: zeman.zoltan@gtk.szie.hu

A. Rudskoi et al. (eds.), *Digital Transformation and the World Economy*, Studies on Entrepreneurship, Structural Change and Industrial Dynamics,
https://doi.org/10.1007/978-3-030-89832-8_2

1 Introduction

The outburst of information technology and their dissemination across all segments of the economy fueled research studies into the nature of information and applied aspects of using information and Big Data. Obviously, most studies were related to the system data architecture, algorithms of implementing various web services, information, and data coding (McGovern et al., 2003). Business information models became an independent and essential line of research due to their significance for solving practical tasks (West, 2011). Particular attention was paid to developing and modeling business processes, when accumulating data at the strategic, tactic, and operational levels, information models aimed to form a single integrated information model of an enterprise (Scheruhn et al., 2015). With increasing complexity of tasks to be solved and the extensive diffusion of information technology into the day-to-day life of most consumers, more importance is added to automatic summarization—the method of Big Data processing which implies abstracting a text within the multidimensional category space and reveals the main features and principles of using and comprehending a language (Hai, 2016). Undoubtedly, the studies related to the nature of information and its practical usage are the most widespread. However, recent decades have been characterized by creating highly efficient digital technologies, intelligent computers, and robots capable of generating large-scale changes in production forces, which greatly surpass achievements of the Third Industrial Revolution. Therefore, the concept of Industry 4.0 is no coincidence (Kagermann et al., 2013). The basic infrastructure for Industry 4.0 is the Industrial Internet of Things (Greengard, 2015), which represents the digital platform ensuring efficient interaction of all industrial objects on the basis of the Internet. Along with this, a multifunctional digital information technology—Blockchain—aimed at reliable record-keeping of assets and their transactions has emerged. Blockchain technology is destined to become a reliable economic framework for the Internet to deal with online payments, a decentralized digital exchange of assets, issuance and execution of "smart contracts" (Swan, 2015). The Internet technologies make the production process fully automated, from manufacturing components and assembly to an electronic order and delivery of finished goods, thereby sidelining humans from the industrial sphere. As digital technologies and platforms play a key role in Industry 4.0 and new information society, there is no doubt that the recent epoch is characterized by the transition to "digital economy." Digital economy and Industry 4.0 mark natural development of the information technology sector of the economy which is named Knowledge Economy, only at a higher technological level. The work (Brynjolfsson & Adam, 2010) shows that information and communications technologies are general purpose technologies which take certain time to generate their own technological and economic environment resulting into an increase in labor productivity and growth rates. From our standpoint, a similar effect will emerge in the time of digital economy, as digital technologies are also general purpose technologies, and they are widely applied in all spheres of economy, management, and public life.

2 Amount of Technological Knowledge

In order to calculate how the labor productivity growth is transformed in the growth of the national income, it is necessary to use production functions (Plakunov & Rayackas, 1984). The most simple, appropriate and common form of setting a production function (PF) has proved to be the PF of Cobb-Douglas, put forward in 1928, which signifies the following (Stoleru, 1975):

$$Y = AK^{\alpha}L^{1-\alpha} \tag{1}$$

where Y is the amount of gross domestic product (GDP); K is the amount of fixed (physical) capital; L is labor (a number of blue-collar workers and white-collar workers in the economy); α is a constant parameter; A is a coefficient that characterizes the technical progress (or a technological level of the economy).

Taking the logarithm of both sides of Eq. (1) and using termwise differentiation, we obtain a PF in the intensive form:

$$q_Y = q_A + \alpha q_K + (1 - \alpha)q_L \tag{2}$$

where $q_Y = \dot{Y}/Y$; $q_A = \dot{A}/A$; $q_K = \dot{K}/K$; $q_L = \dot{L}/L$ are growth rates of respective variables, $\dot{Y}$, $\dot{A}$, $\dot{K}$, $\dot{L}$ are time derivatives of respective variables. If we know the contribution of physical capital and labor into growth rates of the economy, which are measured by growth rates of the gross domestic product, formula (2) shows that the remainder $\{q_Y - \alpha q_K - (1 - \alpha)q_L\}$ represents growth rates of the technical progress, which was confirmed by R. Sollow in 1957. According to R. Sollow's assumptions, made in his classical work (Solow, 1957), an increase in capital can cause only a 12.5% increase in gross output per man-hour, whereas 87.5% of the increase is attributed to technological shifts, i.e., technical change.

Returning to Eq. (2), we will highlight that q_Y, q_A, q_K, and q_L are growth rates of output, technical progress, capital, and labor. Methods for calculating accumulation rates of physical capital (q_K) and also growth rates of a number of workers (q_L) in the economy are well developed and available. They can be found, for example, in the book (Barro & Sala-i-Martin, 2004). Hence, we will consider in detail the contribution of ICT into the growth rates of the technical progress. In order to do this, we will use the information model offered in the paper (Yablonsky, 1986).

The core of the model by A. Yablonskiy is the following: assume that there is a law of accumulating technological knowledge S_A, which determines a technological level of manufacturing A. It is expected that the technological knowledge S_A is implemented in the form of inventions, rationalization proposals, developments, etc., while put into tangible forms of patents, licenses, project plans, etc. It is obvious that the growth of the technological level A is determined not only by the growth of the technological knowledge S_A, but also by the extent of practical implementation of this knowledge, which is characterized by fixed capital renovation:

$$\eta = \frac{I_K}{K} \tag{3}$$

where I_K is investments into the fixed capital. Then, A. Yablonskiy accepts the hypothesis that a growth rate of the technological level $\left(q_A = \dot{A}/A\right)$ is proportional to a growth rate of the technological knowledge $\left(q_S = \dot{S}_A/S_A\right)$ with the coefficient η (1.3.3), which allows for the amount of new technological knowledge implementation (Yablonsky, 1986):

$$q_A = \frac{\dot{A}}{A} = \gamma \frac{I_K}{K} \cdot \frac{\bullet S_A}{S_A} \tag{4}$$

where γ is a gauge coefficient.

Formula (4) is incorrect because it does not allow for the ratio of the right and left sides of the equation. It is not difficult to find out that on the left side of Eq. (4) there is the quantity q_A, the dimension of which is $[q_A] = (\text{year})^{-1}$, and on the right hand side—$\left[\frac{I_K}{K} \times \frac{\dot{S}_A}{S_A}\right] = (\text{year})^{-2}$. Therefore, in accordance with the π-theorem of the dimension theory (Barenblatt, 2003), Eq. (4) will be more accurate in the form:

$$q_A = \frac{\dot{A}}{A} = \gamma \sqrt{\frac{I_K}{K} \cdot \frac{\bullet S_A}{S_A}}. \tag{5}$$

This formula for calculating growth rates of technical progress fully complies with the requirements of the dimension theory. Quantity dimensions on both sides from the sign of equality are identical and equal to $(\text{year})^{-1}$. Hence, knowing the pattern of the change of the technological knowledge S_A in ICT, with formula (5) we can easily calculate the contribution of ICT into growth rates of the technical progress, because data that characterize the fixed capital renovation $\left(\eta = \frac{I_K}{K}\right)$, are available in various data banks, for example, on the website (OECD, 2021). We will come back to estimation of a gauge coefficient γ later.

3 Kurzweil's Law of Accelerating Returns for ICT

In the twentieth century, key properties of various technological devices tended to be improved exponentially for a long period of time, e.g., performance of civil aircrafts (in ton-kilometers per hour) or efficiency of light sources (LM/Wt) (Martino, 2020). Besides, it is obvious that any tendency is limited by the upper boundary of a certain kind (Martino, 2020). For example, the efficiency of energy conversion is to reach 100% after all. Then the increasing tendency will stop.

A famous scientist, inventor, and futurist Ray Kurzweil put forward the Law of Accelerating Returns (LAR), which means that key parameters of ICT development also tend to develop exponentially (Kurzweil, 2005, pp. 491–496). Additionally, R. Kurzweil states that as soon as a technology becomes an information technology, it starts to meet LAR. He assumes that a computational speed is the most important example of LAR action, which is connected with the general use of computers to process different data and their key role in improving all-important technological processes. Briefly, we will give the derivation of Kurzweil's formulae that describe an increase in the computational power of computers (Kurzweil, 2005, pp. 491–496).

The computational speed V (measured in a number of operations per second for one unit of price, e.g., for \$1000) is proportional to the amount of the world knowledge, related to designing and creating computing devices W:

$$V = c_1 \cdot W, \quad c_1 = \text{const} \tag{6}$$

On the other hand, we accept a hypothesis that a rate of change for the world knowledge is proportional to the computational speed, i.e.:

$$\dot{W} = c_2 \cdot V = c_1 \cdot c_2 \cdot W, \quad c_2 = \text{const} \tag{7}$$

Indeed, this equation conforms to the conservative forecast, which has a lot of empirical confirmations. Assuming that a growth rate of the world knowledge is proportional to W^{σ}, where $\sigma > 1$, i.e., $\dot{W} = W^{\sigma}$, then there is a solution with singularity:

$$W = \frac{W_0}{(T_C - t)^{\frac{1}{\sigma - 1}}} \tag{8}$$

where T_C is a point of singularity. It is common that under conditions of definitely finite computational resources, it is impossible to imagine an infinite growth of knowledge. Therefore, Eq. (7) should be admitted correct. Its solution is an exponential function (Kurzweil, 2005, p. 492):

$$W = W_0 \exp\left[c_1 c_2 (t - T_0)\right] \tag{9}$$

Later, R. Kurzweil shows that there is even a more rapid exponential growth of computations, connected with exponentially increasing resources N, provided for computations:

$$N = c_3 e^{c_4 t}, \quad c_3 \text{ and } c_4 = \text{const} \tag{10}$$

We still have $V = c_1 W$. The rate of change for the world knowledge is now proportional to the product of the computational speed V and the quantity of provided resources N:

$$\dot{W} = c_2 \cdot N \cdot V = c_1 \cdot c_2 \cdot c_3 \cdot e^{c_4 t} \cdot W \tag{11}$$

The solution to this equation is Kurzweil (2005), p. 493):

$$W = W_0 \exp\left[\frac{c_1 c_2 c_3}{c_4} e^{c_4 (t - T_0)}\right] \tag{12}$$

It leads to the fact that the world knowledge in computer engineering is accumulated at a double exponential speed. R. Kurzweil shows that the double exponential growth of knowledge (12) is also available in an ordinary computer network. Indeed, Eq. (7) for a network of computers will be written in the form of Kurzweil (2005, p. 496):

$$\dot{W} = W + W \ln W \tag{13}$$

where the item $W \ln W$ describes the network effect. The solution to this equation is also a double exponential function:

$$W = \exp\left(e^t\right) \tag{14}$$

Thus, a computational speed of modern computer systems grows in a conservative option according to the exponential law (9), and in multiprocessor computational systems and computer networks it grows even faster—according to the double exponential law (12). However, one of the Microsoft founders Paul Allen and his colleague Mark Greaves put forward several objections to Kurzweil's LAR, the central of which is impossibility to constantly maintain exponential growth (9) of ICT computational power, let alone the double exponential growth (12) (Allen & Graves, 2011). It is well known that the technology of silicon transistors, due to Moore's law and continuous and consistent reduction in their size, has been maintaining the exponential growth of computational power of computers within the last 50 years. Recently, Moore's law has been predicted to come to an end soon. The thing is that the International Technology Roadmap for Semiconductors (ITRS) stipulates a shift to a 7-nm transistor technology in early 2020s, when key elements of electronic circuits will be several atoms of carbon in thickness and it will be hard to reduce their thickness further.

However, Kurzweil points out that Intel and other manufacturers of integrated circuits are already mastering the technologies of three-dimensional transistors and 3D memory. He assumes that the shift to three-dimensional computations will enable maintaining the exponential growth of cost-to-use parameters of computers in the 2020s (Kurzweil, 2012). Here we should agree with R. Kurzweil, because not

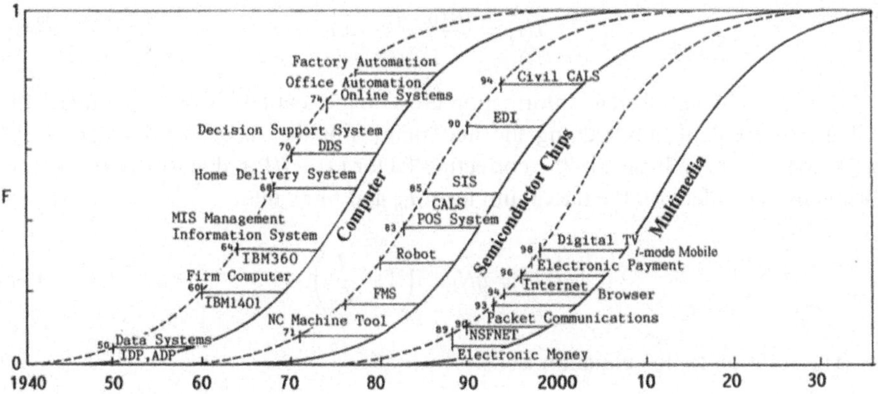

Fig. 1 Development of information technologies. Source: Hirooka (2006)

only the technology of three-dimensional transistors will contribute to it but also the development of nanoelectronics. Therefore, during the life cycle of modern ICTs—till early 2030s (Fig. 1)—we can confidently spread Kurzweil's LAR, which means the exponential growth of ICT performance for a certain unit of price (9), and this growth can be considered as the most proper criterion of progress in the field of ICT improvement. When it comes to the double exponential growth (12), it occurs only for a limited period of time.

4 Isenson-Hartman Model for Describing Informational Dynamics

R. Isenson (1966) and L. Hartman (1966) parallelly published works, which considered information growth. Due to similarity of mathematical models, they are usually considered as a single one (Martino, 2020). Isenson assumes the dependency of the information increase I with time only on two factors—the number of active researchers $N(t)$ and the recognized maximum of information $I_{\max}(I_m)$. He also admits the exponential growth $N(t) = N_0 e^{ct}$, typical for new areas of science and technology in the twentieth century, and writes the following equation for the increase of information without allowing for its recognized maximum:

$$\dot{I}(t) = q \cdot N(t) - q \cdot N_0 e^{ct} \tag{15}$$

where q is an average efficiency coefficient of one active researcher per one unit of time, e.g., per year. This equation has a simple solution:

$$I(t) = \frac{qN_0}{c}(e^{ct} - 1) \tag{16}$$

Hence, at the initial stage information grows exponentially. But it continues only till the moment of approaching the maximum. For the stage of approaching the maximum, Isenson brings in the correcting factor ($1 - I/I_m$), due to which Eq. (15) becomes dependent on the maximum level I_m and turns into:

$$\dot{I}(t) = qN_0 e^{ct}\left(1 - \frac{I}{I_m}\right) \tag{17}$$

The solution to this equation is:

$$I(t) = I_m\left[1 - \exp\left(-\frac{qN_0}{cI_m}e^{ct}\right)\right]. \tag{18}$$

Hence, information, according to Isenson, grows in a S-shaped trajectory, asymptotically approaching the maximum I_m.

L. Hartman assumes from the beginning that the growth of information depends on the amount of existing information, which is significantly different from Isenson's model (15), but more closely corresponds with empirical data on obtaining scientific and technical results:

$$\dot{I} = eI, \quad e = \text{const} \tag{19}$$

This very equation is used by R. Kurzweil to describe the dynamics of knowledge accumulation in ICT in Eq. (7). For the stage of approaching the maximum I_m, Hartman brings in the same correcting factor as Isenson, so Eq. (19) takes the form of:

$$\dot{I} = \varepsilon I\left(1 - \frac{I}{I_m}\right) \tag{20}$$

The solution to this equation is a logistic function:

$$I(t) = \frac{I_m}{1 + \left(\frac{I_m}{I_0} - 1\right)e^{-\frac{\varepsilon}{I_m}(t - T_0)}} \tag{21}$$

As a result, the information also grows in an S-shaped trajectory, asymptotically approaching the maximum I_m.

Isenson-Hartman model shows that it is important to take into account deceleration of the information growth, when approaching the maximum, and a corresponding correcting factor in growth in Eq. (20). This was numerously confirmed empirically. This component of Isenson-Hartman model is valuable concerning correction of Kurzweil's LAR.

5 Models for Forecast Calculations of ICT Contribution into Technical Progress in Resource-limited Settings

We should proceed with the assumption that growth limits of information (knowledge) in ICT are still remote in time, but the moment of approaching the limits of resources in use is close, i.e., human resources.

First option. Let us assume that dynamics of a number of researchers in ICT is known. Let us take the second Kurzweil's in Eq. (11):

$$\dot{W}(t) = k \cdot N(t) \cdot W(t) \tag{22}$$

where k is a gauge coefficient.

Let us assume that $N(t)$, which was growing according to the exponential law (10) at the initial stage, is now approaching its maximum $N_{\max}(N_m)$ according to the logistic law:

$$N(t) = N_0 - 1 + \frac{1 + N_1}{1 + N_1 \exp\left[-\nu(t - T_0)\right]} \tag{23}$$

Here $N_m = N_0 + N_1$, $N_0 = N(t)|_{t=T_0}$.

Substituting Eqs. (23) into (22), we obtain the equation:

$$\dot{W} = k\left\{N_0 - 1 + \frac{1 + N_1}{1 + N_1 \exp\left[-\nu(t - T_0)\right]}\right\}W \tag{24}$$

The solution to this equation is the function:

$$W(t) = W_0 \cdot e^{kN_m(t-T_0)}\left[\frac{1 + N_1 e^{-\nu(t-T_0)}}{1 + N_1}\right]^{\frac{1+N_1}{\nu}k} \tag{25}$$

With the allowance $N_1 > > 1$, we obtain:

$$W(t) \cong W_0 e^{kN_0(t-T_0)} \tag{26}$$

Resulting from the above stated, the amount of knowledge grows exponentially, although it grew faster than the exponent for some time.

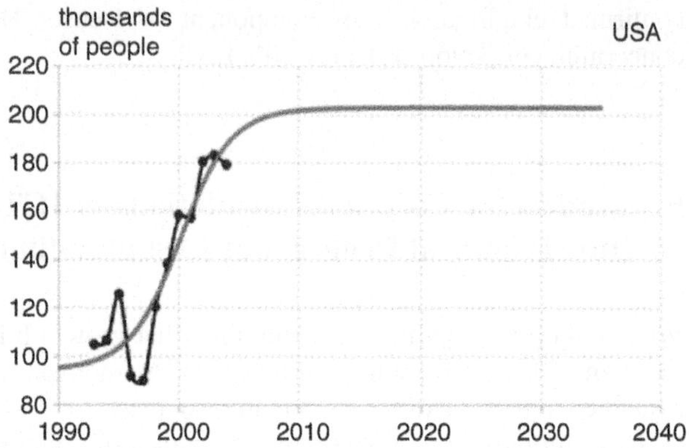

Fig. 2 Dynamics of the researcher number in ICT. Authors' creation based on OECD data (2021)

Equation (24) can be used to forecast growth rates of technical progress. For this purpose, let us use formula (5), in which instead of $(\bullet S_A/S_A)$ we substitute $\left(\dot{W}/W\right)$ from Eq. (24):

$$q_A = \gamma' \left[\frac{I_K}{K} \left\{ N_0 - 1 + \frac{1 + N_1}{1 + N_1 \exp\left[-\nu(t - T_0)\right]} \right\} \right]^{\frac{1}{2}} \quad (27)$$

where $\gamma' = \gamma\sqrt{k}$. Knowing the real dynamics of a number of researchers, who work in ICT in some country, we will be able to determine parameters N_0, N_1, and ν, taking for developed countries T_0=1995—the year when ICT started to influence the economic growth in the most developed countries. Figure 2 shows the researcher number dynamics in ICT in the USA. Resulting from this figure, the number of researchers actually increases by the logistic law and has already reached its maximum—203,000 people (N_0=95,500 people; N_1=107,400 people; N_m=202,900 people; ν=0.465). If we consider that only about 1,200,000 researchers work in the US economy, it becomes clear that every sixth jobs in ICT. The proportion of investments and capital I_K/K for ICT in the USA is given in Fig. 3. As we can see from the Fig. 3, the proportion tends to remain at the level of about 13% after 2000.

To determine the value of the gauge coefficient γ' we used actual data of ICT contribution into growth rates of the technical progress in the second half of the 1990s and obtained $\gamma' = 0.0023$. The forecast of ICT contribution into growth rates of the technical progress in the USA, calculated with formula (27) and shown in Fig. 4. As we can see from this figure, within the next 15 years, the ICT contribution into growth rates of the technical progress will amount to 1.3% on average, with the general percentage from 2 to 3%.

Second option. Let us assume that growth limits of knowledge in spheres of developing, creating, and using ICT are known. Let us consider Eq. (22) again, in which *N*(*t*) grows by the logistic law (23) as before, i.e., in the final form of (24). Then we will limit the information (knowledge) amount *W*, as the maximum limit of knowledge, which a human–computer system can deal with—$W_{\max}(W_m)$. This assumption will be rational because, according to predictions of Kurzweil (2005),

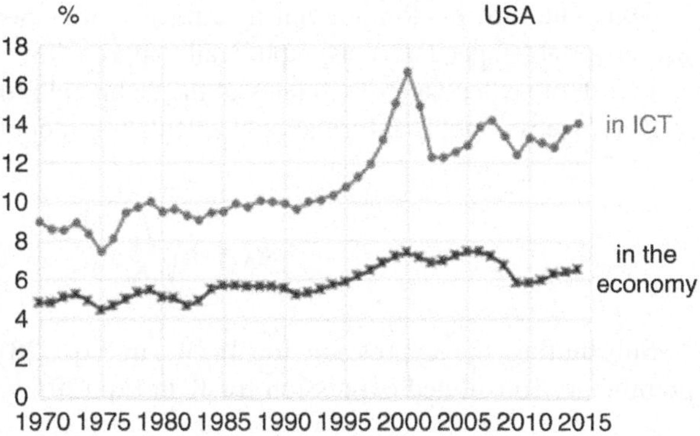

Fig. 3 Proportion of investments and capital. Authors' creation based on OECD data (2021)

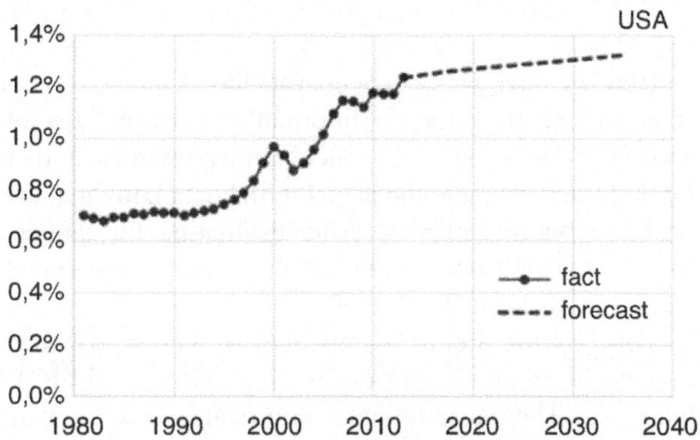

Fig. 4 ICT contribution into technical progress. Authors' creation based on OECD data (2021)

intelligent computers will have reached true intelligence only by the end of 2030s and technological singularity will only begin by 2045. As M. Hirooka showed, the lifecycle of modern ICT will continue only till the beginning of 2030s (Fig. 1). Therefore, we can take into account the movement toward the given maximum W_m by introducing a correcting factor of Isenson-Hartman (1 − W/W_m) into Eq. (27):

$$\frac{\dot{W}}{W} = k\left\{N_0 - 1 + \frac{1 + N_1}{1 + N_1 \exp\left[-\nu(t - T_0)\right\}\left(1 - \frac{W}{W_m}\right)}\right. \tag{28}$$

This equation can be solved in the analytical form and has the following solution:

$$W(t) = \frac{W_m}{1 + \frac{W_m - W_0}{W_0} \exp\left[-\phi(t)(t - T_0)\right]} \tag{29}$$

where $\phi(t) = kW_m\left[\frac{N_m}{N_0 - 1} - \frac{N_1 + 1}{\nu(t - T_0)(N_0 - 1)} \ln \frac{1 + N_1}{1 + N_1 e^{-\nu(t - T_0)}}\right]$.

Thus, the information amount dynamics in this case grows by the logistic law with a variable speed $\phi(t)$, asymptotically approaching the maximum W_m in 2030s.

In order to calculate growth rates of the technical progress, resulting from the use of ICTs, we will apply informational calculation model (5):

$$q_A = \gamma\sqrt{\frac{I_K}{K}\cdot\frac{\dot{W}}{W}} \tag{30}$$

Substituting the expression for $\dot{W}/W$ in Eq. (28), into this formula, with a preliminary substituted expression for W in Eq. (29), we obtain:

$$q_A = \gamma\left\{k\cdot\frac{I_K}{K}\left[N_0 - 1 + \frac{1+N_1}{1+N_1\cdot e^{-\nu(t-T_0)}}\right]\frac{1}{1+\frac{W_0}{W_m-W_0}e^{\phi(t)(t-T_0)}}\right\}^{\frac{1}{2}} \tag{31}$$

Here we have two gauge coefficients (k and γ), one of which k is estimated at the stage of searching for the information growth trajectory $W(t)$ in Eq. (29) and the second γ—at the stage of calculating growth rates of the technical progress q_A in Eq. (31), according to the actual initial data known at the beginning of ICT influence on the economic growth. After estimating the gauge coefficients k and γ, using formula (31) it is possible to calculate forecast growth rates of the technical progress, caused by using ICT till 2030s.

Third option. Let us assume that we know growth rates q_W of the technological knowledge in spheres of developing and creating ICT-products and services, and their use. The most reliable empirical source to determine growth rates of the technological knowledge in ICT is patent statistics. The dynamics of a number of patents, given in ICT, starting form 1982 (start of the rising phase in the 5th KEC based on microelectronic achievements) is presented in Fig. 5 for China and the most developed countries.

As this figure illustrates, all trajectories of patent number growth at the initial stage of ICT active introduction met the exponential law, but with different growth rates and with some gap before the technological leader—the USA. As for China, it became an active participant of this race only in early 2000s, but showed as rapid growth as the leaders. It is also clear that the breakthrough research in this area had been done before middle 2000s. Later this activity stabilized, which is quite natural. Moreover, it is obviously connected with the stabilization of a number of active researchers in this sector. This is shown by the graph in Fig. 2 exemplifying the US growth rates of the technological knowledge in ICT (q_W), equal to the growth rates of the patent number in this sector, calculated for some countries of OECD by approximating the actual growth trajectory of the exponential curve, are given in Table 1.

Earlier we saw that the effectiveness of ICT is greatly influenced by two factors: a number of researchers, working in ICT, and the duration of the exponential growth. It is better to present the values, characterizing these factors, in parts of the general

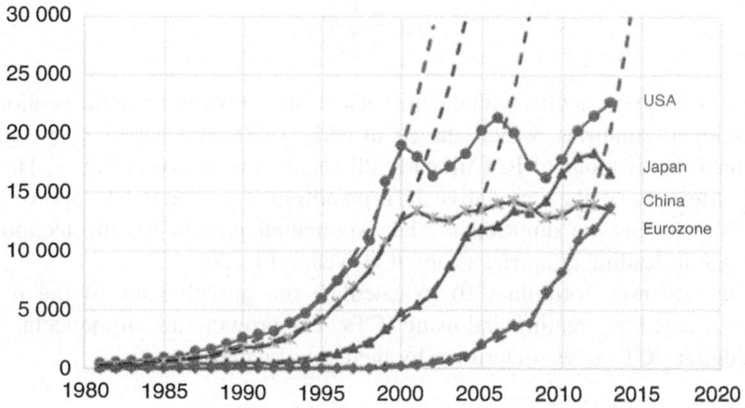

Fig. 5 Dynamics of the patent number in ICT. Authors' creation based on OECD data (2021)

Table 1 Characteristics of ICT contribution into technical progress

Country	q_W	I/K (%)	T_{EG}	τ_{EG}	L_{AW}	L_A	l_A (%)	q_A (%)
USA	0.22	16.7	20	0.40	1100	185	16.8	1.29
Eurozone	0.21	19.0	19	0.38	1080	180	16.7	1.27
Great Britain	0.16	18.4	20	0.40	180	34	18.9	1.30
France	0.23	25.6	20	0.40	250	37	14.8	1.42
Germany	0.21	16.8	20	0.40	360	60	16.7	1.25
Sweden	0.21	18.4	18	0.36	50	10	20.0	1.41
Norway	0.20	18.7	17	0.34	20	5	25.0	1.65
Finland	0.27	15.5	17	0.34	30	6	20.0	1.39
Japan	0.25	25.0	20	0.40	580	70	12.1	1.21
Korea	0.24	15.1	14	0.28	310	55	17.7	0.95
China	0.30	32.0	14	0.28	2900	200	6.9	0.60

number of researchers in the economy L_A (in thousands of people) and the full lifecycle T_{LC} (in years) of the current technological paradigm. Let us designate the part of the researcher number in the ICT sector L_A^{ICT} (in thousands of people) through

$$l_A = \frac{L_A^{ICT}}{L_A} \tag{32}$$

and the part of the duration of the exponential knowledge growth T_{EG} (in years) through

$$\tau_{EG} = \frac{T_{EG}}{T_{LC}}. \tag{33}$$

The ICT lifecycle begins with the microelectronics revolution in the economies of the developed countries, which started in early 1980s and which keeps going as mainstream innovations of ICT till early 2030s, as it is shown in Fig. 1. Therefore, the full lifecycle of the innovative ICT paradigm T_{LC} is equal to approximately 50 years, whereas the duration of the exponential growth for the technological knowledge in leading countries is about 20 years (Fig. 5).

Let us use now formula (30) to calculate the growth rates of the technical progress, caused by creating and using ICTs. The growth rates of the technological knowledge in ICT q_W we determine by the data of patent statistics:

$$q_W \frac{\dot{W}}{W} \tag{34}$$

Consequently, formula (30) will be written as follows:

$$q_A = \gamma \cdot \sqrt{\frac{I_K}{K} q_W} \tag{35}$$

It is obvious that the gauge coefficient γ is proportional to the part of researchers, who work in the ICT sector, and to the part of the exponential growth for the innovative knowledge within the current technological paradigm, i.e.,

$$\gamma = \tau_{EG} \cdot l_A \tag{36}$$

Taking into account (36), we finally obtain the approximate formula for forecast calculations of ICT contribution into growth rates of the technical progress:

$$q_A = \tau_{EG} \cdot l_A \sqrt{\frac{I_K}{K} q_W} \tag{37}$$

All the variables and constant coefficients in this formula were calculated and estimated for some developed countries of OECD and China and were inserted into a table. The table also includes the final results of calculations with formula (44) of growth rates of the technical progress (q_A), ICT products and services their use in different economic sectors. Resulting from the table, the best results were shown by Scandinavian countries—Norway, Sweden, Finland; and France in Europe.

In the present chapter, the authors offer three simple models to forecast calculations of ICT contribution to growth rates of the technical progress. These models use data for growth rates of the technological knowledge in the fields of designing, developing, and applying ICT products and services, and also the relationships between current investments and accumulated capital in the ICT sector. The present chapter shows that growth rates of the ICT technological knowledge can be obtained from the equations which describe Kurzweil's Law of Accelerating Returns for ICT. This law characterizes an exponential growth of various key parameters of ICTs, from a common growth to a double exponential growth. The latter occurs only in certain periods of time, whereas a common exponential growth of ICT technological knowledge is more typical. In this regard, we correct Kurzweil's equations using a limiting factor of Isenson-Hartman. This enables obtaining actual S-shaped trajectories of the technological knowledge, asymptotically approaching the maximum.

In the first model (27), growth rates of the technical progress based on ICT usage are determined by the dynamics of the researcher quantity $N(t)$ in the ICT sector. This model is valuable, as it allows calculating the dynamics of the ICT contribution into growth rates of the technical progress q_A, including a forecast period. The example is provided for the US economy (Fig. 4). The second model (31), along with the given dynamics of the researcher number $N(t)$, uses an S-shaped growth trajectory for the technological knowledge in ICT. Therefore, this model is a generalized modification of the first model.

The third, most simple, model (37) presents growth rates for a number of patents in the ICT field q_W, reflecting growth rates of the technological knowledge, the established number of researchers in the ICT sector l_A and the exponential growth of the patent quantity τ_{EG} in the full lifecycle of the ICT paradigm. This model allows calculating only forecasted estimates of ICT contribution into the technical progress. Applying this model, we calculated the possible forecasted contribution of ICTs into the technical progress in further 10–15 years for 9 countries of OECD and China (Table 1). Unfortunately, we could not fully verify the obtained results, as reliable and accurate information on ICT contribution into productivity and economic growth is unavailable.

Recently, the opinion has been increasingly expressed that the trend observed over the past 40 years of slowing growth rates in the economies of developed countries and the world economy as a whole (Fig. 6) will continue in the twenty-first century, at least during its first half.

In our opinion, the proponents of this view do not take into consideration the consequences of the current NBIC-technological revolution. NBIC technologies (N-nano-, B-bio-, I-info-, and C-cognitive technologies), which are the core of the coming 6th TM (technological mode), will change this trend into an upward one due to the powerful synergy generated by the convergence of nano-, bio-, info-, and cognitive technologies. And the drivers of the coming upward wave of economic growth in the world will be the most developed countries: the USA, China, Germany, and Japan—recognized leaders in the research and development of NBIC technologies.

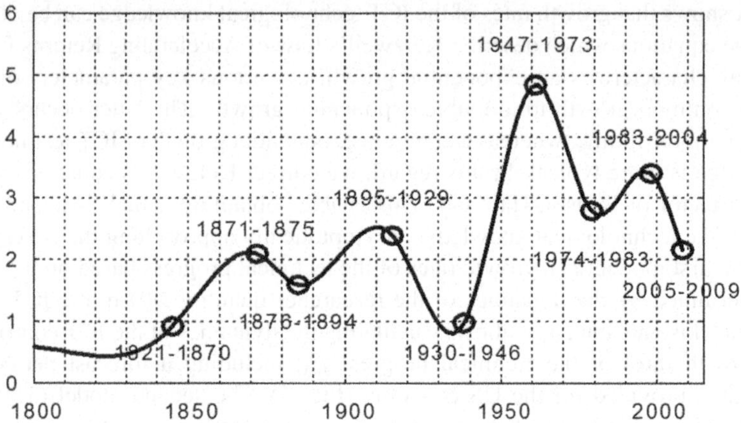

Fig. 6 Trends in the relative average annual growth rate of world GDP, 1800–2009 (%). Authors' creation based on Maddison data (2010)

6 Conclusion

The growth of the technological level is determined not only by the growth of technological knowledge, but also by a degree of practical implementation of this knowledge, characterized by a degree of renewal of fixed capital. In turn, knowing the law of change of the technological knowledge in ICT, we can calculate the contribution of ICT to the rate of technical progress, since the data characterizing the degree of renewal of fixed capital are available in various databases. R. Kurzweil formulated the "Law of Accelerating Returns" (LAR), which implies that the key parameters of ICT development also follow an exponential development trajectory, and as soon as a certain technology becomes an information technology, it begins to comply with this law. The Isenson-Hartman model shows the importance of taking into consideration slowing of information growth when approaching the maximum and the corresponding correction factor, the necessity and importance of which have been confirmed by numerous empirical data. This component of the Isenson-Hartman model is valuable with respect to the Kurtzweil's LAR correction. It should also be noted that the limits of information (knowledge) growth in the field of ICT are still very far, but there comes time to approach the limits on the resources used, in particular—human resources. Three fairly simple models were proposed to forecast calculations of ICT contribution to growth rates of the technical progress. These models use data for growth rates of the technological knowledge in the fields of designing, developing and applying ICT products and services, and also the relationships between current investments and accumulated capital in the ICT sector. It is shown that growth rates of the ICT technological knowledge can be obtained from the equations which describe Kurzweil's Law of Accelerating Returns for ICT. This law characterizes an exponential growth of various key parameters of ICTs, from a common growth to a double exponential growth. The latter occurs only in certain periods of time, whereas a common exponential growth of ICT technological knowledge is more conventional. In this regard, we correct Kurzweil's equations using a limiting factor of Isenson-Hartman. This enables obtaining actual S-shaped trajectories of the technological knowledge, asymptotically approaching the maximum. The calculations based on these models showed that ICT performance is significantly influenced by two factors—the number of researchers involved in ICTs and the duration of exponential growth of knowledge (information) within a particular technical and economic paradigm.

References

Allen, P. G., & Graves, M. (2011, October 2011). The singularity isn't near. *Technology Review Magazine*. Technology Review.

Barenblatt, G. I. (2003). *Scaling*. Cambridge University Press.

Barro, R. J., & Sala-i-Martin, X. (2004). *Economic growth*. MIT Press.

Brynjolfsson, E., & Adam, S. (2010). *Wired for innovation: How information technology is reshaping the economy*. MIT Press.

Greengard, S. (2015). *The internet of things*. The MIT Press.

Hai, Z. (2016). Creative summarization. In *Multi-dimensional summarization in cyber-physical society*. Elsevier.

Hartman, L. M. (1966). In G. A. Steiner & W. Cannon (Eds.), *Technological forecasting / Multinational corporate planning*. Crowel-Collier.

Hirooka, M. (2006). *Innovation dynamism and economic growth. A nonlinear perspective*. Edward Elgar.

Isenson, R. S. (1966). Technological forecasting in perspective. *Management Science, 3*, 70–83.

Kagermann, H., Wahlster, W., & Helbig, J. (2013). *Recommendations for implementing the strategic initiative INDUSTRIE 4.0*. Frankfurt-Main.

Kurzweil, R. (2005). *The singularity is near*. Viking Books.

Kurzweil, R. (2012). *How to create a mind: The secret of human thought revealed*. Viking Books.

Maddison, A. (2010). *World Population, GDP and Per Capita GDP, A.D.1—2003*. www.ggdc.net/maddison

Martino, J. P. (2020). *An introduction to technological forecasting*. Routledge.

McGovern, J., Tyagi, S., Stevens, M., & Mathew, S. (2003). *Java Web services architecture* (1st ed.). Elsevier.

OECD. (2021). *Investment (GFCF) (indicator)*. https://doi.org/10.1787/4537dc58-en

Plakunov, M. K., & Rayackas, R. P. (1984). *Production functions in economic analysis*. Vilnius.

Scheruhn, H.-J., von Rosing, M., & Fallon, R. L. (2015). Information modeling and process modeling. In *The complete business process handbook* (Vol. 1). Elsevier—Morgan Kaufmann.

Solow, M. (1957). Technical change and the aggregate production function. *Review of Economics and Statistics, 39*, 312–320.

Stoleru, L. (1975). *Economic equilibrium and growth*. North-Holland.

Swan, M. (2015). *Blockchain: Blue-print for a new economy*. O'Reilly.

West, M. (2011). *Developing high quality data Models Morgan Kaufmann 2011*. Web browsable version of the HQDM_FRAMEWORK data model.

Yablonsky, A. I. (1986). *Mathematical models in science research*. Publishing House Mysl.

K-Waves and the Innovation-Technological Paradigm of Schumpeter–Mensch–Freeman–Hirooka

Askar Akaev, Tessaleno Devezas, and Andrea Tick

Abstract Kondratiev's long economic cycle has been dubbed one of the most debatable macroeconomic phenomena for over half a century. This paper considers an intrinsic link between Kondratiev's long waves and the Schumpeterian growth paradigm. The research recognizes a significant contribution of such economists as G. Mensch, Ch. Freeman and M. Hirooka in the evolution of the Kondratiev–Schumpeter's theory of innovative cyclical economic development. What is more, this paper thoroughly examines the diffusion of innovations (DOI) theory, together with the Hirooka's innovative paradigm. The research reveals an important role of S. Dubovsky in designing a mathematical procedure used for the assessment of technological capacity. According to the results of the research, Kondratiev–Schumpeter's theory of innovative cyclical economic development can lay a foundation for economists to design comprehensive patterns of economic growth that will address the most recent economic trends. Overall, the underlying idea of this paper is that governments should draw on Kondratiev–Schumpeter's theory while strategizing their long-term economic and financial policies. This is primarily due to the fact that all the parameters of economic trajectory—in disequilibrium within long waves—prove to be reliably predicted and estimated by calculation.

Selected portions of this chapter have appeared previously in Akaev, A. A., & Rudskoi, A. I. (2017). Economic potential of breakthrough technologies and its social consequences. In Devezas, T., Leitão, J., & Sarygulov, A. (Eds.), *Industry 4.0. Studies on entrepreneurship, structural change and industrial dynamics*. Springer. https://doi.org/10.1007/978-3-319-49604-7_2.

A. Akaev
Institute for Mathematical Research of Complex Systems, Lomonosov Moscow State University, Moscow, Russia

T. Devezas (✉)
Atlântica School of Management Sciences, Health, IT & Engineering, Lisbon, Portugal
e-mail: tdevezas@uatlantica.pt

A. Tick
Óbuda University, Budapest, Hungary
e-mail: Tick.Andrea@kgk.uni-obuda.hu

A. Rudskoi et al. (eds.), *Digital Transformation and the World Economy*, Studies on Entrepreneurship, Structural Change and Industrial Dynamics,
https://doi.org/10.1007/978-3-030-89832-8_3

Keywords Long waves · Innovation-technological paradigm · Development strategy

1 Introduction

Public consensus is yet to be built around the macroeconomic phenomenon of Kondratiev's long economic cycle. The debatable character of this phenomenon is reflected in an extensive bibliography, both on the long waves themselves and various theoretical views that either reject or support their existence. The latter viewpoint is represented in the work of Rosenberg and Frischtak (1983), while other researchers doubted the existence of regular long-term economic rhythm due to insufficient proof, in spite of many interesting hypotheses being confirmed (Maddison, 1982). Nonetheless, the interest in the long economic cycle, or the Kondratiev cycle, never faded and was reborn by Sterman, 1985, in another study appealing to the economic crisis of the 1980s. The research largely emphasizes the fact that the very existence of a wide range of self-reinforcing processes, amplifying the inherent economic fluctuations, results in the emergence of a long wave. According to the author, these processes affect many sectors of the economy, including investment, labor market and labor force participation, real interest rate, inflation, debt, savings, consumption rate, and international trade (Sterman, 1985). Perez was the first scientist to observe microelectronics analysis as a tool for estimating the prospects of cutting-edge technologies in terms of facilitating the economy. Based on a long-run analysis of interactions between the technological-economic sphere and the social-institutional structure, Perez reveals a direct link between the long economic cycle and technological progress (Perez, 1985). A later fundamental work by Reijnders, devoted to the history and evolution of long-wave analysis, severely criticized the conventional approach (Reijnders, 1990). Among other works, Kondratiev's theory was supported in a monograph by Freeman and Louçã (2001), on the evolution of economic development in the USA and Europe since 1750 in terms of the long wave theory. This research both heavily criticized macro econometric and cliometric patterns in the history of the economy, and supported a number of approaches outlined in the works of J. Schumpeter and N. Kondratiev (Freeman & Louçã, 2001). Numerous issues related to the Kondratiev cycle were observed in the papers by Silverberg, Atkinson, De Groot, Franses, Gevorkyan, Semmler, and Basu. For instance, problems associated with measuring and modeling long waves in the framework of the general theory of economic dynamics and evolution were investigated in work by Silverberg (2003). Atkinson carried out an analysis of the American economy development over a 150-year period, based on the theory of long waves and its relation to advanced technologies (Atkinson, 2005). The Kondratiev cycle theory has also provided ground for testing the hypothesis of the interrelation between basic innovations and economic growth in modeling cycles of varied duration (De Groot & Franses, 2009). Fundamental mechanisms of economic cycles at different time scales were examined in the work by Bernard et al. (2014), with a particular focus on the theory of long waves. One of the recent studies (Basu, 2016) collected historical data from 20 capitalist countries and confirmed the existence of long waves and phases of their downturn. Among the applied methods of high importance, it is necessary to highlight the wavelet analysis used to detect long-wave models in the global economy based on data on the world GDP growth rate for 1871–2012; as well as the spectral analysis used to assess the interrelation between technological innovations and long waves (Gallegati, 2017; Ozouni et al., 2018). According to the recent studies that claim the rise of the fifth KEC to have occurred in the early 1980s, Kondratiev's theory can also serve as a tool for studying economic crises (Feng, 2018; Tatuzov, 2020).

2 Fundamentals of Kondratiev–Schumpeter's Theory of Innovative Cyclical Economic Development

The theory of long economic cycles, or waves, put forward by the great Russian economist Nikolai Kondratiev was the focus of research in the twentieth century (Kondratiev, 1922, 1935). As early as in the 1920s, Kondratiev looked into the patterns of the world economy development and discovered long cycles of economic growth of around half a century duration, which are called "Kondratiev long economic cycles" (KEC) or "long-wave cycle" (LWC). This paper uses the terms "long-wave cycle" and "Kondratiev long economic cycle" (hereinafter, KEC) as synonyms. Kondratiev identified periods for the first (1780/90–1845/51) and the second (1845/51–1890/96) KECs and assumed that the late 1920s would see a cyclical crisis and depression, which turned out to be confirmed soon in 1920–1930s.

KEC comprises of upturns and downturns, which, for their part, involve the stages of recovery, recession, and depression. Kondratiev comprehensively justified the inherent dependence of economic upturns and their upward stages on the periods of rapid technological development in technological inventions, together with their practical implementation as innovations (innovative products and technologies). According to Kondratiev's theory, the upturn of an upcoming KEC is always preceded by crises, recessions, and depression. Obviously enough, the latter is a two-way street depressing the economy, on the one hand, and stimulating the search for innovations, on the other. This very stage serves as a basis for replacement of obsolete TM, changes in productive assets, improvement of infrastructure and introduction of new technologies and organizational units. And once again, depression is followed by a new KEC.

This relationship is shown in the graph (Fig. 1). It is obvious that technological progress reached its peak in the period from the 1930s to 1960s and then started to decline, which confirms the assumptions made above. Furthermore, we can see that modern industrial society originates from the industrial revolution of the eighteenth

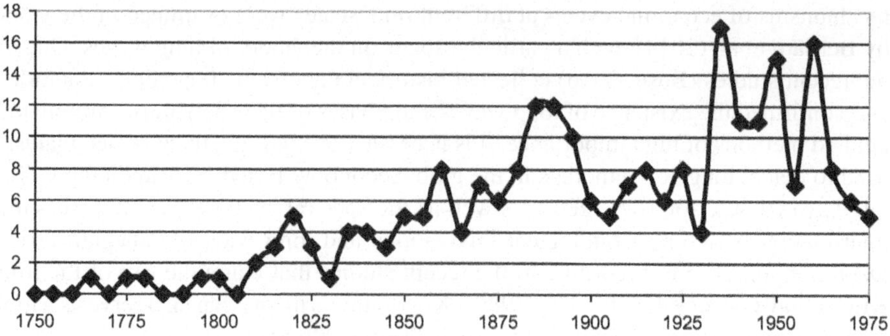

Fig. 1 Technological progress rates (a number of innovations per 5-year period). Source: Silvelberg and Verspagen (2003)

century and five Kondratiev cycles were generated by successive waves of basic innovations, the fourth Kondratiev cycle peaking in (1946–1982).

Kondratiev argued that large cycles are endogenous, i.e., they are inherently typical for the capitalist economy. Significantly enough, Kondratiev was the first to reveal that the wave-like cyclic movements of the economy represent displacement from equilibrium—chased by the capitalist economy. Consequently, a healthy dynamic economy mostly evolves in disequilibrium, whereas classical economic theory claims the opposite. Another brilliant scholar of the twentieth century, J. Schumpeter carried Kondratiev's theory of KEC further and developed an innovative theory of long waves by integrating it into his general innovative theory of economic growth (Schumpeter, 1939). Schumpeter construed cycles as a direct consequence of innovation caused by technological progress, and just like Kondratiev, he considered the cyclical movement as a form of deviation from equilibrium.

It is noteworthy that Schumpeter emphasized that the main force driving the capitalist economy is innovation and entrepreneurship, but not capital in its pure form, as many economists of the time claimed. Schumpeter argued that capital without innovation, initiative, will power, and determination of an entrepreneur is totally powerless and incapable of triggering economic growth. On top of that, Schumpeter believed that spontaneous and haphazard innovations, forming powerful clusters, can cause radical changes in the economy, displacing it from the original equilibrium trajectory, which becomes clearly visible only in stagnation. What is more, the system never returns to its previous state of equilibrium. But another cycle begins, following depression, at a new level of equilibrium.

According to Schumpeter, it is the change in levels of equilibrium that determines the long-term trajectory of economic development and provides the system with dynamic, rather than stationary, equilibrium. Both Kondratiev and Schumpeter recognized three types of equilibrium, and, consequently, three wave-like trends: short-term Kitchin cycles (3–5 years) caused by fluctuations in commodity stocks; medium-term industrial Juglar cycles (7–11 years) and long-term Kondratiev cycles

(30–40 years). As stated by Schumpeter, the superposition of these three waves on the trend trajectory of economic growth provides the overall picture of the market situation within a particular period of time (Schumpeter, 1939).

Schumpeter was the first to assume that innovations are likely to emerge unevenly over time and then spontaneously shape clusters of innovations. Schumpeter distinguished basic and incremental innovations and emphasized the importance of the first in the cyclical dynamics of long waves, considering them the main driving force for the capitalist economy. Due to the fact that the very concept of KEC plays a major role in the innovative theory of Schumpeter, who himself considered KEC the cornerstone of his own theory, we refer to the latter as "Kondratiev–Schumpeter's theory of innovative cyclical economic development."

However, by the time Schumpeter's monograph "Business Cycles" was published in 1939 (Schumpeter, 1939), the developed countries of the West, including the USA, had already adopted the Keynesian doctrine, which encouraged the active involvement of the state in the economy in order to stimulate effective aggregate demand and create favorable conditions for private investors. In such a way, Kondratiev–Schumpeter's theory got outside the mainstream of economics in the middle of the twentieth century.

3 Contribution of Mensch, Freeman, and Hirooka to Kondratiev–Schumpeter's Theory of Innovative Cyclical Economic Development

In 1970–1990 the renewed investigation of KEC provided Kondratiev–Schumpeter's theory with a comprehensive justification, thanks to the work of three outstanding economists of the late twentieth century—G. Mensch (Germany), K. Freeman (England), and M. Hirooka (Japan). Mensch's main achievement was the empirical proof of the fact that a new KEC is launched by self-organized clusters of basic innovations shaped at the depression stage (Mensch, 1979). Mensch dubbed this fact the "trigger effect of depression," meaning that depression incentivizes the innovation process which ensures transition of the economy from stagnation to recovery and then to further dynamic growth. Thereby, Mensch identified the endogenous mechanism of transition from the lowest stage of the cycle—depression to the upward stage—a new KEC. Mensch also determined and justified the endogenous mechanism of the turning point at the peak of the cycle between the upturn and downturn stages, when the existing technologies no longer maintain high rates of economic growth and fail to provide sufficient profit, but, at the same time, new technologies are not yet able to serve as powerful sources of the economic growth. Mensch referred to this situation as "stalemate in technology," implying that it lead to instability and recessions (Mensch, 1979).

Another impressive research was carried out by Freeman, who managed to demonstrate an important role of the innovation diffusion to product markets in the very formation of a cycle. The scholar observed diffusion as a specific mechanism triggering the cycle rise, long enough to cover the entire KEC upturn (Freeman, 1987). Duration of the upturn is determined by the diffusion period, which currently lasts around 20–25 years until the moment when the market is saturated. One more contribution to the Kondratiev–Schumpeter's theory was brought in by Hirooka, who proved the existence of a close correlation between the diffusion of innovations and the upward trends in the KEC. Hirooka was the first to state that diffusion is strictly synchronized with the upward stage of KEC, thus, being completed at the highest peak of the cycle (Hirooka, 2006). While diffusing, all clusters of basic innovations shape new sectors of the economy, mutually reinforcing each other within a particular cluster. Thereby, thanks to the synergistic effect caused by the interaction of innovations within a cluster, powerful cumulative economic growth is being generated.

Among other outstanding achievements, Hirooka also developed an innovation paradigm allowing us to predict the dynamics of emergence and diffusion of innovations in the markets for 20–25 years, even at the very initial stage, when the basic technologies of the future TM are designed (Hirooka, 2006). Moreover, Hirooka analyzed development trajectories of the most promising technologies in the future TM, which have enough potential to form a cluster of basic technologies for the sixth KEC. They include computer technologies, nanotechnologies, biotechnologies and genetic engineering, superconductors and quantum computers, alternative (low-carbon) energy sources, etc. According to Hirooka, all of the abovementioned technologies were commercialized and able to reach their maturity in 2010–2015, which means that during those particular years, the diffusion of innovative products into the markets began, launching the sixth KEC with an upward stage in 2018–2040 (Hirooka, 2006). Hirooka argues that the concept of KEC not only remains valid in the twenty-first century but is even gaining special significance, basically, not without reason, because today, all of Hirooka's predictions are brilliantly confirmed.

Kondratiev–Schumpeter's theory of innovative cyclical economic development is of particular value because it provides an effective mechanism for overcoming the global cyclical crisis and subsequent depression through "launching and stimulating the flow of a new generation of highly efficient basic technological innovations" (Mensch, 1979), in order to replace outdated technologies and forms of production. Significantly enough, this theory, in a certain way, points to the onset of crises and depression and, what is more, implies an innovative paradigm for predicting a new cycle (Hirooka, 2006).

Kondratiev–Schumpeter's theory proved to be highly successful in the 1980s. First of all, at that time, Mensch predicted the cyclical structural crisis of the world economy in the late 1970s at its initial stage. Following this prediction, he correctly identified a peculiar trait of the coming crisis—"stagflation," saying that stagnation would be accompanied by growing prices, i.e., by inflation, and not a decrease—as it used to happen before. Thirdly, Mensch explained that monetary and credit policies were absolutely helpless to pave the way out of the crisis (Mensch, 1979). Consequently, Mensch and other supporters of Kondratiev–Schumpeter's theory suggested mastering new basic innovations based on the achievements of microelectronics and computer science.

In fact, the structural crisis of the world economy in the 1970s, aggravated by oil price shocks, was overcome through a massive transition to energy and resource-saving technologies based on revolutionary tech advances in silicon microelectronics and information technologies (Hirooka, 2006). But even in spite of a number of accomplishments, Kondratiev–Schumpeter's theory once again failed to gain a foothold in the mainstream of economics. This time, scientific leadership was taken over by neoliberals, led by M. Friedman, who was a strong believer in monetary policy as an exclusive tool to suppress inflation. Nonetheless, unfortunate consequences of the neoliberal economic policy were later on fully manifested during the 2008–2009 financial and economic crisis.

4 Diffusion of Innovations and Hirooka's Innovative Paradigm

The process of diffusion of innovations was thoroughly studied by Hirooka (2006), who found that it can be described by Verhulst logistic function:

$$\frac{dy}{dt} = ay(y_0 - y), \tag{1}$$

where y is the demand for the product at the moment t; y_0 is a limit value of the total market; $a$is constant. The solution of this equation is a nonlinear logistic curve described by the equation:

$$y = \frac{y_0}{1 + c\exp\left(-ay_0t\right)}, \quad c = \text{const} \tag{2}$$

In practice, it is customary to express the duration of the innovative product diffusion on the market by the length of time $\Delta\tau$ between $y_{min}/y_0 = 0.1$ and $y_{max}/y_0 = 0.9$, that quite accurately reflects the real-time of diffusion (Hirooka, 2006).

Nonlinear character of the diffusion of innovations (2) implies that every innovation follows the development trajectory that reaches its peak within a specified time span that signals the completion of the life cycle of innovation. This enables us to identify any innovation and determine the temporal segment of its development. M.Hirooka found that the life cycle of innovations reduced gradually: 90 years during the First Industrial Revolution (eighteenth century), and it gradually declined to 25–30 years today.

Some innovations extend beyond one Kondratiev cycle to another, contributing to the emergence of new infrastructures and networks, thereby forming a longer trajectory of development, which M. Hirooka called infratrajectory (e.g., computer in the fourth–fifth KECs). These innovations are referred to as mainstream

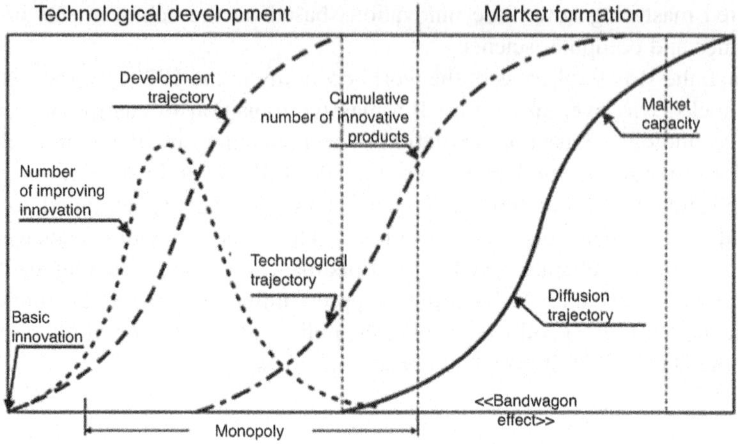

Fig. 2 The structure of innovative paradigm with three trajectories. Source: Hirooka (2006)

innovations; first, they create new markets, and then their wider application contributes to a new infrastructure in the economy. Infratrajectories form particular clusters, each cluster characterized with its core innovation. For example, in the current fifth Kondratiev cycle, such a cluster has been formed by computer technologies. Mainstream innovations also bring about various new applications and institutional changes that contribute to significant market expansion in the subsequent Kondratiev cycle. Mainstream innovations of the forthcoming sixth KEC will be based on information technologies that will form powerful infratrajectories by convergence with nano-, bio-, and cognitive technologies.

M. Hirooka also found that the innovative paradigm consists of three logistic trajectories (Fig. 2): technology, development, and diffusion (Hirooka, 2006). Technological trajectory is a set of "core" technologies relevant to the innovation that emerged as a result of some significant technological invention or scientific discovery. The trajectory of development (development of innovation) is a range of innovative products put out through the application of "core" technologies. The trajectory of development plays an essential role in the innovation paradigm, because it transmits technological knowledge from academic institutions to industries, which results in the establishment of venture enterprises aimed at the industrial development of an innovative product and its marketing. There are more opportunities for venture enterprises in the first 10–15 years of the first half of the development trajectory, since the intensive marketing of the innovative product starts soon after the completion of the technological trajectory and lasts about 25–30 years before the market is saturated.

M. Hirooka was the first to study the trajectory of technology. He showed that it is described by the logistic curve and lasts about 30 years, beginning with some significant discoveries or technological inventions. Hence, the innovative paradigm has a cascade structure with three logistic trajectories spaced from each other at a certain distance that is determined empirically. Thus, the innovation paradigm

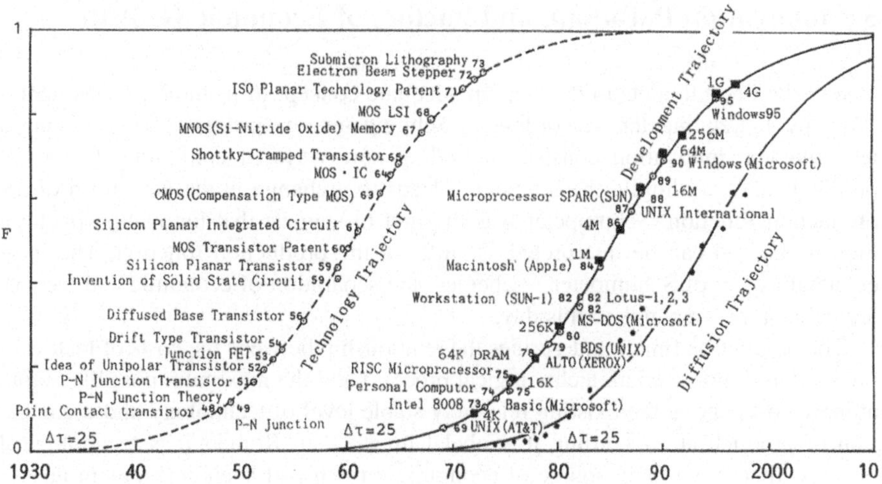

Fig. 3 Innovation paradigm of electronics. Source: Hirooka (2006)

enables us to accurately predict the trajectory of the innovative products diffusion on the market relying on a predetermined trajectory of technology (Fig. 3), which is exemplified by electronics (Hirooka, 2006). Since the latter is 25–30 years ahead of the former, it can easily be built before new products are launched into the market.

Figure 3 shows that the microelectronics technology started in 1948, with the creation of a semiconductor electronic device—the first transistor (J. Bardeen, W. Brattein, W.Shockly), and 25 years later, in 1973, it ended up developing the technology of submicron lithography (IBM) which enables creating integrated microcircuits (microchips) consisting of dozen and hundred millions of transistors. In addition, in 1973, Intel Corporation invented the world's first microprocessor—the Intel 4004—comprised of 2300 transistors on a single silicon crystal. Then in 1974, the world saw the greater Intel-8008 microprocessor with 256 bytes of RAM capable of executing 75 different commands. Consequently, this processor resulted in the first PC. Two years later (1976), S. Wozniak and S. Jobs created the famous Apple—the first Personal Computer produced on a global scale (1977–1978). Thus, we are aware that within 30 years from the emergence of basic technology, innovative products have built new markets.

Thus, Hirooka analyzed the development trajectories of the most prospective technologies of the future, which are likely to form a technological cluster of the upcoming sixth Kondratiev cycle: multimedia, nanotechnology, biotechnology, genetic engineering and regeneration of human organs, superconductors, and quantum computers. He built development trajectories for all these technologies and found that all of them will reach the peak in 2010–2015, which implies their intensive diffusion in the market and the start of the upcoming sixth Kondratiev cycle with the rising wave in 2020–2030.

5 Innovation Paradigm and Factors of Economic Growth

One of the first attempts to develop an adequate concept of technology was undertaken by J. Schumpeter. According to Schumpeter, the process of introducing a technological innovation consists in finding new ways of combining factors of production. Accordingly, the innovation leads to a change in the very form of the production function. Schumpeter was the first to suggest that innovation (technological change) can be interpreted as shifts in the production function. The most essential aspect of Schumpeter's scheme—the separation of economic and technological factors—remains to this day.

The production function describes the relationship between the costs of factors of production (labor, capital, technological process) and the maximum possible output at these costs and at the existing relatively stable level of technology and organization of production. According to Nobel laureate Paul Romer, it is technological progress that is the main source of economic growth and is endogenous in nature, and its acceleration is facilitated by the development of markets (Romer, 1990). Technological progress is an independent factor of production and should be taken into consideration in the production function along with other factors.

M. Brown quite rightly argues, "the relationship between output and costs, and between costs themselves, is determined by the technology that prevails in a given period. Technology is embodied in the production function" (Brown, 1966). Kondratiev and Schumpeter were the first to raise the question of the role of scientific and technological progress in long-term economic development; they also drew attention to the problem of uneven technological progress. In the 40s and 50s, these ideas were put aside—to the forefront came the concept of economic growth, in which technological progress was seen as an important but sustainable factor of development.

Solow and his followers assumed that technological progress develops uniformly at a constant rate. It should be noted that in the middle of the last century, this assumption was fulfilled for quite a long time. In this regard, Jan Tinbergen proposed to write the production function in the following form (Tinbergen & Bos, 1962):

$$Y = A_0 e^{q_A t} K^{\alpha} L^{1-\alpha} \tag{3}$$

However, this contradicted Schumpeter's postulate of an uneven, moreover cyclical development of the innovation and technological process. Supporters of Solow and Tinbergen soon discovered this. Therefore, PF in the form by Tinbergen (3) was further used as an approximate PF, satisfactorily describing the dynamics of real GDP over a certain limited time interval, where $q_A \cong const.$

Time periods within which the parameters of the production function remain unchanged are called technologically homogeneous periods. Identifying technologically homogeneous periods is a rather complex econometric problem. Brown and De Cani developed a procedure for consistent identification of technologically

Table 1 Technologically homogeneous periods for the US economy

1	2	3	4
1890–1906	1907–1920	1921–1939	1940–1960

homogeneous periods and identified such periods for the US economy from 1890 to 1960 (Brown, 1966). They are presented in Table 1.

It should be noted that these periods coincide with the upward (2 and 4) and downward (1 and 3) stages of the Kondratiev cycles.

Thus, dynamization of the Cobb-Douglas production function carried out by Solow (1957) and Tinbergen allowed estimating the value of the intensive growth component equated to the difference between the growth rate of production output and the weighted average sum of the growth rates of labor and capital. This estimate of the contribution of scientific, technological, and organizational progress to economic growth is called the "residual" because the value of the resulting variable, in addition to the intensive component of growth, reflects the imperfection of measurements of output and resources used in production. The "Solow residual" was accepted in official statistics and began to be calculated as an indicator of total factor productivity.

However, already in the 1960s, the idea of uneven technological progress once again gained some popularity, mainly due to the works of Schmookler (1972). The decline in the rate of economic growth in the 1970s stimulated the search for a connection between this phenomenon and long cycles. More and more attention was paid to the problem of uneven economic development over time and to the alternation of periods of high and low economic growth rates.

Unsteady scientific and technological progress in global modeling was studied in detail by Sergei Dubovsky in a series of his works (1989). He also developed a mathematical apparatus for analyzing the unsteady dynamics of STP and obtained an equation linking the rate of average technological level (*A*) with the rate of capital renewal (*I*/*K*) and the efficiency of new technologies (*a*/*A*):

$$q_A = \frac{\dot{A}}{A} = \frac{I}{K}\left(\frac{a}{A} - 1\right), \tag{4}$$

where *I*(*t*)is the movement of investment into fixed (physical) capital; *a*(*t*)is the level of successive technological innovations.

Since Dubovsky's formula (4) has important practical applications, its derivation is given below (1989).

6 Modeling the Technological Level of Production Potential

From the set of economic macro indicators that characterize an economic system, we can distinguish two subsets: absolute indicators (GDP, physical capital, working capital, the number of employees, etc.) and specific indicators (productivity, capital-labor ratio, power available per worker, resource costs per unit of final products, etc.). If the first group of indicators characterizes the scale of development of the object (quantitative level), part of the indicators of the second group characterizes the technological level of development of the system (qualitative level). Macro indicators of the second group are the averaged characteristics of new technologies, which are recognized as effective for implementation.

Theoretical birth of technology is the moment of its generation by scientific research potential, and the operational birth is the moment of its implementation in production funds. If we count the productive age of technology from its second birth, it coincides with the age of production funds, so to solve the problem, it is necessary to use the distribution of production funds by age.

This distribution is described by the following relations (Dubovsky, 1988, p.9):

$$\begin{aligned} \frac{\partial \rho}{\partial t} + \frac{\partial \rho}{\partial \tau} &= -\mu(t,\tau)\rho \\ \rho(t_0,\tau) &= \rho_0(\tau); \\ \rho(t,0) &= I(t), \end{aligned} \tag{5}$$

Where t is the current time; τ is the age of the funds; $\rho(t, \tau)$ is distribution of the funds by age; $\rho_0(\tau)$ is distribution of the funds by age at the initial given time t_0 (given function); $I(t)$ is introduction of new funds at time t (given function); $\mu(t, \tau)$ is the coefficient of disposal of the funds (given function).

If we take $\mu(t, \tau) = \mu(t)a$ then at $\rho(t, \infty) = 0$ the well-known equation for fixed capital $K(t) = \int_0^\infty \rho(t,\tau)d\tau$ follows from (1.2.1):

$$\dot{K}(t) = I(t) - \mu(t,\tau)K(t). \tag{6}$$

Let us denote any of the indicators of the technological level of an economic system with different-age funds and technologies as $a(t - \tau)$. If distribution of funds by age is given by function $\rho(t, \tau)$ then by definition the average technological level of an economic object (system) with capital $K(t)$ is given by the expression:

$$A(t) = \int_0^\infty \frac{\rho(t,\tau)a(t-\tau)}{K(t)} d\tau. \tag{7}$$

Differentiating this expression over time, taking into consideration the equality $\partial a/\partial t = -\partial a/\partial \tau$ and relations (5) and (6), we obtain the following Eq. from (7):

$$\frac{\dot{A}(t)}{A(t)} = \frac{I(t)}{K(t)} \times \frac{a(t-0) - A(t)}{A(t)}, \tag{8}$$

where all the terms of the equation make clear economic sense: $\dot{A}/A$ is the growth rate of the average technological level of the entire economic system, I/K is the rate of renewal of production potential (fund); $\{a(t-0) - A(t)\}/A(t)$ is the relative excess of the newest technological level $a(t-0)$ over the average technological level $A(t)$, i.e., the quality of the newest technology. This expression is the sought Dubovsky formula (4).

So, Eq. (8) is a formal description of the fact that the rate of STP, measured as the growth rate of macro indicators of the technological level, is determined by the rate of renewal of production potential and the relative economic efficiency of newly introduced technologies.

7 Technological Progress and Economic Growth

According to the macroeconomic description by means of the production function, it is shown (Dubovsky, 1984, p.40) that:

$$\text{a)}\ \frac{\partial Y}{\partial K} = (1-\alpha)\frac{Y}{K};\quad \text{b)}\ \frac{\partial Y}{\partial A} = \frac{Y}{A};\quad \text{c)}\ \frac{\partial Y}{\partial L} = \alpha\frac{Y}{L} \tag{9}$$

Here α is the share of labor remuneration in the final product. The following hypotheses were accepted:

1. The amount of labor resources is determined by the condition of profit maximization.
2. For Hicks-neutral technical progress, the hypothesis of linear homogeneity is accepted (9 b).
3. For Harrod-neutral technical progress (labor-saving), it is accepted that $Y = \frac{\partial Y}{\partial A}A + \frac{\partial Y}{\partial K}K$

Equations (9) are equivalent to the Pfaffian equation under hypothesis 2:

$$\frac{dY}{Y} = (1-\alpha)\frac{dK}{K} + \alpha\frac{dL}{L} + \frac{dA}{A}. \tag{10}$$

This equation at $u_L = const$ has the first integral in the form of the well-known Cobb-Douglas PF with a Hicks-neutral technical process:

$$\frac{Y}{Y_0} = \left(\frac{K}{K_0}\right)^{1-\alpha}\left(\frac{L}{L_0}\right)^{\alpha}\frac{A}{A_0} \tag{11}$$

If we accept hypothesis 3, we get the equation:

$$\frac{dY}{Y} = (1-\alpha)\frac{dK}{K} + \alpha\frac{dL}{L} + \alpha\frac{dA}{A}, \tag{12}$$

having at $\alpha = const$ the first integral in the form of a PF with a labor-saving TP

$$\frac{Y}{Y_0} = \left(\frac{K}{K_0}\right)^{1-\alpha}\left(\frac{L}{L_0}\frac{A}{A_0}\right)^{\alpha} \tag{13}$$

Equations (10) and (12) allow giving an economic interpretation of the technological level indicator A. When $Y/K = \text{const}$, i.e., during the development regime with constant return on funds (return on capital) from Eqs. (10) and (12), we get the following expressions for the growth rate of the technological level:

$$\text{a)} \quad \frac{\dot{A}}{A} = \alpha\left(\frac{\dot{Y}}{Y} - \frac{\dot{L}}{L}\right); \quad \text{c)} \quad \frac{\dot{A}}{A} = \frac{\dot{Y}}{Y} - \frac{\dot{L}}{L}. \tag{14}$$

In the second case, the rate is higher. Both variants are true for unchanged conditions of economic development. Simple estimation formulas for the rate of economic growth follow directly from here:

$$\text{a)} \quad q_Y^{(1)} = \frac{\dot{Y}}{A} = \frac{1}{\alpha} \times \frac{\dot{A}}{A} + \frac{\dot{L}}{L}; \quad \text{c)} \quad q_Y^{(2)} = \frac{\dot{Y}}{Y} = \frac{\dot{A}}{A} + \frac{\dot{L}}{L}; \tag{15}$$

Since the future digital economy will have a low or even negative job growth rate, the growth rate of the economy, according to formulas (15) will be mainly determined by the rate of technological progress.

The countries with the highest rates of STP tend to have the highest rates of economic growth. It would seem that the spread of technology around the world should lead to a leveling off TP rates, but this is prevented by the strong differentiation of countries in terms of the capital-labor ratio. Technologies developed in developed countries are oriented, as a rule, to the high cost of jobs and high professional level of the workforce. These technologies cannot be massively used in countries with a 15–20-fold lag in terms of capital. Therefore, programs focused on affordable capital-labor ratios are of great importance for developing countries.

Due to the synergistic effect of multiple innovative paradigms in a large innovation cluster, the prosperity of developed countries has grown exponentially. GNP in the US has increased 30-fold over the past 100 years, and in Japan 80-fold. Energy consumption also grew proportionally. The cumulative growth of innovation and the effect of its synergy is the most important proof that the innovation process is the main engine of economic development. No other interpretation is able to assess the cumulative contribution to the cause of constant economic growth. Briefly, the interrelated emergence of clusters of innovations is the true cause of the great Kondratiev cycles.

Innovations are conceived in developed countries, pushing them to an even higher level of development. Developing countries, using old technology, manufacture products of lower quality. Taking advantage of the available innovations, developing countries reach the same level of technology and start exporting their products. There is a competition between developing and developed countries, that is, a struggle to reduce costs and improve quality. This is the situation concerning the innovation paradigm, in terms of international STP. As innovation develops, the relationship between the inventor country and the countries that use that innovation changes. This is because countries that imported foreign technology had lower labor costs, such as China. Therefore, individual countries can turn from developing to advanced vanguard countries through successful borrowing and effective use of advanced technological innovations. This requires the development of the economy based on innovation at an annual rate of about 8–10% within two or three decades. A number of countries, including Japan, South Korea, Singapore, Malaysia, and finally China, followed this path in the twentieth century.

8 Long Waves and Innovation Paradigms: Practice of Economic Development

Actually, the economic slowdown coincides with the decrease in the number and effectiveness of innovative technologies, which is confirmed by the reduced share of gross investment in the world GDP (Fig. 4) over the period of 1965–2005, as well as the lower effectiveness of macroeconomic investment measured in US dollar GDP

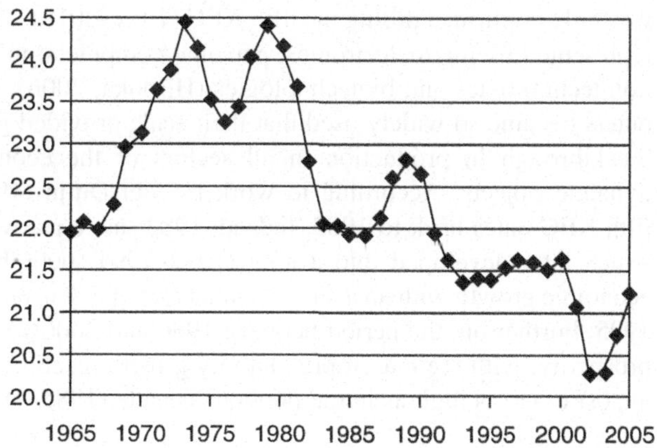

Fig. 4 Dynamics of gross fixed investments (% world GDP). Authors' creation based on World Bank data (2010)

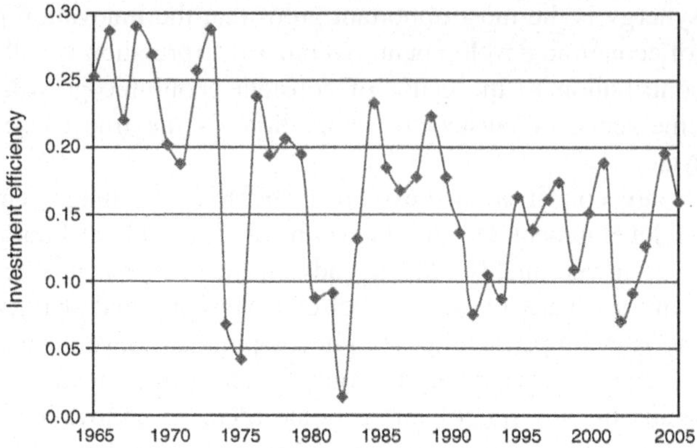

Fig. 5 Dynamics of investment efficiency, USD/USD. Authors' creation based on World Bank data (2010)

growth to US dollar investment (Fig. 5). At the beginning of the fifth Kondratiev cycle (1980s), the world entered the information age that will reach its peak by the end of the sixth Kondratiev cycle (about 2050). Perhaps then there will be a new technological revolution with breakthrough innovations (Yakovets, 2004), which may start a new era of long-term technological and economic growth, likewise the one seen in the middle of the twentieth century.

The rising cycle stage covers a period of the long-term (20–25 years) prevalence of active market when it develops dynamically and successfully overcomes minor recessions. The downward cycle stage implies the period of the low economy (10–12 years—duration reduced in the twentieth century), characterized by sluggish economic activity and depression, despite local upswings. As a result, the world economy develops erratically, regularly falling into deep crises. That is due to the fact that the commercial potential of current innovations gets exhausted, and entrepreneurs start losing profits.

Kondratiev–Schumpeter's theory of innovative cyclical economic development was fully confirmed during the fifth KEC (1982–2018). The core of the fifth TM was represented by microelectronics, personal computers, information and communication technologies and biotechnologies (Hirooka, 2006). Microprocessors and computers became so widely used that their scale provided grounds for a technological breakthrough in production in all sectors of the economy and management of dynamic objects. According to work by van Duijn (1983), the beginning of the fifth KEC dates back to 1982. Indeed, 1982 saw a recovery in the world economy, which later developed into a long (1982–1994) period of stable and fairly rapid economic growth with an average annual rate of 3.4%, ending with a slight decline in 1995. Further on, the period between 1996 and 2006 was characterized by genuine prosperity, with the rate of productivity growth reaching 2.8% per year, which was almost twice as high as in the previous decade (1985–1995).

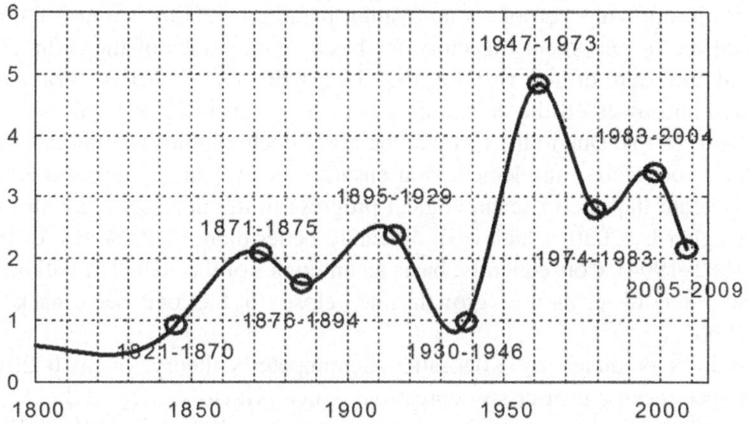

Fig. 6 Dynamics of relative annual average growth rate of the world GDP, 1800–2009 (%). Authors' creation based on World Bank data (2010)

Undoubtedly, these achievements resulted from the widespread use of ICTs as well as an unprecedented surge in investments. This explains the phenomenon of spikes in the labor productivity growth of the late 1990s in the developed countries. In early twenty-first century, the global market for ICT products exceeded 1 trillion US dollars. At that point, developed countries started talking about the birth of a new "knowledge economy." However, by the mid-2000s, productivity growth triggered by ICT came to its end. According to Mensch, this meant that the fifth KEC had reached its peak, which required a new search for innovations and next-generation products. In 2006–2007, the OECD countries started to experience a decline in economic growth, which marked the transition from upward trend of the fifth KEC to the downward one. Thus, 2004–2006 became the peak turning point for the fifth KEC. As expected, the period of the upward trend of the fifth KEC amounted to 22–24 years (1982–2006).

Less than 3 years later, an unexpected financial and economic crisis of 2008–2009 hit the world. The severity of the crisis greatly resembled the one of 1929 that preceded the Great Depression in the 1930s, and therefore was called the "Great Recession." As suggested in the paper (Akaev et al., 2011), global cyclical financial and economic crises are typically presaged by the explosive growth of prices for such highly liquid commodities as oil and gold. Additionally, the paper referred to above provides a nonlinear dynamic model for predicting the specific time of a crisis. Using this model, we successfully predicted the date of the second wave for the global financial crisis 9 months before it actually broke out on August 4, 2011, with an error of only two weeks. Apart from that, we demonstrated that the crisis of 2008–2009 could have also been predicted in advance. Fluctuations described above are clearly visible in the dynamics of the relative average world GDP growth rate per year (Fig. 6), which correlates well with the rates of technological growth over the same period (Fig. 1).

Later on, applying Hirooka's innovation paradigm (2006), we also thoroughly described the development trajectory for basic technologies of the sixth TM, and predicted the start of the rise for the sixth KEC (2017–2018). Moreover, we calculated and assessed the economic potential of the NBIC technologies (Akaev & Rudskoi, 2015). Due to the fact that the NBIC-technologies are mutually convergent, their cooperative implementation ensures a significant synergistic effect that will accelerate the rate of technological progress in the developed countries up to 3%, or higher by 2030, which is significantly better than the 2.3% rate of the fifth KEC (1982–1994). Consequently, basic technologies of the sixth TM will be able to provide a record economic growth rate, close to the one seen back in the 1950–1960s.

Indeed, as predicted by Kondratiev–Schumpeter's theory, in 2010–2016, the world experienced a post-crisis depression, which primarily affected the developed countries. The global economic recession reached its bottom in 2013–2014, then entering the recovery associated with the development of innovative products based on NBIC and other digital derivatives. As a result, 2017 was marked by the synchronized growth of the world's leading economies. According to the IMF, in 2017 all eight of the world's largest economies (USA, China, Japan, Germany, India, Russia, France, and the UK) grew by more than 1.5% (IMF, 2018). In general, the global economy also grew by 3.8% in 2017, in comparison with 3.2% in 2016. Later on, 2018 witnessed the synchronized growth of GDP in almost all 45 countries monitored by the OECD. As the IMF states, this happened twice in the last 40 years, and previously the periods of such synchronized growth used to last several years. For instance, the world economy grew at the rate of 4% annually in 1984–1989 and 2004–2007, i.e., at the very start of the upturn and at the peak of the upward trend in the fifth KEC. Obviously enough, since 2018, we have been observing the rise of the sixth KEC, which is expected to last approximately thirty years.

Overall, these ideas raise the following question: will the current synchronized growth in developed economies be stable over the medium term? Back in their classic works, Kondratiev and Schumpeter noted that the economic growth in the initial recovery of the KEC is highly susceptible to various risks that make the situation increasingly unstable. As a result, many scholars recommended governments to assist entrepreneurs in order to settle the situation down actively. Among major impediments to sustainable economic recovery, it is crucial to distinguish: huge accumulated debt of governments, households, corporate, and financial sectors; widening gap between the real economy and the financial sector; accelerating growth of excessive income inequality; acute lack of consumer demand; instability of financial system; heightened protectionism from developed countries, resulting in trade wars and severe environmental threats. What makes the solution more difficult to develop is the fact that in can only be done through joint effort, for example, at the G20 summits. Unfortunately, this time the parties involved are less eager to collaborate, unlike back in 2008–2009, when the G20 countries successfully cooperated their efforts, thereby preventing devastating financial consequences. But today, constructive cooperation between the G20 member-states in hindered by numerous trade and ideological conflicts. Therefore, the rise of the sixth KEC is expected to be highly unstable and may be interrupted by minor recessions, although not as severe ones as the 2009 "Great Recession."

Nonetheless, in terms of new TM, the positive contribution of the Covid pandemic should not be neglected. The pandemic exposed major existing shortcomings in many areas of public life and, particularly in public administration and healthcare. What is even more important, it triggered the launch of innovative technologies of the Fourth Industrial Revolution—the function previously performed by wars and conflicts. The entire past decade has been marked by vast debate over the issues associated with digitalization of economy and management, transition to a flexible working week, and partly to remote work, active use of telemedicine in healthcare, big data and AI in diagnosing and prescribing, etc. Then, the pandemic did break out, literally forcing the implementation of these ideas into practice and leaving no alternative to either governments or the private sector. In a close to wartime conditions, many fundamental changes have become feasible, and the widespread use of digital technologies has begun.

According to Kondratiev–Schumpeter's theory, the sixth KEC rise in the 2020s will result from the diffusion of innovative technologies and products of the Fourth Industrial Revolution into the economy (Schwab, 2016; Schwab & Davis, 2018) in the face of exacerbating disequilibrium and unstable economic growth. Consequently, the economic policy of states should promote the wide implementation of innovations in the economy and maintain dynamic stability at high growth rates. Transition to a new TM requires large-scale investments in fixed production capital, as well as in innovative technologies and modernization of the economy based on IT. Despite the fact that private investment is a direct driver of the economic growth and job creation, the most enabling environment is created by public investment in the public sector, in particular, in education and new infrastructure. Investment in education is a top priority here because successful development and commercialization of IT products of the sixth TM are impossible without specialists that are possessed of adequate competencies and digital skills.

When it comes to developing countries, they should first and foremost strengthen their ICT infrastructure dynamically. ICTs accelerate the emergence of innovative goods and services based on the NBIC technologies, as well as encourage the development, production, and marketing of digital technologies. The fifth KEC had already witnessed the ICT revolution, when the Internet took its leading role as a key technology of the information era and a major factor in increasing productivity and competitiveness, thereby, allowing the spread of new networks in business. ICTs are now becoming the backbone infrastructure technologies linking the fifth (1982–2018) and the sixth KEC (2018–2050) in the global economy (Hirooka, 2006). In their turn, NBIC technologies revolutionize ICTs by greatly increasing their productivity. Countries with a highly developed ICT infrastructure show higher economic growth rates, which leads to a conclusion that the role of ICTs will keep on gaining particular significance in the next decade.

9 A Rising Phase of Kondratiev's Sixth Long Wave: Mainstream Innovations and Technological Convergence

Using Hirooka's innovation paradigm (Fig. 7), we will try to forecast the beginning of the rising phase of Kondratiev's sixth Economic Cycle (KEC). We definitely know the beginning of the development trajectory of nanotechnologies: 1985 marked the discovery and synthesis of fullerenes, which are carbon compounds C_{60} composed of 60 carbon atoms in the form of a hollow sphere, and is considered to be the first nanostructure. 1986 is when the atomic force microscope (AFM) was invented. AFM enables imaging and manipulating single atoms. AFM is the main tool for creating new nanostructures and their measurements (Williams & Adams, 2007). Leading countries did their best in the abovementioned areas and showed enormous achievements. E.g., in the area of creating new nanostructures only carbon-related achievements are the following: 1991 marked the discovery of carbon nanotubes with the great potential for a number of industries; 2004 marked the discovery of graphene, a one-atom-thick carbon film, likely to be a mostly prospective material for nanoelectronics. As a whole, nanomaterials, or smart materials, with their unique properties can be used in almost every sphere of human activity, bringing about innovations and breakthroughs (Rudskoy, 2007).

Besides, nanotools constantly evolved and progressed, resulting into the invention of such essential nanotools as computerized scanning probe microscopes (SPM) for high-precision online imaging and manipulating nanoparticles; optical tweezers for three-dimensional picking up and manipulating nanostructures. Nanomanipulators with piezoelectric motors enable smooth, controllable manipulations in any directions. Summing up, we can argue that nanotools have reached perfection and revealed great opportunities for researchers and scientists to create new nanostructures, measure their properties, find new practical applications. The industrial application of nanotools contributes to producing nanoparticles and nanomaterials in amounts that could satisfy the market demand (Williams & Adams, 2007).

Thus, it is obvious that nanotechnologies (nanomaterials and nanotools) are successfully evolving. According to Hirooka's innovation paradigm, the trajectory will reach saturation approximately in 2016 (30 years after AFM invention in 1986) and shortly afterward the technological trajectory will result in the large-scale diffusion of innovation nanoproducts onto markets. This will lead to the economic upturn in the developed countries and later the global economy. The paper (Akaev et al., 2009) confirms on the basis of the Schumpeter–Kondratiev theory of innovative cyclical economic development that the current slowdown will be prolonged and last till 2017–2018, when the rising phase of the sixth KEC starts.

A new innovation paradigm contributes to developing innovative products and establishing new industries. However, it is extremely important to provide a stream of innovations into existing industries, which will increase the added cost in these industries and ensure higher productivity throughout the economy. The transition of technologies from new industries to conventional ones results in the convergence of technologies and the evolution of innovation paradigms. Hence we can identify two directions in the development of major innovations. The first is the establishment of a new industry to produce innovative products. The second is the penetration into the conventional industries, which triggers the increase in productivity and the invention of new products through technological convergence. Innovations ensure considerable economic growth in case they are universal and permeate a lot of economic areas. During the fourth and the fifth Kondratiev cycles, such a universal innovation were computers and electronics (microprocessors). The most outstanding example is the convergence of electronics and metal-cutting machines, which has led to the invention of high-precision efficient CNC metal-cutting machines.

It should be noted that the automobile industry was significantly improved by the adoption of electronics. Electronic components are used in today's cars to check engines, control driving etc. Generally, microprocessors have revolutionized production technology in all industries ranging from metal-cutting machines to cars and planes. The first microprocessor Intel 8088, launched in 1973, was a simple modified chip that can be regarded as a "founding father" of the Information Era based on extremely powerful and cheap microelectronics. Intel 8088 was the foundation for the first commercial IBM PC in 1981. The technological convergence of computers with the industries of steel, cement, chemicals resulted into a quality leap in these industries. Thus, innovations will embrace the whole economy and its institutions via mechanisms of converging technologies and institutional changes. It is important that institutions should meet the tasks at every stage. Accordingly, the usage of major technologies of the sixth KEC in the conventional industries shall be the center of attention, and the stimulation of this process shall be a priority. Today the usage of nanotechnologies is limited to household, medical, agricultural, and power engineering areas, i.e., conventional industries.

The fruitful convergence of technologies in the sixth KEC can be exemplified by the convergence of NBIC technologies with the technologies of 3D printing. The latter, known as additive manufacturing, has revolutionized manufacturing, technology, design, medicine, because this process is cheap, user-friendly, environmentally friendly and waste-free. 3D printing is widely used in the production of supporting elements for planes, major parts for spacecraft engines. NASA experts predict that in the near future, it will be possible to apply 3D printing in weightlessness using robotic spiders for building structures of dozens of meters in diameter and hundreds of meters in length. Raw materials for 3D printing can include a variety of powders, fibers, minerals, and other materials. In a short time, we will see amazing uses of 3D printing in medicine: printing human organs, intervertebral cartilage printing, remodeling injured bones etc. Using unique properties of NBIC technologies will allow establishing 3D industry that is able to manufacture diverse customized and personalized products. Moreover, diversification of products is a prerequisite for sustainable economic development.

As it was mentioned before, computers became the mainstream innovation as early as the fourth KEC, bringing to life the digital world, software, microelectronics, Internet, multimedia etc., which interact, strengthen, and enrich each other. All the above-listed is the foundation for the area of information and communication

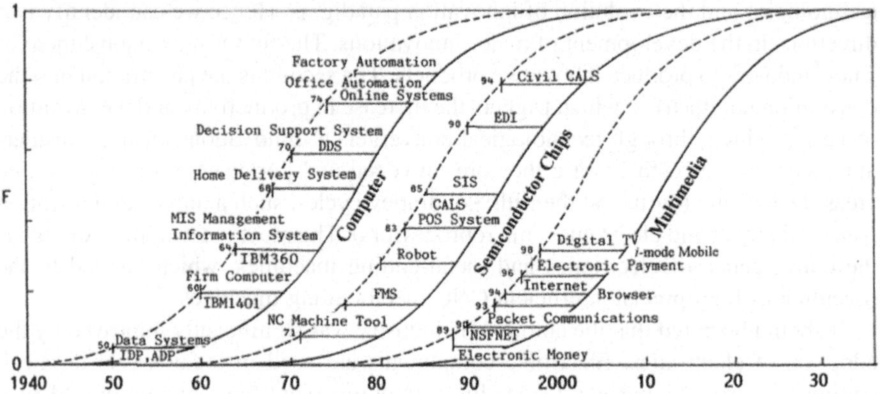

Fig. 7 Development of information technologies. Source: Hirooka (2006)

technologies (ICT). M. Hirooka calculated and built the ICT innovation paradigm that is shown in Fig. 7 (Hirooka, 2006). ICT—the greatest achievement of the twentieth century—is one of the major resources for economic development in the twenty-first century. In the early twenty-first century, the global ICT market exceeded \$1 trillion with steady growth within the boundaries 10% per year. These growth rates for this market are expected to be maintained at least till 2020. As Fig. 7 shows, their life cycle will continue till the 2030s. That will be the time when NBIC technologies will have reached a peak.

Information and communication technologies are getting mainstream technologies, infratrajectories that connect the fifth and sixth technological modes, fifth, and sixth KEC in the global economy. ICT transform traditional technologies not only by changing their properties, but also completely modifying them. This is related to unlimited opportunities that ICT provide to process large arrays of information using the most powerful supercomputers and relevant software. These are the computer technologies that have contributed to the success of genetic engineering, which has revolutionized agriculture.

The information technological revolution has occurred. Computer technologies have transformed telecommunications. The Internet and networks have become the backbone of today's global society. The Internet is not only a current technological innovation, and it is a key technology of the Information Age. The Internet has become a fundamental factor for the increase in productivity and competitiveness, which enables setting up new network businesses, hereby establishing a new form of economy. Using the Internet by private companies has become common in OECD countries, e.g., in 25 countries, over 89% of companies have access to the Internet and more than a half of them their own websites. Highly developed countries have recently charted their course toward the Intelligent Internet of Things, based on Wi-Fi protocol and promotion of the mobile Internet.

Due to the innovation breakthrough in 1980s–1990s, information economic and technological indicators became dominant, and the developed world moved into the post-industrial era. According to the economists (Jorgenson & Motohashi, 2005), ICT made a contribution to the 20–40% growth of GDP in the developed countries in the middle 2000s, with ICT amounting to 70–80% in the positive dynamics of the aggregate factor productivity. Annual ICT costs rose by 5–6% throughout the world. ICT costs reach 9–20% in companies' revenues and account for 5% of their capital. ICT costs in the GDP amount to 7–10% for the developed countries (Sweden—9%, Great Britain—8%, USA—8%, Japan—7%), the developing countries have less percentage (India–3%, Brazil—5.5%, Russia—3%).

In the general opinion, as it was stated in the introduction, the economic impact of ICT use is determined by not only investments in ICT, but by investments in the ICT-related system of complementary assets, namely in the formation of the respective organizational and human capital. Actually, the comprehensive survey undertaken by Bresnahan, Brynjolfsson and Hitt found evidence for complementarity between ICT, on the one hand, and organizational capital, human capital and product innovations, on the other hand (Bresnahan et al., 2002).

Investments in ICT products and services lead to capital deepening with higher labor productivity. However, this is not typical for every country. The comprehensive empirical research, conducted by the Economist Intelligence Unit, showed that ICT could contribute to the economic growth only in the case of reaching a certain vantage point (EIU, 2003), i.e., ICT had to reach a critical amount before making a significant impact on the country's economy. Therefore, countries with highly developed ICT infrastructure tend to experience faster economic growth. Among these countries are Scandinavian countries—Denmark, Norway, Finland, and Sweden. They are the countries which showed the greatest contribution to the rise in labor productivity from 1996 to 2006. Countries, especially developing ones, with ICT development indices lower than the vantage point have either zero ICT effect or a negative effect.

Today it is obvious that ICT play a dominant role in a new Kondratiev economic wave and higher economic growth rates, followed by achievements in nanotechnologies, biotechnologies, genetic engineering, creation of new materials, adoption of alternative energy sources and aerospace engineering. ICT provide the growth in creating innovative products and services based on NBIC technologies in their manufacturing and selling. Using ICT, the developed countries aspire to ensure high automation and optimization of manufacturing processes to reduce power and material consumption. The most outstanding achievements in this sphere belong to USA. Compared to 1997, the consumption of power in mechanical engineering halved in 2003. Within the same period in the processing industry, this indicator reduced by a third, whereas the US GDP reduced by 15%. The consumption of materials in the same period in mechanical engineering decreased by 25%, in the processing industry—by 20%, GDP went down by 10% (Survey of Current Business, 2005, pp. 51–57).

ICT speed up economic development, as countries tend to get integrated into the global economy, which results in the increase in living standards and economic activity of the population. ICT can help developing countries to improve accessibility and quality of education, to accelerate the usage of scientific, technological, and organizational achievements accumulated in the developed countries. However, first of all, the developing countries should develop their ICT infrastructure in order to reach the vantage point that leads to economic growth, technology borrowing and usage of NBIC technologies and innovative products.

10 Conclusion

Recession periods cause an interest in those theories which are not mainstream ones and are not supported by most economists. This is relevant to the report to the Club of Rome published in 2008 (von WeiZsäcker et al., 2008), which was continued in the book (Füchs, 2016). The newly published book assumes that the next Kondratiev wave will be a green wave, and "digitization in combination with AI will play a key role in the transition to the GreenGrowth—ecologically sustainable economic development" based on smart logistics, smart cities, smart energy, smart agriculture and smart things (Naumer, 2020). We expect Kondratiev–Schumpeter's theory, as one that provides the most adequate description of non-equilibrium and uneven cyclical economic development, to be the mainstream economic theory and to become the foundation for the real-world economic policy conducted by target governments. We do not contrast Kondratiev–Schumpeter's theory and other economic theories—Neo-Keynesianism, Neoclassical synthesis, Monetarism etc., but we are convinced that Kondratiev–Schumpeter's theory should be a firm backbone which will allow combining measures proposed by other classical theories and specified by a particular situation in particular periods (LWC phases and stages). Our key idea is that governments when working out their economic and financial policies, have to rely on the innovative cyclical theory of Kondratiev–Schumpeter as the basic long-term development strategy. Significantly, all the parameters for the trajectory of economic development under conditions of non-equilibrium within LWC can be truly forecasted and assessed via calculations. However, the selection of priorities for an economic policy depends on an LWC phase.

References

Akaev, A., Pantin, V., & Aivazov, A. (2009). *Analysis of the dynamics of the movement of the world economic crisis on the basis of the theory of cycles.* Report at the First Russian Economic Congress. Moscow: Lomonosov Moscow State University.

Akaev, A. A., & Rudskoi, A. I. (2015). A Mathematical Model for Predictive Computations of the Synergy Effect of NBIC Technologies and the Evaluation of its Influence on the Economic Growth in the First Half of the 21st Century. *Doklady Mathematics, 91*(2), 182–185.

Akaev, A. A., & Rudskoi, A. I. (2017). Economic potential of breakthrough technologies and its social consequences. In T. Devezas, J. Leitão, & A. Sarygulov (Eds.), *Industry 4.0. Studies on entrepreneurship, structural change and industrial dynamics*. Springer.

Akaev, A. A., Sadovnichiy, V. A., & Korotaev, A. V. (2011). Huge rise in gold and oil prices as a precursor of a global financial and economic crisis. *Doklady Mathematics, 83*(2), 243–246.
Atkinson, R. (2005). *The past and future of America's economy: Long waves of innovation that power cycles of growth*. Edward Elgar.
Basu, D. (2016). *Long waves of capitalist development: An empirical investigation*. Working Paper No. 2016-15. Amherst, MA: University of Massachusetts.
Bernard, L., Gevorkyan, A., Palley, T., & Semmler, W. (2014). *Long-wave economic cycles: The contributions of Kondratieff, Kuznets, Schumpeter, Kalecki, Goodwin, Kaldor, and Minsky*. Almanac: Kondratieff waves: Juglar—Kuznets—Kondratieff.
Bresnahan, T., Brynjolfsson, E., & Hitt, L. (2002). Information technology, work-place organization and the demand for skilled labor. *Quarterly Journal of Economics, 117*(1), 339–376.
Brown, M. (1966). *On the theory and measurement of technological change*. Cambridge.
De Groot, B., & Franses, P. H. (2009). Cycles in basic innovations. *Technological Forecasting and Social Change, 76*(8), 1021–1025.
Dubovsky, S. V. (1984). *Processes of global development: Modeling and analysis*. Collected works of the All-Russia Scientific Research Institute of System Studies, issue 3.
Dubovsky, S. V. (1988). *System modeling: Models and methods*. Collected works of the All-Russia Scientific Research Institute of System Studies, issue 20.
Dubovsky, S. V. (1989). *Non-stationary scientific and technological progress in global modeling. System modeling: Models and methods*. vol. 20, 20–50. VNIISI.
EIU. (2003). http://www.microsoft.com/Rus/Government/analytics/EUI/part1.mspx
Feng, G. (2018). On the economic long wave. *China Political Economy, 1*(2), 181–206.
Freeman, C. (1987). *Technology policy and economic performance: Lessons from Japan*. Pinter Publishers.
Freeman, C., & Louçã, F. (2001). *As time goes by: From the industrial revolutions to the information revolution*. Oxford University Press.
Füchs, R. (2016). *Intelligent Wachsen: Die grüne Revolution*. Hanser.
Gallegati, M. (2017). *Structural cycles in world economic growth: Long waves dating chronology*. In: Conference: Association Française de Science Economique Meeting (AFSE).
Hirooka, M. (2006). *Innovation dynamism and economic growth. A nonlinear perspective*. Edward Elgar.
IMF. (2018). *World economic outlook database*. International Monetary Fund.
Jorgenson, D., & Motohashi, K. (2005). Information technology and the Japanese economy. *Journal of the Japanese and International Economies, 19*(4), 460–481.
Kondratiev, N. D. (1922). *The world economy and its conditions during and after the war*. Regional department of the State Publishing House.
Kondratiev, N. D. (1935). The long waves in economic life. *Review of Economics and Statistics, 17*(7), 105–115.
Maddison, A. (1982). *Phases of capitalist development*. Oxford University Press.
Mensch, G. (1979). *Stalemate in technology*. Cambridge University Press.
Naumer, H. J. (2020). *Ecologically-oriented growth—Green wave of growth*. Allianz Global Investors GmbH.
Ozouni, E., Katrakylidis, C., & Zarotiadis, G. (2018). Technology evolution and long waves: Investigating their relation with spectral and cross-spectral analysis. *Journal of Applied Economics, 21*(1), 160–174.
Perez, C. (1985). Microelectronics, long waves and world structural change: New perspectives for developing countries. *World Development, 13*(3), 441–463.
Reijnders, J. (1990). *Long waves in economic development*. Edward Elgar.
Romer, P. M. (1990). Endogenous technical change. *Journal of Political Economy, 98*(5), 71–102.
Rosenberg, N., & Frischtak, C. R. (1983). Long waves and economic growth: A critical appraisal. *The American Economic Review, 73*(2), 146–151.
Rudskoy, A. I. (2007). *Nanotechnology in metallurgy*. Publishing House "Science".
Schmookler, J. (1972). *Patents, invention and economic change*. Harvard University Press.

Schumpeter, J. A. (1939). *Business cycles. A theoretical, historical and statistical analysis of the capitalist process*. McGraw-Hill Book Company.

Schwab, K. (2016). *The fourth industrial revolution*. WEF.

Schwab, K., & Davis, N. (2018). *Shaping the fourth industrial revolution*. WEF.

Silvelberg, G., & Verspagen, B. (2003). Breaking the waves: A Poisson regression approach to Schumpeterian clustering of basic innovations. *Cambridge Journal of Economics, 27*, 688–690.

Silverberg, G. P. (2003). *Long waves: Conceptual, empirical and modelling issues*. Working Paper, Volume/Issue 15. UNU-MERIT Research Memoranda.

Solow, M. (1957). Technical change and the aggregate production function. *Review of Economics and Statistics, 39*, 312–320.

Sterman, J. D. (1985). *The economic long wave: Theory and evidence*. Massachusetts Institute of Technology.

Survey of Current Business. (2005, February). *Current business* (pp. 51–57). Bureau of Economics Analysis.

Tatuzov, V. (2020). Contemporary global economic crisis: Some conclusions for Russia and BRICS (taking into account Kondratieff long waves). *BRICS Journal of Economics, 1*(2), 25–40.

Tinbergen, J., & Bos, H. C. (1962). *Mathematical models of economic growth* (1st ed.). McGraw-Hill.

van Duijn, J. J. (1983). *The long wave in economic life*. George Allen and Unwin.

von WeiZsäcker, E. U., Hargroves, K., Smith, M. H., Stasinopoulos, P., & Desha, C. (2008). *Factor five: Transforming the global economy through 80% improvements in resource productivity*. Earthscan.

Williams, L., & Adams, W. (2007). *Nanotechnology*. McGraw-Hill.

World Bank. (2010). *World Development Indicators Online*. World Bank. http://web.worldbank.org/WBSITE/EXTERNAL/DATASTATISTICS/0,contentMDK:20398986-pagePK:64133150~piPK:64133175-theSitePK:239419,00.html.

Yakovets, Y. V. (2004). *Epic innovation of the 21st century*. Economy.

Assessment of the Quality of Growth of National Economies in the Context of Digital Transformation

Bulat Khusainov, Asset Nussupov, Sholpan Kaimoldina, and Aleksandr Shirov

Abstract The purpose of the study is to assess and analyze the impact of digitalization indicators (factors) on the quality of growth of developed and developing countries. As a novelty, it is presented an assessment of the impact of digitalization indicators on nontraditional measures of the pace and quality of economic growth for national economies. The methodology used is the econometric modeling of the impact of ICT sector indicators on the dynamics and determinants of the quality of growth of national economies based on panel data. The authors conducted a meaningful analysis of the obtained calculations and suggest further research of the relationship and interdependence of the quality of economic growth and digital transformation at the national and intercountry levels.

Keywords The quality of growth · National economies · Digitalization · An econometric model

1 Introduction

Economic growth is one of the most striking issues of theory and practice. World economics is constantly devoting much attention to this issue. The fact is reasserted in vast foreign studies. Economic growth is not a goal in itself. It is among the necessary conditions for improving the welfare of the population. Most theoretical and applied researches focus on the clarification of quantitative growth parameters.

B. Khusainov (✉)
JSC Economic Research Institute, Almaty, Kazakhstan

A. Nussupov · S. Kaimoldina
JSC Economic Research Institute, Nur-Sultan, Kazakhstan
e-mail: asset.nussupov@gmail.com; Sh.Ibraimova@eri.kz

A. Shirov
Institute of Economic Forecasting of the Russian Academy of Sciences, Moscow, Russia

A. Rudskoi et al. (eds.), *Digital Transformation and the World Economy*, Studies on Entrepreneurship, Structural Change and Industrial Dynamics,
https://doi.org/10.1007/978-3-030-89832-8_4

The quality of growth is more important than its pace. Indeed, in recent decades, there was remarkable progress in developing countries, especially in China. However, stagnation and rollback were observed, even in countries with the highest growth rates of the economy. These serious discrepancies and sharp setbacks bring us to adequate idea of elements that promote development. There is a general observation that inclusiveness, which means a fair distribution of benefits from economic growth across different population groups, is a key enabler of growth.

The issue of the quality of growth attracts the attention of researchers for a long time, since the 1970s of the last century. However, substantive research of "quality of growth" phenomenon had started at the turn of the twentieth and twenty-first centuries (World Bank, 2000). Most scientific papers investigate the traditional characteristics of the quality of growth. However, the determinants of the quality of growth may differ significantly for various groups of countries in different periods of their development. In recent years, interest in the quality of economic growth issues has been significantly increasing. This is primarily caused by uneven pace of development of different countries: the slowdown in the growth rate of developed economies and progress in developing countries and emerging markets, as well as the nature of the quality of their growth. Despite the abundance of early research, the problem of growth quality is still insufficiently studied. As a result, the definition of "quality of growth" in the scientific literature has not been yet strictly defined.

There are ambiguous and contradictory views on the nature of economic growth and its quality in the scientific literature. Proponents of rapid growth dynamics note the positive dynamics of the main macroeconomic indicators. This allows channeling more funds to social programs and challenges of environmental problems. Another part of the researchers claims that high growth rates do not lead to a rapid improvement in the well-being of all segments of the population and more associated with the aggravation of social, environmental, and political problems. The issue of the distribution of national wealth, depending on the state policy, is highly important. This determines the extent of accumulated national wealth which leads to an increase in the well-being of the country's population. A single-sided focus on economic growth entails ambiguous consequences, in particular, a low level of growth quality. The latter fact leads to a high level of income and wealth inequality both within national economies and between countries.

The problem of income and wealth inequality will be exacerbated by the growing influence of a new driving force—digitalization. It is digitalization, which is among the typical manifestations of globalization (Khusainov, 2012), that plays a key role in modern economic relations. In addition, a lot of talks appeared about "scaling down" of the globalization. Meanwhile during the pandemic dominant impact of digitalization on all aspects of economic and social developments on a global and regional scale was observed. The time when "old" economy, that used information and communication technologies as a tool for achieving its goals, has gone. Today, these technologies are changing the world on their own in accordance with their needs, influencing the dynamics and quality of growth of national economies. This has necessitated the relevance of this study.

2 Theories of Economic Growth and Phenomenon of "The Quality of Growth"

Before the analysis of "the quality of growth" phenomenon and its determinants let us start with a brief overview of theoretical views on economic growth.

From a chronological point of view starting position for modern theories of growth have begun from the work of F. Ramsey (1928) that, as R. Barro mentioned, was "for several decades ahead of its time" (Barro, 1994, p.10). The problem of intertemporal optimization of the households, which was studied by Ramsey gave impetus not only to growth theory but also to the theory of business cycles, consumption, prices, and assets. Neoclassical model of economic growth obtained the most complete view in the works of R. Solow (1956, 1996, 2000) and T. Swan (1956). A significant part of modern economic growth theories were aimed at endogeneity of exogenously set parameters of economic growth in the Solow model (Barro & Sala-i-Martin, 2015). Starting from the advent of Solow-Swan growth model these aspects represent one of the most promising areas of economics.

The regularity of the evolution of economic growth theories is obvious. The factors of economic growth and development are also evolving. Indeed, over the past few centuries, various schools and theories of economic growth have emerged. We believe that this movement will continue, which is predetermined by the advent of modern interpretations of knowledge-based economic development, digitalization (knowledge economy, digital economy). The centuries-old history of economic science, based on theoretical research and empirical observations, has created many models of growth and development. Undoubtedly, the models that were used for long-term forecasts are of particular interest. These are Keynesian (neo-Keynesian) models that highlight the value of the growth of autonomous demand, especially investment demand. Others are classical (neoclassical) models that have a long tradition.

Thus, one of the central elements of the neoclassical model is the use of the "technical progress" parameter (TP). The priority merit in substantiating the essence of economic growth and its dependence on certain set of factors, including scientific and technical (scientific and technological) progress, belongs to S. Kuznets. Model that he formulated (Kuznets, 1960) was formalized by M. Kremer (1993) and is well-known as the Kuznets-Kremer model. Later alternative endogenous models of economic growth associated with TP were proposed by K. Arrow (1962), P. Romer (1986). Afterward there were specifications of the last two models related to the introduction of additional variables. Analyzing these models, A. Akaev and V. Sadovnichy note that "all of them turned out to be useless for predicting TP in the information and digital era" (Akaev & Sadovnichii, 2021). Authors have developed their own original mathematical model for calculating labor productivity in the digital economy, where the symbiosis of "man + intellectual machines" is widely used.

It is clear that over time new interpretations and theoretical views on the problem of economic growth and especially on the phenomenon of "the quality of growth" are appearing.

Why economic growth matters? What should be the rates and boundaries of economic growth? At first glance, the questions are simple, but the answers to them are not so obvious. In reality, everything is much more complicated. First, the growth of gross domestic product (GDP) is interpreted as the rate of its change over time. The growth rate does not reflect the quality of economic growth and as a result does not reflect the level of well-being of the country's population. Secondly, at certain stages of the development of the national economy high growth is essential. It is widely known that there are countries in the world with annual growth rates at 14–15 percent for many years. The most striking and illustrative example is the fast-growing economy of China. For the last twenty years, the average annual growth rate of the Celestial Empire was almost 8.8 percent. Another example is the economy of India, where over the same period the average annual growth rate was 8.2 percent. It is worth to be added that the emerging markets of South Asia are experiencing the same high growth rates. In the Post-Soviet region, the economy of Kazakhstan has demonstrated one of the highest growth rates in the last 20 years, the average annual growth rate was 5.3 percent. Third, while analyzing quantitative growth indicators, it is necessary to consider a comparison base. The lower the base of the comparison period is, the higher the growth will be. For example, a comparative analysis of the growth rates of more than 200 countries of the world conducted by authors showed that high growth rates are common to some poorly developed countries, as well as small island states. Moreover, high rates can be observed in countries with currently depressing economies (Afghanistan, Iraq, etc.).

Economic growth rates could be high but with decreasing real level of population's material, social and other resources endowment at the same time. Paradoxically, even with minimal economic growth nations' welfare and the average life expectancy can grow due to the adequate redistribution of resources. Eloquent examples are the economies of many developed countries, where a fairly high level of quality of life is observed.

Despite the importance of the GDP as an indicator, it does not meet a number of pressing questions on the socioeconomic situation of individual groups of the population. For example, most of important indicators are not very clear to the broad masses of the population. Calculated as averages for the whole country or a large territory, they do not reflect the actual processes happening locally: in small cities and settlements.

The overall growth of GDP per capita may concurrently accompany an increase in inequality within a society. There are ample evidence for that. If inequality increases, there will be growing discrepancy between the average income and the median income (the income of a representative individual, that is, the one who is in the middle of the ranked population). This approach more accurately determines the profitability per person. Indeed, in many cases, GDP data give the impression that the economy is working much better than most citizens feel. Thus, the GDP per capita indicator cannot accurately characterize the profitability, since it is calculated for the "average person," smoothing out the differentiation of profitability by individual groups. While there is an intensive growth of the wealth of some groups and a decrease in the income of others, GDP can also grow with the impoverishment of a significant mass of the population. This process is common for developing countries.

The problem of the discrepancy between the macroeconomic measurements of the reality appeared in economics long time ago. But it has been fully presented in the scientific community quite recently. The shortcomings of calculating GDP according to the System of National Accounts (SNA), widely recognized by economists, are described in detail in the Report of the Commission on the Measurement of Economic Performance and Social Progress (Stiglitz et al., 2009). In addition to the problems and shortcomings of the SNA statistics, the Report suggests some ways to improve the system of economic measurements. The main recommendations of the Commission suggest shifting focus from measurements that characterize production to indicators aimed at measuring people's well-being. In particular, it is proposed to develop a kind of "indicator panel," which includes indicators in eight areas that reflect various aspects of the welfare and quality of life of the population: (1) Living standards (income, consumption, wealth, inequality in their distribution). (2) Health. (3) Education. (4) Personal activities, including work, leisure. (5) Social relations and mutual relations. (6) Participation in political life and governance. (7) A sense of insecurity, both economically and physically. (8) The state of the environment (current and future). Undoubtedly, this does not mean a total rejection of the SNA indicator system.

As a result of the generalization of a significant number of foreign, Soviet, and Russian studies concerning the quality of growth (Tenyakov, 2016, 2018) the following approaches to assessing the quality of growth are identified:

- *Structural*: The quality of growth is assessed as the optimality of structural characteristics: growth rates, proportions between industries and output components-consumption, accumulation, exports, etc.
- *Resource based*: The quality of growth is defined as the productivity of primary resources.
- *Ecological*: The quality of growth is characterized by the consequences of growth for the surrounding environment.
- *Social*: The quality of growth is manifested in reducing social inequality and improving the quality of life of the population.

It is clear that the quality of growth cannot be characterized by one parameter. In our opinion, in each of these approaches, the performance of the quality of growth of national economies should be determined by the reflecting indicators.

The analysis of many studies conducted in the course of the study shows that the "quality of growth" is often understood as a type of economic growth that contributes to reducing poverty, structural inequalities, protecting the environment, and supporting the growth process itself (López et al., 2008).

At the beginning of the twenty-first century, in order to ensure the applied nature of theories and their practical application, factors of its intensity, sustainability, and inclusiveness started being associated with the concept of "economic growth." The economic growth might be sustainable and effective in reducing poverty, however, it should be inclusive. The latter is defined as increasing the growth rate and volume of the economy by ensuring equal conditions for investment and expanding productive employment opportunities. Attempts to measure inclusive growth remain limited. Inclusive growth can be conceptually considered outside the traditional boundaries of poverty and should also reflect changes in the size and distribution of neither the poor nor the rich, but the middle class.

The quantitative assessment of "decent work" is an interesting indicator, which researchers consider to be the main measure of the impact of education on the quality of life. This approach is proposed by the International Labor Organization. Decent work is a multidimensional concept that includes different characteristics and assessments of ensuring the economic and social security of employees and their families, which reflects the relationship between paid work and other activities. In this context, it is necessary to assess the level of precariousness (instability) of employment. We should add that precariousness which has become an important characteristic of modern development and is inherent in many countries bring risks of destroying human resources from rising unemployment. It also has significant cultural and political consequences, increasing social instability in society as a whole. The measurement of precariousness is a difficult task, despite the considerable history of the study of this phenomenon and the great attention to this problem. This can be linked to the multidimensional nature of this phenomenon, which manifests itself in the form of nonstandard employment, informal employment, non-guaranteed employment, urgent nontraditional labor relations, flexible staffing mechanisms, new forms of employment, etc.

Thus, GDP, which is still being used to measure the dynamics of growth, was a good indicator for the economy of the twentieth century. But it is becoming less appropriate for the economy of the twenty-first century, in which other determinants play a decisive role—social, environmental, as well as increasing digitalization. Along with this, the quality of their growth becomes instrumental for assessing the development of national economies.

3 Quality of Growth and Digital Transformation

One of the most important trends in the global development of the last decades is the emergence and rapid spread of the digital economy. The related processes such as digitalization and digital transformation are making an increasing impact on the global and national economies. For the first time, the concept of the digital economy appeared in the mid-1990s. Since then, it has evolved to reflect the rapidly changing nature of technologies and their use by consumers. In the last few years, more attention has been paid to the ways of distributing digital technologies, services, products, methods, and skills in different countries. This process is often called digitalization, defined as the transition of a business to the use of digital technologies, products, and services. Digital products and services contribute to faster changes in a wider range of sectors and are not limited to those high-tech sectors that were previously in the spotlight. Reflecting this change, the study (UNCTAD, 2019) focused on "digitalization" and "digital transformation," i.e., on the ways in which digital products and services are increasingly disrupting traditional sectors with the aim to study various cross-industry trends of digitalization. This is especially true for developing countries and emerging markets, where the digital economy affects traditional industries (agriculture, tourism, transport). Indeed, the most important economic changes may occur thanks to the digitalization of traditional sectors, and not due to the emergence of new sectors that use digital technologies.

A significant number of works are devoted to the digital transformation in all spheres. Thus, in the work (Basaev, 2018) the main directions of such a transformation and its consequences for the world economy are identified. A number of Russian researchers (Litvinceva et al., 2019; Litvinceva & Karelin, 2020) consider the process of digital transformation and the effects caused by it in the territorial context, assessing the impact of digital factors on production and the quality of life of Russian regions population.

The conceptual foundations and practical experience of the formation of the digital economy in national systems are studied in a large number of works. Therefore, we focus on the works that investigate scientifically based and methodological issues of assessing the quality of growth of national and regional economic systems. Chinese scientists (Long & Ji, 2019) conducted an original study assessing the quality of economic growth of the 31 provinces of mainland China for the period of 1997–2016. To do this, they used an unconventional indicator "Genuine Progress Indicator" (GPI), significantly improving the assessment of environmental and social costs. The authors argue that China attaches great importance to the quality of economic growth. It is justified in the official documents adopted by the Government of the Celestial Empire. In other words, China has abandoned the blind pursuit of macroeconomic indicators and payed more attention to the quality and sustainability of the growth of the national economy. The study showed the following results. First, the GPI per capita has declined in some provinces; according to the authors this poses a threat to social well-being and sustainability. Secondly, the "relative threshold effect" (introduction to social services provision is slower than the expansion of economic scales) was found in many provinces. Third, resource consumption and environmental pollution, especially water pollution and carbon emissions, will lead to significant losses of well-being. Despite the fact that this work is not directly related to the assessment of the impact of digitalization indicators on the quality of growth the nontraditional indicators used are of undoubted interest.

Yalmaev et al. (2019) studied an important role in determining the new quality of growth of national entities in the digital economy. The purpose of this research is to justify the prospects for ensuring a new quality of growth of national systems in the digital economy and to develop scientific recommendations for their practical implementation. In the research process, developed countries from the G7 and developing countries from the BRICS were studied. According to the authors, the digital economy should be considered as a tool for ensuring a new quality of growth of national systems and a source of social, environmental, and economic benefits. The research indicate that currently the potential of the digital economy in ensuring a new quality of growth of national systems is not fully realized. The authors state that the formation of the digital economy is one of the most striking and popular trends of the modern world economic system and at the same time one of its most controversial manifestations. The external goals of the emergence of the digital economy, related in particular to the acceleration of growth rates, often contradict the internal goals. The latter include ensuring a new quality of growth by improving the standard of living of the population (human development), innovative, and sustainable (stable, balanced, with low environmental costs) development. The authors argue that the digital modernization of the economy should not be a goal in itself. Indeed, the governments of many countries redistribute public resources in their favor, refusing to implement socially significant projects. This is especially true for developing countries. The benefits of overcoming the gap with developed countries can only be seen at the macroeconomic level. These benefits may be very limited, although the key priority of reducing the imbalances in the development of the global economic system is to equalize the quality of human life and create benefits for everyone. According to the authors, the digital economy has the potential not only to quantitatively accelerate the pace of economic growth, but also to improve its quality.

In the context of our study, the work (Grigorescu et al., 2021) was of most interest, where the impact of human capital and digitization on the well-being of the population in eleven countries of Central and Eastern Europe (CEE) is analyzed. The authors chose this group of countries to understand how digitalization and the transformations it causes in human capital contribute to improving well-being in the CEE countries. This allowed to determine the gap between CEE and the developed economies of the European Union. The results of the study confirmed that the digitalization of the economy and the developed human capital will eventually contribute to public well-being. The authors are convinced that technological changes are associated with transformational shifts in the measurement of human capital. Firstly, in terms of technology creation and development, and secondly, in terms of the role of the user of these new technologies. Unlike other studies, the Human Development Index is used here. According to the authors, use of the Index reflects the influence of education and health as the most important factors for improving human capital. The Index also reflects the indicator of Internet access, which determines the ability of human capital to use digital technologies at the workplace and beyond.

In the process of digital transformation, its effects and their distribution by the levels of development of national economies are important. Therefore, our study attempts to determine the impact of digital indicators (factors) on the dynamics and quality of growth in developed and developing countries.

Each wave of technological progress is associated with an increase in inequality between developed and developing countries: with an increase in inequality in access to products, social services, and public goods—from education to health

Table 1 NNI/PPP per capita in various regions of the world, 1990–2019 (in constant dollars 2019)

Region	1990	2000	2010	2015	2019	2019/1990
World (average)	8944	10,152	12,853	14,534	15,650	175.0
Africa	3480	3571	4636	4904	4917	141.3
Asia	5428	5934	9414	11,619	13,219	243.5
Australia and New Zealand	26,609	33,074	37,974	38,881	40,629	152.7
Europe	24,818	29,724	33,357	34,574	37,480	151.0
Latin America	9069	11,095	13,193	14,277	13,772	151.9
Middle East	13,181	15,128	18,590	20,098	20,286	153.9
South America	9367	10,798	13,809	14,857	13,888	148.3
Northern America	24,818	29,724	33,357	34,574	37,480	157.5

Source: Calculated and compiled by the authors according to the World Inequality Database https://wid.world/data/ (the date of the request June 20, 2021)

care, from information and communication technology (ICT) infrastructure to electrification. Developing countries face three main challenges in their efforts to ensure equal access to the benefits of advanced technologies (UNCTAD, 2021):

- *High-income poverty*—Many people in developing countries cannot afford new goods and services, especially in rural areas; in this case, the obstacles are not technical, but economic and social in nature.
- *Digital gap*—Many advanced technologies are designed for a stable high-speed wired connection to the Internet, but almost half of the world's population still does not have a connection to it; many developing countries lack the necessary digital infrastructure, and for most of their population the cost of the Internet is prohibitively high.
- *Absence of training*—In developing countries basic and standard training is on average 10–20 percentage points lower than in developed countries (in developed countries, 65% of the population have basic computer literacy; in developing countries—46%).

To assess the well-being of the population, we use in our study the concept of national income. The indicator of Net National income (NNI) is found as GDP minus consumption of fixed capital (depreciation of capital) plus net foreign income. NNI is more important because it takes into account the depreciation of fixed capital, which is not an income for anyone. It also takes into account the share of domestic production that is transferred to the owners of foreign capital (including the principle of offshore wealth). For example, a country with a large GDP, but a significant depreciation of capital and an outflow of foreign capital does not have much income to distribute among its citizens (World Inequality Lab, 2020).

Our comparative analysis of NNI/PPP per capita (PPP—Purchasing Power Parity) over the past three decades clearly demonstrates how inequality between regions of the world has increased over these years (Table 1).

Australia and New Zealand, North America, and Europe, being developed economies, have the highest NNI values per capita. In Asia, Africa, the Middle East,

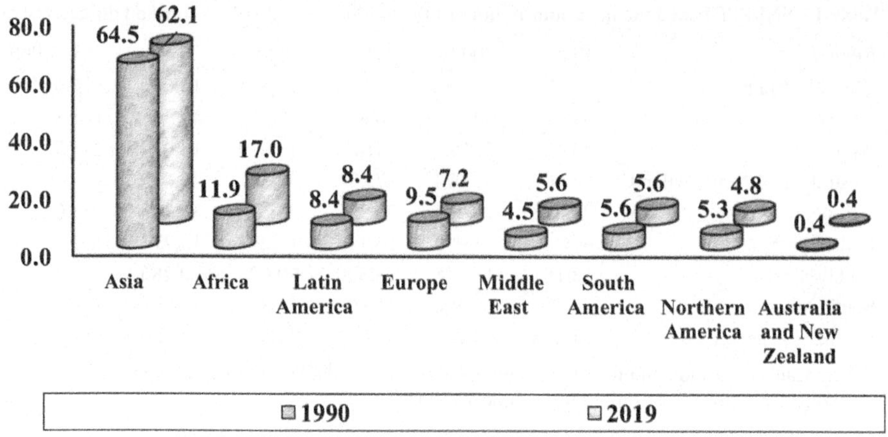

Fig. 1 Distribution of the population by regions of the world, 1990–2019 (as a percentage of the world population). Source: Authors'

Latin, and Southern Europe, where mainly developing countries are concentrated, this indicator is noticeably lower. At the same time, the highest growth rates of NNI are typical for Asia (growth by 2.4 times), and the lowest in Africa (growth by 1.4 times), which is lower than the world average (once).

An informative analysis of the population distribution by the world regions shows that three-quarters of the world's population live in middle-income countries. Most of the world's population lives in Asia, Africa, Latin and South America, the Middle East, where mainly developing countries are located, 95% of the population lived in 1990, and 98.7% in 2019. In Australia and New Zealand, Europe and North America, where developed economies are concentrated, this indicator was 15.1 and 12.3 percent, respectively (Fig. 1).

As for the geography of digitalization, in most regions of the world in 2020 more than 90% of the population had access to a mobile broadband network (3G or higher). In developed economies, 97% of the population is covered by 4G mobile communications, in developing countries—82.2%. Africa and the CIS countries are the regions experiencing the largest gap, where 23% and 11% of the population respectively, do not have access to a mobile broadband network. It is noteworthy that in 2020 Africa achieved a 21% growth in the 4G deployment process, while in all other regions of the world, growth was insignificant.

Globally, about 72% of urban households had Internet access at home in 2019, which is almost twice as much as in rural areas (about 38%). The gap between urban and rural areas in developed countries is small, but in developing countries urban access to the Internet is 2.3 times higher than access in rural areas. In Africa, only 28% of households in urban areas have Internet access at home. But this is still 4.5 times higher than in rural areas, which is 6.3%. In other regions of the world, household Internet access in urban areas ranged from 70 to 88 percent, and access in rural areas ranged from 37 to 78 percent. A similar picture arises for households

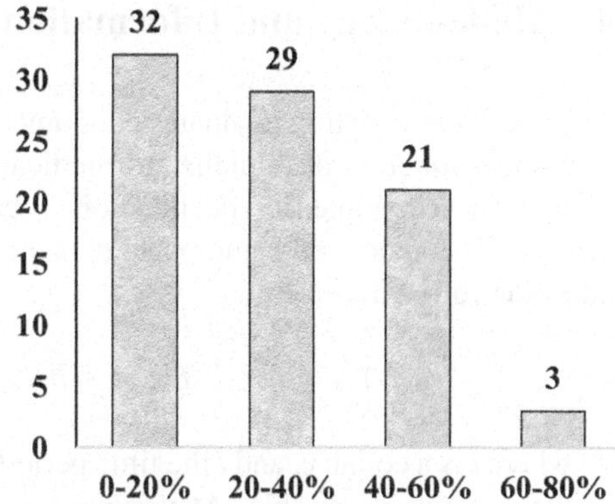

Fig. 2 Distribution of the economy by the share of population having standard skills, 2017–2019. Source: Authors' creation

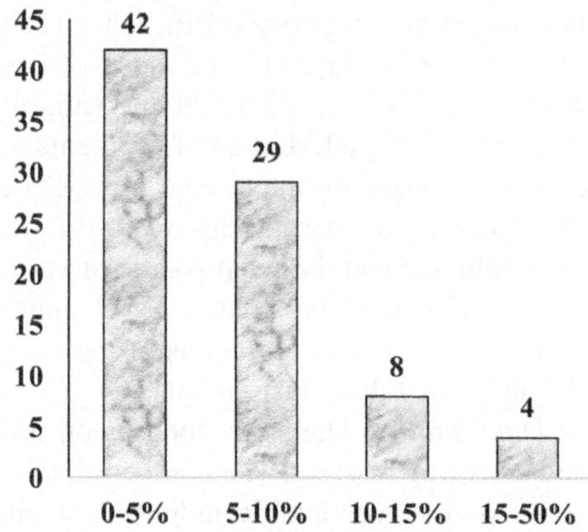

Fig. 3 Distribution of the economy by the share of population having advanced skills, 2017–2019. Source: Authors' creation

that own a computer. However, since computers are no longer the main gateway to the Internet, across the board, the percentage of households with a computer is less than the percentage of households with Internet access (Measuring digital development. Facts and figures, 2020).

Low ICT skills remain an obstacle to full participation in the digital society. The self-assessment of individual ICT skills can be subjective. Therefore, ICT skills are measured based on whether a person has recently performed a specific activity that requires a certain level of skills. The distribution of the economy by the share of their population with standard and advanced skills is presented in Figs. 2 and 3.

It was observed (Facts and Figures, 2020) that in 40% of the countries where data were available, less than 40% of individuals reported that in the last three months they performed one of the activities attributable to basic skills, for example, sending an email with an attachment. In 70% of countries, less than 40% of people have completed one of the standard components of skills, for example, creating an electronic presentation using software. In only 15% of countries, more than 10% of people have written computer programs using a specialized programming language in the last 3 months.

4 Methodology and Information Base

The empirical equation evaluates economic growth and/or its quality characteristics as a linear function of digitalization indicators for developed and developing economies. The econometric specification is based on the Solow growth model. The equation is constructed using panel data, so that the original regression specification takes the following form:

$$ln\, Y_{i,t} = a + b_1 Lnx_{i,1} + b_2 Lnx_{i,2} + \ldots + b_n Lnx_{i,n} + \varepsilon_{i,t} \quad (1)$$

where *i* is a country, and *t* the time period. *LnY* denotes logarithm of the real value of the dependent variable. At various stages of the study, the following variables were used as the *y* variable: net national income (NNI/PPP) per capita according to purchasing power parity (PPP); labor productivity according to PPP; employment precarization (instability), the index of cross-country inequality of national economies; $Lnx_{i,\ n}$ is a set of logarithmic variables characterizing ICT.

The Generalized Method of Moments (GMM) is used as part of the analysis. All results are based on the system of GMM estimator, which uses variations of variables both between countries and within countries (over time). Thus, this estimate takes into account the main source of variation in ICT variables (i.e., cross-country differences). In general, the GMM approach uses a set of internal instruments derived from past observations of measurement variables, conducting several validation tests of these instruments.

Data quality. The study focuses on 36 developed and 46 developing countries and emerging markets. The number of countries depends on the qualitative dynamic series of macroeconomic indicators available primarily in the World Inequality Database, and digitalization indicators from the ITU-D ICT database and the World Development Indicators Database. The outcome indicator NNI/PPP per capita in constant dollars in 2019 is used from the World Inequality Database for the period 1985–2019. Statistical data on labor productivity (PPP, in constant dollars 2017), export of ICT services (as a share of the total volume of services) are taken from the World Development Indicators Database for the period 1991—2019. The number of mobile cellular subscribers, income from ICT services and investments in ICT services (in current US dollars) are taken from the ITU-D ICT database.

Given that digitalization leads to an increase in income inequality, the index of cross-country inequality is used. It is based on the development of the concepts of cross-country, international and global inequality as set out in the works of B. Milanovich (Milanovic, 2005, 2012). The development is expressed in their influence on the growth dynamics of national economies (Khusainov et al., 2017), where the impact of cross-country and international inequality on the economic growth of national economies was carried out for the first time.

The concept of cross-country inequality focuses on heterogeneity among countries worldwide. The corresponding indicator is based on statistical data on inequality calculated on the basis of GDP or average incomes obtained during household surveys in all countries of the world without taking into account the specific weight of the population. The value of applying the concept of cross-country inequality is based on the fact that it is the state, not people, that should have an equal weight in assessing the equitable distribution of the benefits of globalization.

In calculating cross-country inequality, countries are taken as the unit of observation. The Gini coefficient is calculated using the following formula:

$$G_1 = \frac{1}{\mu}\frac{1}{n^2}\sum\nolimits_{i=1}^{n}\sum\nolimits_{j>1}^{n}(y_j - y_i), \tag{2}$$

where G_1 is the coefficient of cross-country inequality, y_j and y_i are the gross national income (GNI) of countries j and i, n is the number of countries, μ is the global average value of GNI.

To calculate the coefficient of cross-country inequality in absolute and relative terms, the country indicators of GNI/PPP in international dollars of 2011 are used. The calculations were carried out from 1985 to 2018 with the indicators of 132 countries, where continuous dynamic series in the World Development Indicators Database were available. As one of the potential determinants of the quality of growth of the national economy, we used the indicator of employment precariousness (instability).

As noted earlier (please see Chap. 2 of this article), the assessment of the level of precariousness is a complex methodological problem. As a result, there is no generally accepted method for measuring it. Therefore, the level of precariousness (as a percentage of total employment) is defined as the sum of the shares of self-employed and unemployed, based on the International Labor Organization estimates, for the period 1991–2019.

5 Results

The econometric model (1) was implemented using the capabilities of the R programming language. The first part of the study focused on net national income per capita in purchasing power parity (NNI/PPP). The hypothesis about the influence of ICT indicators on the dynamics of this indicator, which in our case is the real growth of national economies, was tested.

The empirical results of the model show the following. It is noteworthy that for developed economies all five indicators of the ICT sector used are significant. However, only "Mobile-cellular telephone subscriptions" has a positive influence on the dynamics of NNI/PPP. The coefficients of the other four indicators are in a negative range. It is clear that the indicators used are not the main factors of the growth of national economies. This has, to some extent, led to a negative value of these coefficients. In the process of calculations, the need to remove the constant in equation (1) was determined. It is not possible to make a proper assessment of the relationship between endogenous and exogenous variables. In particular, in each case, the constant value was very significant and demonstrated the absence of a statistical relationship between the growth rates of NNI/PPP and the digitalization indicators. In other words, it has "closed" the entire desired relationship.

In any case, the negative coefficient value of ICT indicators is the subject of future research. What is important is that the hypothesis that there is a statistically significant relationship between the dynamics of NNI/PPP and the digitalization indicators has been empirically confirmed. Sargan-Hansen statistics show that the digitalization indicators used in the model are reliably identified. This is confirmed by its high value (p-value $= 0.027$). The Wald test rejects the null hypothesis about the absence of a statistical relationship between endogenous and exogenous variables with a probability of 46%.

For the developing countries and emerging markets, two of the five ICT indicators used do not show statistical significance. This is the revenue and export of ICT services. The Wald test rejects the null hypothesis that there is no statistical relationship between the studied variables with a probability of 51% (Table 2).

In the second part of the study, the hypothesis of the impact of ICT indicators on the labor productivity in PPP was tested. For this purpose, the model reflected in Eq. (1) was also used. For a group of developed countries, there is a statistically significant relationship between labor productivity and mobile cellular subscribers and the value of ICT services exports at the level of 5%. Three other digital indicators do not demonstrate this relationship. For the other three digitalization indicators, such a relationship is not observed. The Sargan-Hansen statistics show that the exogenous indicators selected for analysis are identified (29.095). The Wald criterion confirms the null hypothesis about the absence of a statistically significant relationship with a probability of about 25% (p-value $= 0.0001$).

For developing economies and emerging markets, a statistically significant relationship was revealed for investments in the ICT sector with a one-year lag and the mobile cellular subscriptions. The other three digitalization indicators showed a statistically insignificant relationship with labor productivity. Nevertheless, with a probability of 40%, it can be argued that the choice of exogenous variables is carried out correctly (Table 3).

The third part of the study assessed the impact of ICT indicators on the level of precariousness (instability) of employment in developed and developing economies. For both groups of countries, a statistically significant relationship was found only for one indicator—investment in the ICT services. The Wald test allows us to reject the null hypothesis that there is no statistically significant relationship between the level of precariousness of employment and indicators of digitalization with a probability of 33% for two groups of countries (Table 4).

Finally, in the final part of the study, for the first time, an assessment of the impact of digitalization indicators on the cross-country inequality, based on data from 132 countries of the world, was carried out. Undoubtedly, this is the novelty of this study.

For a group of developed economies, the employment in the ICT services sector, the number of mobile cellular subscribers, and the ICT services export have a significant impact on cross-country inequality. The reliability of the identified

Table 2 Empirical assessment of the relationship between NNI/PPP dynamics and the ICT indicators for two groups of countries

Indicators	Estimate	SE	z-Value	Pr(>|z|)
Developed countries ($n = 36$)				
Ln Inv <1>	−0.0185111	0.0068524	−2.7014	0.0069047**
Ln subscr	0.0334570	0.0059961	5.5798	2.408e-08***
Ln emp	−0.0153257	0.0045264	−3.3858	0.0007097***
Ln rev	−0.0049250	0.0020262	−2.4307	0.0150691*
Ln exp	−0.0031820	0.0011872	−2.6803	0.0073566**
Time period—35 years; number of observations—1188				
Sargan–Hansen test: chisq (18) = 31.19955 (p-value = 0.027294)				
Wald test for coefficients: chisq (5) = 46.0818 (p-value = 8.7404e-09)				
Developing countries ($n = 46$)				
Ln Inv <1>	−0.01273254	0.00316693	−4.0205	5.808e-05***
Ln subscr	0.03737316	0.00694678	5.3799	7.452e-08***
Ln emp	−0.00756926	0.00186096	−4.0674	4.754e-05***
Ln rev	−0.00080946	0.00072094	1.1228	0.2615
Ln exp	0.00073921	0.00069189	1.0684	0.2853
Time period—35 years; number of observations—1516				
Sargan–Hansen test: chisq (18) = 29.47148 (p-value = 0.042913)				
Wald test for coefficients: chisq (5) = 51.21492 (p-value = 7.8148e-10)				

Note: Ln—logarithm, Inv <1>—investments in the ICT sector with a time lag of one year, subscr—mobile cellular subscriptions, emp—Full-time equivalent telecommunication employees, Rev—ICT services income, exp—ICT services export; ***, **, *—significance at the level of 1%, 5%, and 10%, respectively

relationships is confirmed at the level of 1%. For the second group of countries, a statistically significant relationship was revealed between two exogenous variables—the employment in the ICT sector and the mobile cellular subscribers. The reliability of empirically established relationships is also at the level of 1%. The Wald test allows us to reject the null hypothesis that there is no statistically significant relationship between the level of precariousness. The Wald coefficient is 319 and 172 for developed and developing economies, respectively (Table 5).

The obtained statistical estimates of the constructed and implemented econometric model are the initial results for a meaningful analysis of the given research.

6 Conclusion

This work is part of a study aimed at identifying new determinants of the quality of growth of national economies. It should contribute to the search and explanation of the phenomenon of "quality of growth" in the background of increasing world digital transformation. The role and importance of digitalization were especially crucial in the context of the covid pandemic. Meaningful analysis of many studies, a

Table 3 Empirical assessment of the relationship between the labor productivity dynamics and the ICT indicators for two groups of countries

Indicators	Estimate	SE	z-value	Pr(>|z|)
Developed countries ($n = 36$)				
Ln Inv <1>	−0.00653126	0.00455668	−1.4333	0.151761
Ln subscr	0.04793398	0.01495990	3.2042	0.001355**
Ln emp	−0.00713912	0.00439255	−1.6253	0.104103
Ln rev	−0.00145245	0.00096625	−1.5032	0.132793
Ln exp	−0.00253944	0.00092215	−2.7538	0.005890**
Time period—35 years; number of observations—1369				
Sargan–Hansen test: chisq (18) = 31.19955 (p-value = 0.027294)				
Wald test for coefficients: chisq (5) = 46.0818 (p-value = 8.7404e-09)				
Developing countries ($n = 46$)				
Ln Inv <1>	−0.0103853	0.0032318	−3.2135	0.001311**
Ln subscr	0.0676235	0.0123724	5.4657	4.612e-08***
Ln emp	0.0097453	0.0084451	1.1540	0.248514
Ln rev	−0.0025469	0.0054617	−0.4663	0.640991
Ln exp	0.0036950	0.0028405	1.3008	0.193323
Time period—35 years; number of observations—1516				
Sargan–Hansen test: chisq (18) = 29.47148 (p-value = 0.042913)				
Wald test for coefficients: chisq (5) = 51.21492 (p-value = 7.8148e-10)				

Note: Ln—logarithm, Inv <1>—investments in the ICT sector with a time lag of one year, subscr—mobile cellular subscriptions, emp—full-time equivalent telecommunication employees, Rev—ICT services income, exp—ICT services export; ***, **, *—significance at the level of 1%, 5%, and 10%, respectively

small part of which is presented in this chapter, allows us to conclude that the problem of the quality of growth of national economies is still far from being solved. And this is while researchers have been dealing with the problem of the quality of economic growth for at least half a century. Obviously, the most scientific papers are focused on the traditional characteristics of the quality of growth. But the determinants of the quality of growth vary significantly for different groups of countries at various time periods. Now there is a unique opportunity to focus on the study of the relationships and interdependencies between the pace and quality of growth and digital transformation.

The main objective of this study was to identify a statistically significant relationship between the indicators of the ICT sector and individual parameters of national economies, as well as cross-country inequality. In all cases, the obtained econometric estimates were statistically significant, empirically confirming the hypotheses during the study.

It is extremely important to use nontraditional indicators to measure the speed of economic growth. The econometric assessment of the impact of digitalization indicators on the dynamics of net national income of developed and developing economies has been empirically proven. The negative coefficients of the ICT sector indicators on net national income demonstrate an asymmetric effect of influence.

Table 4 Empirical assessment of the relationship between the level of precariousness (instability) of employment and the ICT indicators of for two groups of countries

Indicators	Estimate	SE	z-Value	Pr(>|z|)
Developed countries ($n = 36$)				
Ln Inv <1>	0.00985761	0.00424082	2.3245	0.0201*
Ln subscr	−0.00266527	0.00177699	−1.4999	0.1336
Ln emp	0.00165778	0.00169800	0.9763	0.3289
Ln rev	−0.00135299	0.00134420	−1.0065	0.3142
Ln exp	−0.00042994	0.00088863	−0.4838	0.6285
Time period—29 years; number of observations—972				
Sargan–Hansen test: chisq (18) = 33.0571 (p-value = 0.016427)				
Wald test for coefficients: chisq (5) = 8.977067 (p-value = 0.10998)				
Developing countries ($n = 46$)				
Ln Inv <1>	0.00985761	0.00424082	2.3245	0.0201*
Ln subscr	−0.00266527	0.00177699	−1.4999	0.1336
Ln emp	0.00165778	0.00169800	0.9763	0.3289
Ln rev	−0.00135299	0.00134420	−1.0065	0.3142
Ln exp	−0.00042994	0.00088863	−0.4838	0.6285
Time period—28 years; number of observations—1193				
Sargan–Hansen test: chisq (18) = 33.0571 (p-value = 0.016427)				
Wald test for coefficients: chisq (5) = 8.977067 (p-value = 0.10998)				

Note: Ln—logarithm, Inv <1>—investments in the ICT sector with a time lag of one year, subscr—mobile cellular subscriptions, emp—full-time equivalent telecommunication employees, Rev—ICT services income, exp—ICT services export; ***, **, *—significance at the level of 1%, 5%, and 10%, respectively

Firstly, the values of these coefficients are not large; secondly, in almost all economies of the world, the main growth factor is domestic (consumption and investment) and external (foreign trade balance) demand; third, the deterrent effect could be minimized by adding the main growth factors to the model (1). This is the subject of future research.

The digital divide between countries and regions of the world will be a catalyst for increasing inequality between them. Researchers strongly consider that polarization will occur primarily in the sphere of income and capital. As a result, inequality will affect many areas of the global and national economies. In this context, the undoubted novelty of this study is in the assessment of the impact of digitalization indicators on the dynamics of changes in cross-country inequality. The qualitative results of the assessment of the presence of a significant relationship of inequality between countries and indicators of digitalization also require serious research. We were not able to find such studies among the many works related to inequality.

Employment precariousness is a complex and obscure phenomenon. It cannot depend on a single, albeit very important, sector of national economies. However, with the development of digital transformation and elimination of traditional professions, the problem of employment precariousness will become more and more pressing. Therefore, obtained preliminary estimates are the first step in this direction.

Table 5 Empirical assessment of the relationship between the cross-country inequality dynamics and the ICT indicators of for two groups of countries

Indicators	Estimate	SE	z-Value	Pr(>|z|)
Developed countries ($n = 36$)				
Ln Inv <1>	0.00252473	0.00129315	1.9524	0.0508922
Ln subscr	−0.01176560	0.00248406	−4.7364	2.175e-06***
Ln emp	0.00789805	0.00230223	3.4306	0.0006022***
Ln rev	−0.00058325	0.00078118	−0.7466	0.4552909
Ln exp	−0.00483687	0.00048535	−9.9657	<2.2e-16***
Time period—34 years; number of observations—1224				
Sargan–Hansen test: chisq (18) = 34.91905 (*p*-value = 0.0096766)				
Wald test for coefficients: chisq (5) = 319.0287 (*p*-value = < 2.22e-16)				
Developing countries ($n = 46$)				
Ln Inv <1>	1.0323e-02	6.2144e-03	1.6611	0.0966941
Ln subscr	−1.5791e-02	2.0018e-03	−7.8884	3.061e-15***
Ln emp	2.0313e-03	5.7842e-04	3.5117	0.0004452***
Ln rev	4.6047e-04	3.7786e-04	1.2186	0.2229853
Ln exp	2.3849e-05	2.7067e-04	0.0881	0.9297878
Time period—34 years; number of observations—1564				
Sargan–Hansen test: chisq (18) = 41.33206 (*p*-value = 0.0013697)				
Wald test for coefficients: chisq (5) = 172.0733 (*p*-value = <2.22e-16)				

Note: Ln—logarithm, Inv <1>—investments in the ICT sector with a time lag of one year, subscr—mobile cellular subscriptions, emp—full-time equivalent telecommunication employees, Rev—ICT services income, exp—ICT services export; ***, **, *—significance at the level of 1%, 5%, and 10%, respectively

In our study, only a few indicators of digitalization were used. Skeptics may argue that they do not reflect all the processes of digital transformation. However, the use of only five indicators of the ICT sector, we consider, does not diminish the significance of the obtained results. Selection of these indicators is determined by the availability of high-quality statistical data available in international sources. For a more complete study, it is necessary to consider the structural changes of national economies, in particular, the share of ICT sector's added value in various countries. We were not able to find such information on the analyzed countries. As a result, it was not possible to build high-quality dynamic series that are not discrete in nature and have a long time period.

Acknowledgments This research is funded by the Science Committee of the Ministry of Education and Science of the Republic of Kazakhstan (Grant No. AP08856289).

References

Akaev, A. A., & Sadovnichii, V. A. (2021). The human component as a determining factor of labor productivity in the digital economy. *Studies on Russian Economic Development, 32*, 29–36.

Arrow, K. J. (1962). The economic implications of learning-by-doing. *Review of Economic Studies, 29*, 155–173.

Barro, R. J. (1994). *Economic growth and convergence*. ICS Press, International Center for Economic Growth Publication.

Barro, R. J., & Sala-i-Martin, H. (2015). *Ekonomicheskij rost*. BINOM.

Basaev, Z. V. (2018). Cifrovizaciya ekonomiki: Rossiya v kontekste global'noj transformacii. *Mir novoj ekonomiki, 12*(4), 32–38.

Grigorescu, A., Pelinescu, E., Ion, A. E., & Dutcas, M. F. (2021). Human capital in digital economy: An empirical analysis of Central and Eastern European Countries from the European Union. *Sustainability 2021, 13*.

International Telecommunication Union. (2020). Measuring digital development. Facts and figures 2020.

Khusainov, B., Nussupov, A., & Zhangalieva, K. (2017). Koncepcii neravenstva i nacional'nye ekonomiki: ocenka i vliyanie. *Ekonomika i statistika, 2*, 42–51.

Khusainov B. D. (2012). Globalizaciya, Transnacionalizaciya, Integraciya. Monografiya. Otvet. redaktor professor Oksfordskogo universiteta Piter Oppengejmer. Almaty.

Kremer, M. (1993). Population growth and technological change: One million B.C. to 1990. *The Quarterly Journal of Economics, 108*, 681–716.

Kuznets, S. (1960). Population change and aggregate output. In *Demographic and economic change in developed countries*. Princeton University Press.

Litvinceva, G. P., & Karelin, I. N. (2020). Effekty cifrovoj transformacii ekonomiki i kachestva zhizni naseleniya v Rossii. *Terra Economicus, 18*(3), 53–71.

Litvinceva, G. P., Shmakov, A. V., Stukalenko, E. A., & Petrov, S. P. (2019). Ocenka cifrovoj sostavlyayushchej kachestva zhizni naseleniya v regionah Rossijskoj Federacii. *Terra Economicus, 17*(3), 107–127.

Long, X., & Ji, X. (2019). Economic growth quality, environmental sustainability, and social welfare in China—Provincial assessment based on genuine progress indicator (GPI). *Ecological Economics, 159*, 157–176.

López, R. E., Thomas, V., & Wang, Y. (2008). The quality of growth: Fiscal policies for better results (IEG Working Paper).

Milanovic, B. (2005). *Worlds apart: Measuring international and global inequality*. Princeton University Press.

Milanovic, B. (2012). Global inequality: From class to location, from proletarians to migrants. *Global Policy, 3*(2), 125–134.

Ramsey, F. P. (1928). A mathematical theory of saving. *The Economic Journal, 38*, 549–559.

Romer, P. M. (1986). Increasing Returns and Long-Run Growth. *Journal of Political Economy, 94*, 1002–1037.

Solow, R. M. (1996). Perspektivy teorii rosta. *Mirovaya ekonomika i mezhdunarodnye otnosheniya, 8*, 25–32.

Solow, R. M. (2000). *Growth theory: An exposition*. Oxford University Press.

Solow, R. M. A. (1956). Contribution to the theory of economic growth. *The Quarterly Journal of Economics, 70*, 65–94.

Stiglitz, J., Sen, A., & Fitoussi, J.-P. (2009). Report by the commission on the measurement of economic performance and social progress.

Swan, T. W. (1956). Economic growth and capital accumulation. *Economic Record, 55*, 334–361.

Tenyakov, I. M. (2016). Podhody k ocenke kachestva ekonomicheskogo rosta. *Voprosy politicheskoj ekonomii, 4*, 61–73.

Tenyakov, I. M. (2018). Sistema faktorov ekonomicheskogo rosta: rossijskie osobennosti. *Dissertaciya na soiskanie uchenoj stepeni d. e. n.* Moskva, MGU.

UNCTAD. (2019). Digital Economy Report 2019. Value creation and capture: Implications for Developing Countries. Geneva: UNCTAD.
UNCTAD. (2021). Technology and Innovation Report 2021. Catching technological waves Innovation with equity. Geneva: UNCTAD.
World Bank. (2000). The Quality of Growth (2000). Washington, DC: World Bank.
World Inequality Lab. (2020). Distributional National Accounts Guidelines. Methods and concepts used in the World Inequality Database.
Yalmaev, R., Shalaev, V., Giyazov, A., & Tashkulova, G. (2019). The Perspectives of Provision of New Quality of Growth of Economic Systems in the Digital Economy. In *Digital Economy: Complexity and Variety vs. Rationality* (pp. 30–38). Springer International Publishing.

Digital Transformation and Growth Models

Askar Akaev, Nabi Ziadullaev, Askar Sarygulov, and Alexander Petryakov

Abstract The digital transformation of economic systems has become an established trend. One piece of evidence for this is that some of the empirical laws formulated by N. Kaldor, which accompanied the process of long-term economic growth in the twentieth century, have ceased to act. Another feature of modern development is that digital technologies, having an intensive labor-saving property, which makes their use "toxic" for the labor market. This fact raises the importance of assessing the potential number of jobs, taking into account technological substitution under various scenarios of real wage formation. In close connection with such an assessment is the determination of the gross product and the level of decline in aggregate consumer demand caused by a reduction in the number of jobs and the increasing role of intelligent machines in the economy. For a more accurate description of the above features of modern economic development, we have proposed a set of economic growth models that take into account the new stylized facts of economic development formulated by J. Stiglitz and T. Piketty. The developed models are verified using the US statistics.

Keywords Digital transformation · Economic system · Mathematical model

A. Akaev
Institute for Mathematical Research of Complex Systems, Lomonosov Moscow State University, Moscow, Russia

N. Ziadullaev
Tashkent State University of Economics, Tashkent, Uzbekistan

A. Sarygulov · A. Petryakov (✉)
Saint Petersburg State University of Economics, Saint-Petersburg, Russia
e-mail: dept.cfr@unecon.ru

A. Rudskoi et al. (eds.), *Digital Transformation and the World Economy*, Studies on Entrepreneurship, Structural Change and Industrial Dynamics,
https://doi.org/10.1007/978-3-030-89832-8_5

1 Introduction

In the twentieth century, there were a number of empirical laws accompanying the process of economic growth, which were to be valid in the long term. N. Kaldor (1961) formulated a number of them, but not all of them remain valid at present. A number of works devoted to the central issue of economics—the distribution of income between factors of production and the distribution of income and welfare among people, taking into account the widespread diffusion of artificial intelligence (AI) (Korinek & Stiglitz, 2017; Stiglitz, 2016)—showed that it is necessary to use new models. One reason for this rethinking has been the rapid growth of the NBIC technology sector (Bainbridge & Roko, 2006; Roco, 2011).

The technologies of the fourth industrial revolution have become a new reality, which makes it possible to fully automate the manufacturing process of products, practically crowding out people from the sphere of production and even services. Digital technologies have an intensive laborsaving property, which makes them "toxic" for the labor market. The utilization of digital platforms, computers, and robots at a large scale will accelerate the process of technological replacement of labor by capital in the coming decades.

In relation to today, negative expectations for the labor market are largely associated with the development of digital technologies, where the effects of wide automation are estimated to be from an employment reduction of 9% in the European economy (Arntz et al., 2016) to 47% in the US economy (Frey & Osborne, 2017). The acute discussion of this issue is also largely due to the growing income inequality over the past 30 years (Piketty, 2014; Stiglitz, 2012) and the long-term downtrend in the manufacturing share (OECD, 2017) in developed countries.

The McKinsey Global Institute experts' forecast (2017) shows that by 2055, half of the existing jobs around the world can be eliminated due to full automation of production.

One of the consequences of digital technologies development is a decrease in average wages (Brynjolfsson & McAfee, 2014), which is due to the widespread use of information and communication technologies, and as a result, their gradual reduction in cost. Acemoglu and Restrepo (2017) noted that the use of industrial robots between 1990 and 2007 in local US labor markets had reduced employment and wages: one robot per thousand workers reduces the employment-to-population ratio by about 0.18–0.34 percent and reduces wages by about 0.25–0.5 percent. According to other estimates for the EU countries, one robot per thousand workers reduces the level of employment by 0.16–0.2 percent (Chiacchio et al., 2018). The use of industrial robots on a global economic scale also poses significant threats: the obtained estimates indicate a long-term reduction in employment by about 1.3% (Carbonero et al., 2018). The impact of automation on labor market transformation is lasting: automation is very good for economic growth and very bad for equality (Berg et al., 2018).

Not all assessments are so pessimistic. Analyzing the American labor market for the period from 1850 to 2015, Atkinson and Wu (2017) argue that the level of professional outflow in the USA is now at a historic low, and no more than 10% of jobs in the US economy are exposed to a real threat of automation. In many cases, machines replace and complement human labor; they add value to tasks requiring the unique abilities of workers (Autor, 2015). Autor and Dorn (2013) noted that due to the imbalance of technological progress when it is impossible to replace routine tasks with information technology, there is an increase in wages and employment in the low-skilled services sector. Some researchers in Europe are also not inclined to dramatize the consequences of widespread job automation (Arntz et al., 2016; Pouliakas, 2018). In Germany, according to research, no more than 13–15 percent of employees are at risk of automation (Arnold et al., 2016; Dengler & Matthes, 2018). OECD researchers also tend to believe that no more than 10% of those employed in the American economy are at risk of automation (Nedelkoska & Quintini, 2018). Exploring the practical application of robots and AI (Vermeulen et al., 2018), a team of authors notes that this is "a common structural change." Analyzing German industrial practice regarding the use of robots from 1994 to 2014 (Wolfgang et al., 2018), the authors note that the use of robots resulted in job losses in manufacturing, but this was offset by successes in the business services sector.

An important attribute of the digital economy is a qualitatively new role of technological progress contributing to an uneven increase in productivity of the main factors of economic growth (capital and labor). At the same time, the fourth industrial revolution, along with the complete production automation and acceleration of the growth of productivity and GDP, may have very negative social consequences. One of the possible effects is the sharp reduction in the number of middle-class jobs and a further increase in income inequality in society. Therefore, a scenario in which the reduction of the middle class can lead to social upheaval in developed countries is possible.

Due to the growth of total factor productivity (TFP), national income (GDP) will also grow. However, empirical evidence over the past 40 years shows that median income in a number of developed countries stopped growing as far back as the 1980s, although until then, it had grown proportionally to productivity for decades (Brynjolfsson & McAfee, 2014). This process accelerated after the 2000s. If stagnation of the median salary was observed before 2000, now it has already begun to decline, although TFP in developed economies has been growing steadily all this time (Brynjolfsson & McAfee, 2014). Such inequality is increasing because of a growing gap a) between labor income and capital income and b) between high-income and low-income families (Leipziger & Dodev, 2016). Referring to the data on the US economy, they emphasize that the share of domestic income that goes to wages has been declining since the early 1970s, since the share that goes to capital has increased. This trend in the ever-decreasing share of gross domestic income earmarked for labor (wages) since its peak in 1970 explains the expansion of inequality in the USA in recent decades.

One of the options for maintaining aggregate demand at the level of potential output of goods and services may be the introduction of a universal basic income (UBI) for all adult citizens. In a number of states, such as Switzerland and Finland, the idea of UBI has not find widespread support (Gotev, 2016; Valero, 2019). In the

Netherlands, experiments, although they do not have a direct reference to basic income, are being carried out in about twenty municipalities. Similar projects are under development in Denmark, France, Catalonia, Scotland, Corsica, and Portugal (De Wispelaere & Haagh, 2019). In February 2017, the European Parliament voted with 328 votes against using UBI to offset losses from the use of robots in the labor market. However, the idea of basic income is gaining considerable popularity among the public: support for basic income in the last wave of the European Social Survey (ESS) averages to just over 50 percent (Lee, 2018). The idea of UBI is negatively perceived by US researchers (Hoynes & Rothstein, 2019; Kearney & Mogstad, 2019), although they admit that the motivation for using UBI is a labor market situation, where adequate wage and income growth is not provided for a long time for those workers who are at the bottom of the income distribution curve.

Our research is devoted to the development of mathematical models describing the influence of digital transformation on the economic system. The models consider human capital, the new nature of technological progress in the digital economy, and capital income as endogenous factor. In addition, we present the simplest model for determining the unconditional basic income (UBI), which provides a balance of real demand and supply in the economy. The US economy data from 1982 to 2018 is used to verify developed models and to forecast dynamics of the US GDP, employment and UBI needed.

The paper is organized into the following sections that build off each other. Section 1 provides an overview of the literature on digital transformation and modern economic development studies. The data and the set of models are presented in Sect. 2. Section 3 contains models' validation, analysis of the results and the main points of discussion. The last section concludes the research with recommendations for future analysis.

2 Stylized Facts and the Model Theoretical Foundations

A number of recent works (Korinek & Stiglitz, 2017; Stiglitz, 2016) showed that new models must take into account the following: firstly, human capital in the production function; secondly, the new nature of technological progress in the digital economy, which will be determined mainly by the amount of technological information necessary for the production of goods and services; thirdly, capital income, which should be considered as an endogenous factor in describing the growth of the physical capital share in national income.

In the twentieth century, there were a number of empirical laws accompanying the process of long-term economic growth and N. Kaldor (1961) was the first to formulate a number of them. The following Kaldor laws are of interest for our further analysis: (a) the ratio of physical capital to output is approximately constant; (b) the shares of labor and physical capital in national income are approximately constant; (c) the wages of workers grow in proportion to labor productivity.

Stiglitz (2016) formulated new stylized (empirical) facts in the modern economy development, and some of them differ from the Kaldor laws. Among them are the following: (a) the average wage no longer grows in proportion to productivity, so the share of capital is growing; (b) there is growing inequality, both in terms of wages and capital income, as well as growing inequality in general.

Stiglitz only needed a small technical modification of classical models in order to take into account new empirical facts. Nevertheless, his models made it possible to formulate new theoretical foundations that explain the stagnation of workers' wages in recent decades, despite productivity and GDP continuing to grow. In Korinek and Stiglitz (2017), AI is seen as an absolute form of technological progress, replacing skilled workers and leading to technological unemployment. The same work also analyzed how technological labor substitution affects the workers' wages in the short and long term. It is shown that in the general case, the addition of machine labor creates a redistribution of income from human labor to additional factors.

T. Piketty studied new trends in capital accumulation, economic growth and income inequality, which emerged at the beginning of the twenty-first century and obtained interesting results. First, Picketty showed that capital intensity of developed countries followed a large U-curve and at the beginning of the twenty-first century and returned to maximum values close to those observed at the end of nineteenth at (Piketty, 2014, Ch. 2, 3). The return of capital intensity in developed countries in the twenty-first century to its maximum value means that it is now stabilizing again, at least until the middle of the century (Piketty, 2014, Ch.5). Therefore, it follows that in the first half of the twenty-first century, Kaldor's first empirical regularity remains valid.

Kaldor's second empirical regularity will cease to operate in practice in the twenty-first century: the share of capital income in GDP will not remain constant but will grow, as Piketty (2014) shows. Piketty suggests that the share of capital income at the global level will reach 30–40% by the middle of the current century, i.e., a level close to the indicators of the eighteenth–nineteenth centuries (Piketty, 2014, Ch.6). As for the share of labor, it should accordingly fall. For example, in the USA, the share of labor in GDP has already fallen from 65% to 55% between 1970 and 2015. This was precisely the reason for the stagnation of the workers' wages observed during this period.

Kaldor's third regularity ceased to work since the mid-1970s, when the growth paths of labor productivity and real average wages of workers diverged: the first continued and continues to grow steadily, while the second—at first stagnated, and from the beginning of the twenty-first century started to decline (Ford, 2015).

B. Arthur (1996) was the first to note that in the high-tech sectors of the knowledge-based economy, there are increasing returns to scale, while in traditional industries, including manufacturing, decreasing returns to scale remains dominant. As changes took place, the main mechanisms determining the behavior of the economy have shifted: from decreasing to increasing returns to scale.

We also took into account the presence of long waves in the economy, although not all economists support the theory of long waves, primarily because of the difficulty of confirming their regular nature. Among economists who share this theory, there is no consensus regarding the periodization of these waves, but the prevailing opinion is that the rise of the 4th cycle was seen in 1948–1973 (Van Duijn, 2006). In this regard, we will adhere to the same periodization, assuming that the rise of the 5th cycle occurred at the beginning of the 1980s, approximately between 1982 and 2019.

Based on the above and taking into account the new stylized facts established by Stiglitz and Piketty, we have proposed models to forecast the dynamics of potential jobs, employment of people in the economy, as well as the dynamics of UBI required to ensure a guaranteed level of aggregate demand. These models can serve as a useful complement to the theoretical results obtained by J.Stiglitz and T. Piketty.

3 Data and Model

3.1 Data

The main data used in our set of models are data on GDP (Y), physical (K) and human capital (H), labor (L) and technological progress (A).

The numerical values of production factors (K, L) and GDP (Y) for the US economy were taken from the US Bureau of Economic Analysis (2020b, 2020c, 2020d). TFP data (A) was taken from the University of Groningen and the University of California. The human capital (H) data was obtained from an article by M. Christian (2017).

Auxiliary data involved in our calculations include data from the International Federation of Robotics (2019) on the number of robots and statistics on the US population dynamics (US Bureau of Economic Analysis, 2020a).

3.2 The Basic Model of Long-Term Economic Growth

As a basic model for describing long-term economic growth, we adopted a modified neoclassical model (Mankiw et al., 1992), which takes into account human capital:

$$Y(t) = \gamma \times K^{\alpha}(t) \times H^{\beta}(t) \times \left[A(t) \times L_p(t)\right]^{1-\alpha-\beta+\delta} \qquad (1)$$

where $Y(t)$—gross domestic product (GDP); $K(t)$—physical capital; $H(t)$—human capital; $A(t)$—technological progress; $L_p(t)$—potential number of jobs in the economy; α and β—physical and human capital shares in GDP; δ—parameter characterizing increasing returns to scale ($\delta > 0$); γ—constant rate factor.

We introduced the parameter δ into the production function in Eq. (1) to account for the increasing returns generated in high-tech science-intensive sectors of the economy according to Arthur (1996).

Kaldor's second regularity means that in Eq. (1) α and β, characterizing the shares of physical and human capital, as well as $(1 - \alpha - \beta + \delta)$, characterizing the share of effective labor, are constant values.

Kaldor's third regularity is formalized in the form:

$$\bar{w}(t) = a_0 \times A(t) \tag{2}$$

where $\bar{w}(t)$ —current average workers' wage; a_0—normalization coefficient. Such an increase in workers' wages was observed in the "golden era" of the global economy (1950–1970).

In order to take into account the new empirical pattern of increasing capital income share in GDP, we propose an endogenous calculation mechanism for $\alpha(t)$, taking advantage of the fact that the marginal product of labor is equal to the real wage rate in a perfectly competitive market (Kurzenev & Matveenko, 2018, Ch.3):

$$\frac{\partial Y}{\partial L} = \frac{W}{P} = w \tag{3}$$

where W—nominal wage; P—price level. Accordingly, the marginal product of capital is generally equal to the interest rate r (average return on capital) plus the capital depreciation rate (Kurzenev & Matveenko, 2018, Ch.3):

$$\frac{\partial Y}{\partial K} = r + \mu_K \tag{4}$$

Since the production function is given in Eq. (1), for the real wage rate in Eq. (3), we obtain the formula:

$$w = \frac{\partial Y}{\partial L} = [1 - \alpha(t) - \beta(t) + \delta]\frac{Y_P}{L_P} \tag{5}$$

where Y_P—potential GDP. The formula for calculating the combined physical and human capital share in national income is below:

$$\alpha(t) + \beta\,(t) = 1 + \delta - \frac{wL_p}{Y_p} \tag{6}$$

Calculating the marginal product of capital in Eq. (4) for the production function in Eq. (1), we obtain:

$$\begin{aligned} &a)\ r + \mu_K = \tfrac{\partial Y}{\partial K} = \alpha \tfrac{Y}{K};\\ &b)\ \alpha = (r + \mu_K) \times \sigma_K \end{aligned} \tag{7}$$

It follows that the physical capital share in GDP is proportional to the average return on capital (r) and capital intensity of income (σ_K). This, according to Piketty

(2014), is the first fundamental law of capitalism that defines the national income distribution between capital and labor.

Based on the equality of the net marginal products of physical and human capital (Barro & Sala-i-Martin, 2003), in accordance with the production function in Eq. (1), $\frac{\partial Y}{\partial K} = \alpha æ_K = \frac{\partial Y}{\partial H} = \beta æ_H$, we get the ratio:

$$\alpha = \beta \frac{æ_H}{æ_K} \tag{8}$$

Therefore, from formula in Eq. (6), using relation in Eq. (8), we can distinguish the dynamics of the physical capital share:

$$\tilde{\alpha} = \alpha(t) = \frac{æ_H}{æ_H + æ_K}\left(1 + \delta - \frac{wL_p}{Y_p}\right) \tag{9}$$

Thus, the inclusion of human capital in in Eq. (1) allows us to assess the physical capital share in national income in Eq. (9) more accurately.

3.3 The Basic Model of Long-Term Economic Growth

The accumulation of capital and innovative technologies of the 4th industrial revolution will become the driving force of economic development. Capital growth was the most important feature of capitalism in the nineteenth–twentieth centuries. It will accelerate in the twenty-first century, according to Piketty.

We assume that Kaldor's first empirical law is formalized as follows:

$$\begin{aligned} &\text{a) } K = \sigma_K \times Y, \;\; \sigma_K = \text{const};\\ &\text{b) } Y = æ_K \times K, \quad æ_K = \text{const} \end{aligned} \tag{10}$$

where σ_K—physical capital intensity ratio; $æ_K$—physical capital productivity ratio.

For human capital, similar equations are obtained:

$$\begin{aligned} &\text{a) } H = \sigma_H \times \; Y, \sigma_H = \text{const};\\ &\text{b) } Y = æ_H \times H, \quad æ_H = \text{const} \end{aligned} \tag{11}$$

where σ_H—human capital intensity ratio; $æ_H$—human capital productivity ratio.

The movement of physical $K(t)$ and human $H(t)$ capital is described by the classical equation of capital accumulation (Kurzenev & Matveenko, 2018, Ch.3; Barro & Sala-i-Martin, 2003, Ch.1):

$$\begin{aligned} &a)\ \dot{K}(t) = I_K(t) - \mu_K \times K(t); \\ &b)\ \dot{H}(t) = I_H(t) - \mu_H \times H(t) \end{aligned} \tag{12}$$

where $I_K(t)$ and $I_H(t)$—gross investment in physical and human capital; μ_K and μ_H—physical and human capital depreciation rates.

Since $I_K(t) = s_K \cdot Y(t)$, $I_H(t) = s_H \cdot Y(t)$, where s_K and s_H—the rate of investment in physical and human capital, respectively, Eq. (12) are transformed in:

$$\begin{aligned} &a)\ \dot{K}(t) = s_K \times Y(t) - \mu_K \times K(t); \\ &b)\ \dot{H}(t) = s_H \times Y(t) - \mu_H \times H(t) \end{aligned} \tag{13}$$

Given Kaldor's first empirical regularity in Eq. (10), Eq. (13) will be simplified further:

$$\begin{aligned} &a)\ \dot{K}(t) = (s_K \times æ_K - \mu_K) \times K(t); \\ &b)\ \dot{H}(t) = (s_H \times æ_H - \mu_H) \times H(t) \end{aligned} \tag{14}$$

The solution of differential Eq. (14) has the form:

$$\begin{aligned} &a)\ K(t) = K_0 \times \exp\left[(s_K \times æ_K - \mu_K) \times (t - T_0)\right]; \\ &b)\ H(t) = H_0 \times \exp\left[(s_H \times æ_H - \mu_H) \times (t - T_0)\right] \end{aligned} \tag{15}$$

where K_0 and H_0—physical and human capital volumes at the initial moment T_0.

Therefore, in the first half of the twenty-first century, there will be an exponential increase in accumulated capital. However, given that, in accordance with the theory of long waves, at its lower stage, the effect of capital saturation should occur in the 2020–2030, the accumulation of capital will occur along the logistic path:

$$K(t) = \frac{K_1}{1 + u_K \times \exp\left[-\vartheta_K \times (t - T_0)\right]} \tag{16}$$

where K_1, u_K and ϑ_K are constant parameters.

Similarly, to describe the process of human capital accumulation, we obtain the following equation:

$$H(t) = \frac{H_1}{1 + u_H \times \exp\left[-\vartheta_H \times (t - T_0)\right]} \tag{17}$$

where H_1, u_H and ϑ_H are constant parameters.

Knowing the trajectory of capital accumulation in Eq. (16) and using relation in Eq. (10b), we can calculate the growth trajectory of potential output:

$$\mathrm{Y_p(t) = æ_K \times K(t)} \tag{18}$$

We use the set of Eqs. (15)–(17) to predict the physical and human capital dynamics in the first half of the twenty-first century.

3.4 The Model of the Dynamics of Technological Progress in the Era of the Digital Economy

Next, we need to decide on a model for calculating technological progress $A(t)$, which is expressed by the total factor productivity (TFP) of capital and labor. TFP plays the key role in economic development and provides for more than 60% of productivity growth (Easterly & Levine, 2019).

In Akaev and Sadovnichy (2018), we derived a formula for calculating the rate of technological progress for the era of the digital economy:

$$\begin{aligned} &\text{a) } q_{Ad}(t) = \frac{\dot{A}_d(t)}{A_d(t)} = \xi\sqrt{\psi_d(t) \times \dot{g}(t)}; \\ &\text{b) } \psi_d(t) = \frac{I_d(t)}{K_d(t)};\ S_d(t) = S_{do} \times \exp[g(t)] \end{aligned} \tag{19}$$

where $A_d(t)$—technological progress (TFP) in the era of the digital economy; ξ—calibration factor ($\xi = 0.07$); $I_d(t)$—current investment in fixed assets $K_d(t)$ of information and digital industries; $S_d(t)$—volume of technological production knowledge (information) in the digital economy, which is growing exponentially. Therefore, $\dot{g}(t)$ represents the growth rate of technological production information.

In Akaev and Sadovnichy (2018), we showed that the function $\psi_d(t)$ can be approximated by a linear function and extrapolated for predictive purposes:

$$\begin{aligned} &\psi_d(t) = \psi_0 + \psi_1 \times (t - T_0); \\ &T_0 = 1982; \psi_0 = 0.09; \psi_1 = 0.002 \end{aligned} \tag{20}$$

The growth rate of production technological information $\dot{g}(t)$ for the forecast period of 2020–2030 is described by the following function (Akaev & Sadovnichy, 2018):

$$\begin{aligned} &\text{a) } \dot{g}(t) = \frac{1}{\varsigma_g} \times \left(1 - \frac{e^{-\rho \times \varsigma_g \times g(t)}}{1-\rho} + C_1 \times e^{-\varsigma_g \times g(t)}\right)^{-1}; \\ &\text{b) } C_1 = e^{\varsigma_g \times g_1}\left(\frac{1}{\nu_1} - 1 + \frac{e^{-\varsigma_g \times g_1}}{1-\rho}\right); \end{aligned} \tag{21}$$

$$\text{c) } t = \varsigma_g \times g(t) + \frac{e^{-\rho \times \varsigma_g \times g(t)}}{\rho(1-\rho)} - C_1 \times e^{-\varsigma_g \times g(t)} + C_2;$$

$$\text{d) } C_2 = \frac{1}{\nu_1} - 1 - \varsigma_g \times g_1 - \frac{1}{\rho} \times e^{-\rho \times \varsigma_g \times g_1}$$

The values of all parameters included in the above formulas were estimated in Akaev and Sadovnichy (2018):

$$g_1 = 5.3; \varsigma_g = 14; \rho = 0.008; \nu_1 = \frac{1}{14} \tag{22}$$

Solving the differential Eq. (19a) with respect to $A_d(t)$, we get:

$$A_d(t) = A_{do} \times \exp\left\{\xi \times \int_t^{To} \sqrt{\psi_d(\tau)\dot{g}(\tau)}d\tau\right\} \tag{23}$$

Since the functions $\psi_d(t)$ and $\dot{g}(t)$ are given, we can calculate the growth path of technological progress $A(t)$ in the era of the digital economy using formula (23).

3.5 *Models of Employment and Income, Taking into Account Technological Substitution of Jobs*

Substituting relations in Eqs. (10) and (11) in formula (1) and resolving it with respect to $L(t)$, we obtain the following formula for calculating employment:

$$L(t) = \lambda \times \frac{K(t)^{\frac{1-\tilde{\alpha}-\tilde{\beta}}{1-\tilde{\alpha}-\tilde{\beta}+\delta}}}{A(t)}, \lambda = \left(\frac{æ_K^{1-\beta} \times æ_H^{\beta}}{\gamma}\right)^{\frac{1}{1-\tilde{\alpha}-\tilde{\beta}+\delta}} \tag{24}$$

Here λ—constant normalization factor. In this formula, the parameters $æ$, γ, δ are constant, and the share of expanded capital $\tilde{\alpha} + \tilde{\beta}$ in GDP will increase in accordance with the formula (6). Therefore, the parameters $\tilde{\alpha}$ and $\tilde{\beta}$ are marked with an $\tilde{\alpha}$ (i.e. combining grave-acute-grave) at the top, indicating that they are variable. If in formula (24), we fix the constant current values to $\tilde{\alpha} = \alpha_0$ and $\tilde{\beta} = \beta_0$, then the formula can be used to forecast the dynamics of the potential number of jobs in the economy.

Having predicted growth paths of potential GDP (Y_p) and potential jobs L_p, we can calculate the growth of the total share of physical and human capital $\widetilde{\alpha} + \widetilde{\beta}$ depending on the given growth scenarios of the real worker's wage rate (w) using formula (6). Two practically interesting scenarios come to mind: first, empirical growth and second, growth proportional to labor productivity. The first scenario is based on the continuation of the trend in the movement of the wage rate that has developed over the past decades. In the second scenario, the real salary paid by firms is determined by the formula (Blanchard, 2016, Ch.3), which expresses Kaldor's third law in Eq. (2):

$$w = \frac{A}{1+\eta}; \eta \geq 0 \tag{25}$$

where η—cost overrun. If markets were perfectly competitive, then $\eta = 0$. We will describe this scenario as hypothetical.

Next, we consider the impact of the technological substitution of jobs. Their reduction due to the intensive use of robots will occur in various sectors of the economy, the growth of which can be predicted using the logistic function:

$$\mathrm{R(t)} = \mathrm{R_1} + \frac{\mathrm{R_2}}{1 + \mathrm{u_R} \times \exp\left[-\vartheta_\mathrm{R} \times (\mathrm{t} - \mathrm{T_{BR}})\right]} \tag{26}$$

where R_1, R_2, u_R, ϑ_R—constant parameters.

Automation using robots increases the demand for more skilled labor. However, the overall balance is negative for employment and wages: they are both declining, as it is claimed in Acemoglu and Restrepo (2017). The empirical laws for the US economy established by Acemoglu and Restrepo are formalized as follows:

$$\begin{aligned} &\text{a) } \mathrm{L_H(t)} = \mathrm{L_p(t)} \times \{1 - \varepsilon_\mathrm{L} \times [\mathrm{R(t)} - \mathrm{R_0}]\}; \\ &\text{b) } \bar{\mathrm{w}}(\mathrm{t}) = \bar{\mathrm{w}}_0 \times \{1 - \varepsilon_\mathrm{w} \times [\mathrm{R(t)} - \mathrm{R_0}]\} \times \exp\left[\bar{\mathrm{q}}_\mathrm{p} \times (\mathrm{t} - \mathrm{T_0})\right] \end{aligned} \tag{27}$$

where $L_H(t)$—jobs (number) occupied by people; $\bar{w}_0$—average annual employee wage; $\bar{q}_p$—average projected inflation; R_0—the number of robots operating in the economy at the time T_0; $\varepsilon_L = (0.18 + 0.34) \cdot 10^{-7}$ и $\varepsilon_w = (0.25 + 0.5) \cdot 10^{-7}$—empirical coefficients.

Thus, we will have the following equations for calculating the dynamics of increasing the total capital share in Eq. (6) and the physical capital share in Eq. (9), according to the two scenarios:

1. empirical

$$\begin{aligned} &\text{a) } \widetilde{\alpha}_e + \widetilde{\beta}_e = 1 + \delta - \bar{w}_0 \times \{1 - \varepsilon_w \times [R(t) - R_0]\} \times \exp\left[\bar{q}_p \times (t - T_0)\right] \times \tfrac{L_p}{Y_p}; \\ &\text{b) } \widetilde{\alpha}_e = \tfrac{æ_H}{æ_H + æ_K}\left[1 + \delta - \bar{w}_0 \times \{1 - \varepsilon_w \times [R(t) - R_0]\} \times \exp\left[\bar{q}_p \times (t - T_0)\right] \times \tfrac{L_p}{Y_p}\right] \end{aligned} \tag{28}$$

2. hypothetical

$$\begin{aligned} &\text{c) } \widetilde{\alpha}_w + \widetilde{\beta}_w = 1 + \delta - \tfrac{A(t)}{1+\eta} \times \tfrac{L_p}{Y_p} \times \exp\left[\bar{q}_p \times (t - T_0)\right]; \\ &\text{d) } \widetilde{\alpha}_w = \tfrac{æ_H}{æ_H + æ_K}\left\{1 + \delta - \tfrac{A(t)}{1+\eta} \times \tfrac{L_p}{Y_p} \times \exp\left[\bar{q}_p \times (t - T_0)\right]\right\} \end{aligned} \tag{29}$$

By substituting dependencies in Eqs. (28a) and (29c) alternately into formula (24), we obtain forecast trajectories L_{pe} and L_{pw} for the growth in the number of real jobs in the US economy, corresponding to the two scenarios adopted above. Further, using the formula (27a), we calculate the predicted trajectories of the number of jobs for people L_{He} and L_{Hw}.

Therefore, if $\bar{w}(t)$ is the nominal average forecast wage of one employee, then the forecast of the dynamics of the total income of all workers employed in the economy can be calculated using both empirical laws in Eq. (27):

$$\bar{Y}_{ph}(t) = \bar{w}(t) \times L_H(t) \tag{30}$$

In order to establish a relationship between the private households' incomes $\bar{Y}_{ph}(t)$ in Eq. (30) and the real aggregate demand for goods and services, we turn to the main economic identity:

$$Y = C + I + G + NX \tag{31}$$

where *C(t)*—total household consumption; *I(t)*—gross investment; *G(t)*—government spending; *NX(t)*—net exports.

Assuming that in this equation $C(t) = c\bar{Y}_{ph}$ (*c*—households average consumption coefficient), $I = s \cdot Y$, $G = \tau \cdot Y$ (τ—average tax rate) and $NX = 0$ (case of balanced foreign trade), we obtain the following relationship linking aggregate real demand for goods and services (Y_{rd}) and real total annual household income $\bar{Y}_{ph}$:

$$Y_{rd}(t) = c' \times \bar{Y}_{ph}(t); \; c' = \frac{c}{1 - s - \tau} \tag{32}$$

The question arises, how can consumer demand be ensured at the level of potential output of goods and services? We have already noted above that one of the solution options is the introduction of UBI. To assess the UBI, first, it is necessary to calculate the predicted dynamics of population growth, which can best be set by the logistic function:

$$N(t) = N_1 + \frac{N_2}{1 + u_N \times \exp[-\vartheta_N \times (t - T_{bN})]} \tag{33}$$

where N_1, N_2, u_N, ϑ_N—constant parameters, T_{bN}—year of the beginning of the population growth dynamics approximation.

We also approximate the dynamics of the UBI by the logistic function:

$$r_b(t) = \frac{r_{bo}}{1 + u_b \times \exp[-\vartheta_b(t - T_{b0})]} \tag{34}$$

where r_{b0}, u_b, ϑ_b—constant parameters; T_{b0}—year of UBI commencement.

The total UBI received by the entire adult population is determined by the formula:

$$Y_{Nb}(t) = \phi \times N(t) \times r_b(t) \tag{35}$$

where ϕ—coefficient taking into account the adult population receiving UBI ($\phi \leq 1$). Then, the aggregate demand of households, taking into account both labor income $\bar{Y}_{ph}$ in Eq. (30) and UBI in Eq. (35):

$$Y_{rdb}(t) = c'[\bar{Y}_{ph}(t) + Y_{Nb}(t)] \tag{36}$$

So, we have compiled the model of economic growth in Eq. (1), taking into account both physical and human capital, and endogenous formation mechanisms of physical and human capital shares in national income in Eq. (6), as well as technical progress (Eqs. 19 and 23). We use the model to forecast the potential GDP and the number of jobs under given scenarios of the wage rate changes and the level of UBI necessary to ensure the sustainability of the economy.

4 Results and Discussion

4.1 Results

The article (Christian, 2017) presents a study on the assessment of the US economy human capital from 1975 to 2013, and therefore calculations using H are limited to this period.

The verification of the production function (1) for the US economy in the period from 1982 to 2013 are presented in Table 1:

The approximation of US GDP using the formula (1) is presented in Fig. 1. Actual values are marked in black, simulated in red.

Table 1 Results of calculations for the model (1)

Parameter Estimates	Accuracy ratings
$\gamma = 0.101$; $\alpha = 0.439$; $\beta = 0.183$; $\delta = 0.081$	The average approximation error is 0.59%; Normalized coefficient of determination 0.964

Source: calculated by the authors based on data from M. Christian (2017), US Bureau of Economic Analysis (2020b, 2020c, 2020d), The University of Groningen and University of California, Davis (2020)

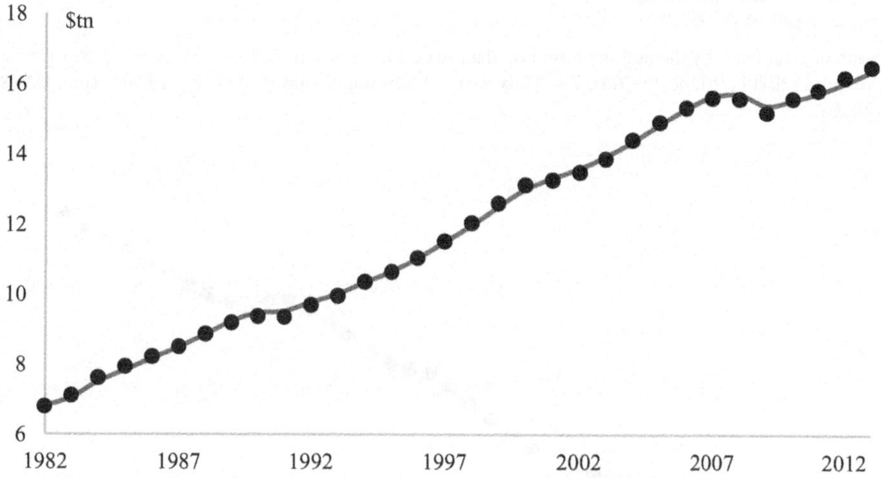

Fig. 1 US GDP growth dynamics (1982–2013). Source: Authors' creation

Table 2 Estimates of the model (1) parameters quality

Parameters	Standard error	*t*-statistic
α	0.0587	8.832
β	0.0282	4.986
δ	0.0176	25.028

Source: calculated by the authors based on data from M. Christian (2017), US Bureau of Economic Analysis (2020b, 2020c, 2020d), The University of Groningen and University of California, Davis (2020)

Table 2 shows the parameters' statistical estimates for production factors (significance level of 95%).

Based on data for the $K(t)$ (from 1982 to 2018) and for the $H(t)$ (from 1982 to 2013), coefficient estimates were obtained for capital accumulation models in the twenty-first century. The results are summarized in Table 3:

By extrapolating in accordance to formula (15b) for 2014–2018, using values of human capital and taking into account available statistical data on other production factors, Fig. 1 can be supplemented with simulated GDP values (highlighted in green in Fig. 2).

Table 3 Calculation results for capital accumulation models (15–17)

Parameter Estimates	Accuracy ratings
$\sigma_K = 3.31$; $\ae_K = 0.302$; $\mu_K = 0.035$; $s_K = 18.6\%$ $K_1 = 163.6$ trillion dollars; $u_k = 1.782$; $\vartheta_k = 0.038$ $\sigma_H = 13.12$; $\ae_H = 0.076$; $s_H = 29.5\,\%$; $\mu_H = 1.04\%$ $H_1 = 567.5$ trillion dollars; $u_H = 1.399$; $\vartheta_H = 0.02$	R^2 are close to 1; The observed F-test values are more than critical (significance level of 95%)

Source: calculated by the authors based on data from M. Christian (2017), US Bureau of Economic Analysis (2020b, 2020c, 2020d), The University of Groningen and University of California, Davis (2020)

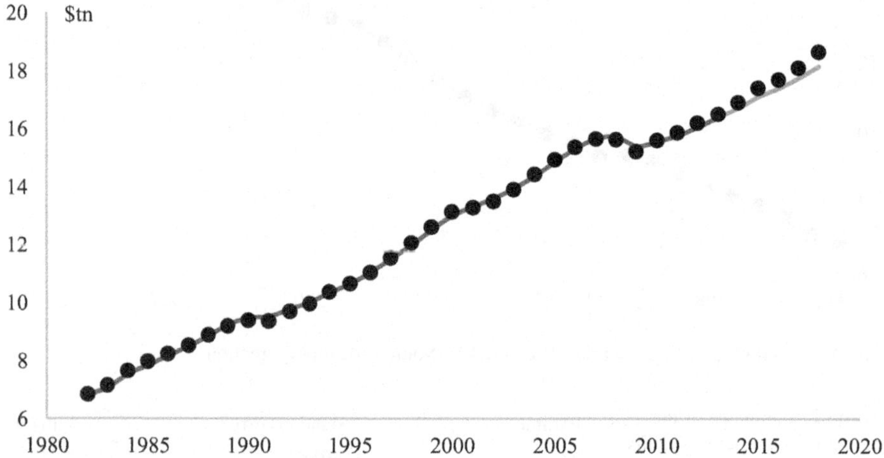

Fig. 2 US GDP growth dynamics (1982–2018). Source: Authors' creation

Let us note that we do not present the results for the technological progress model (19–23), since it was studied in detail in Akaev and Sadovnichy (2018).

According to the International Federation of Robotics (2019), on the number of robots operating in the US economy, the parameters values of Eq. (26) were found: $R_1 = 0.17$ million; $R_2 = 17.5$ million; $u_R = 132$; $\vartheta_R = 0.121$; $T_{BR} = 1995$.

The predicted dynamics of the potential number of jobs in the US economy as a whole is $L_p(t)$ and, for the two varying scenarios $L_{pe}(t)$ and $L_{pw}(t)$, which are calculated by formula (24), are shown in Fig. 3a. The corresponding trajectories of the number of employees, taking into account production and management robots—L_{He} and L_{Hw}, are presented in Fig. 3b.

Predicted growth paths of potential US GDP until 2030, calculated using the formula (1) under various scenarios of the labor employment reduction L_{pe}, L_{pw}, L_{He}, L_{Hw}, (see Figs. 3a, 3b) and accelerated capital accumulation K (16), are presented in

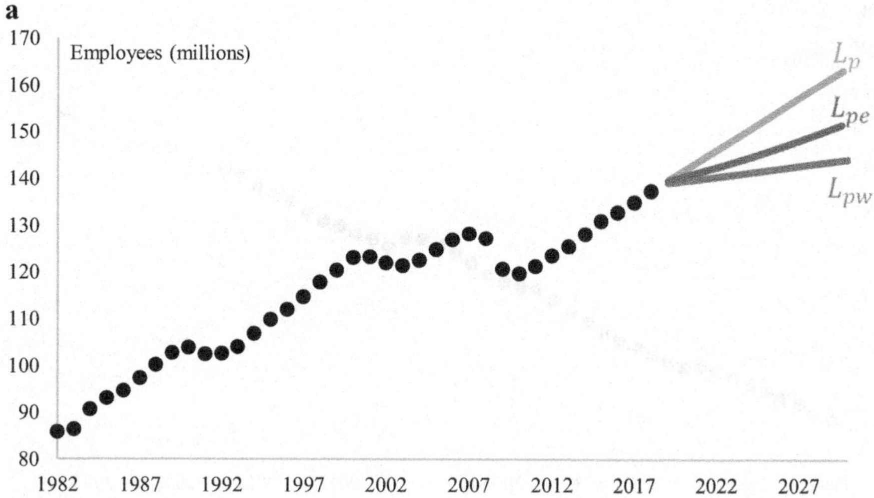

Fig. 3a Forecasts of the number of employed in the US economy, taking into account technological substitution of jobs (L_p—potential number of employees; L_{pe}, L_{pw}—number of employees in the empirical and hypothetical scenarios). Source: Authors' creation

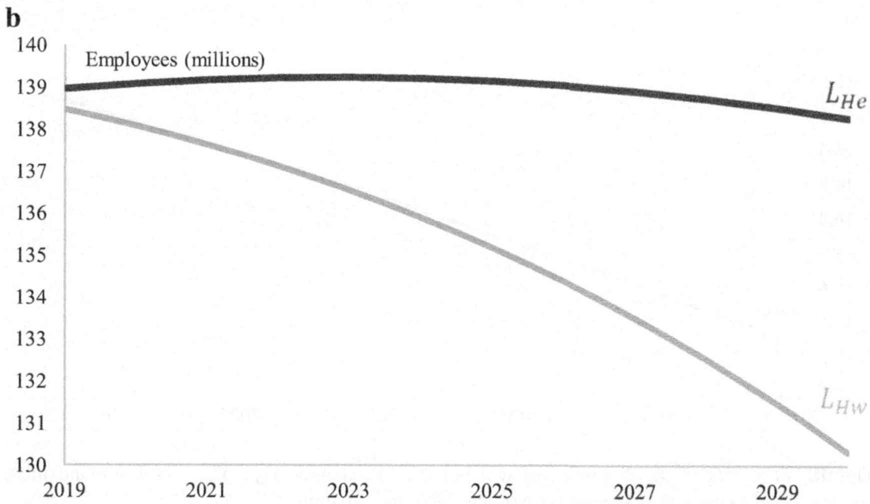

Fig. 3b Forecasts of the number of employees in the US economy, taking into account production and management robots (L_{He}, L_{Hw}—number of employees in the empirical and hypothetical scenarios). Source: Authors' creation

Figs. 4a and 4b. Note that the current values for USA hold as follows: $c = 0.82$; $s = 0.18$; $\tau = 0.11$; $c' = 1.16$.

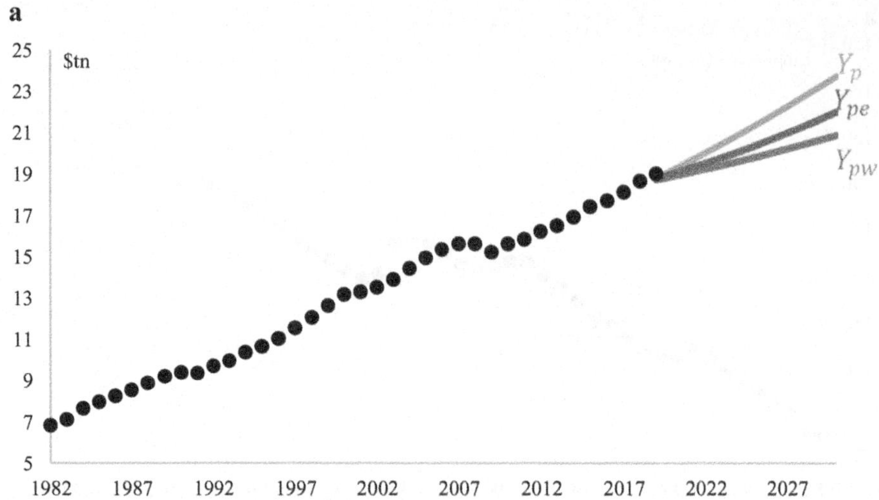

Fig. 4a Forecasts of GDP dynamics taking into account technological substitution of jobs (Y_p—potential GDP; Y_{pe}, Y_{pw}—GDP in the empirical and hypothetical scenarios). Source: Authors' creation

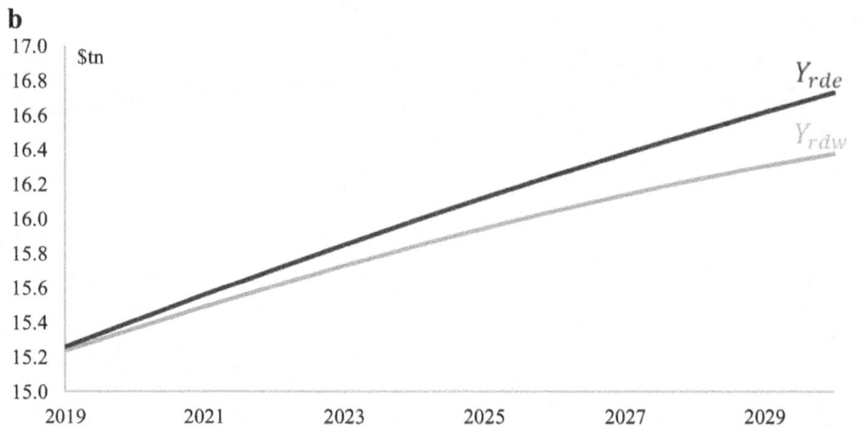

Fig. 4b Forecasts of the dynamics of real household demand (Y_{rde}, Y_{rdw}—real demand in the empirical and hypothetical scenarios). Source: Authors' creation

According to estimates, the GDP potential value (Y_p) for 2030 is 23.7 trillion dollars with the number of employees L_p equal to 164.1 million jobs. Table 4 shows the US economy forecasts for 2030 under the considered scenarios.

To describe the dynamics of the US population growth, the numerical values of the parameters are determined: $N_1 = 0.009$ million people; $N_2 = 617.76$ million people; $u_N = 2.93$; $\vartheta_N = 0.018$; $T_{bN} = 1950$.

Table 4 USA Economic Forecast 2030

Indicator	Scenario	
	Empirical	Hypothetical
Number of employees (million), including:		
technological substitution of jobs	152.2	144.3
production and management robots	138.3	130.3
GDP, taking into account technological substitution of jobs (trillion dollars)	22	20.9
Households real demand (trillion dollars)	16.7	16.3

Source: calculated by the authors based on data from M. Christian (2017), International Federation of Robotics (2019), US Bureau of Economic Analysis (2020b, 2020c, 2020d), The University of Groningen and University of California, Davis (2020)

a

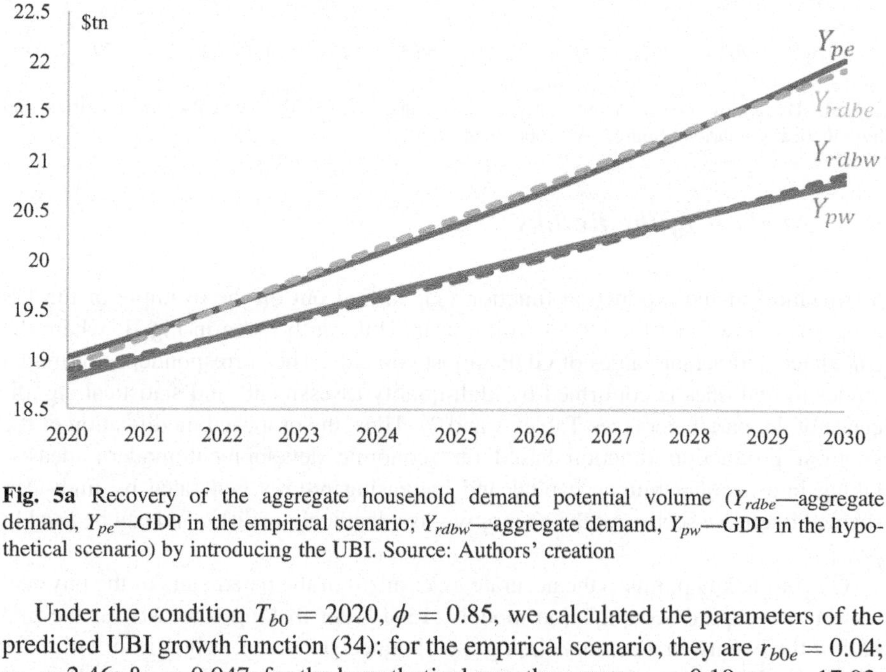

Fig. 5a Recovery of the aggregate household demand potential volume (Y_{rdbe}—aggregate demand, Y_{pe}—GDP in the empirical scenario; Y_{rdbw}—aggregate demand, Y_{pw}—GDP in the hypothetical scenario) by introducing the UBI. Source: Authors' creation

Under the condition $T_{b0} = 2020$, $\phi = 0.85$, we calculated the parameters of the predicted UBI growth function (34): for the empirical scenario, they are $r_{b0e} = 0.04$; $u_{be} = 2.46$; $\vartheta_{be} = 0.047$; for the hypothetical one, they are $r_{b0w} = 0.19$; $u_{bw} = 17.03$; $\vartheta_{bw} = 0.018$

The growth trajectory of the aggregate household demand, including UBI in Eq. (36) and the growth curve of the UBI itself in Eq. (34) are presented in Figs. 5a and 5b.

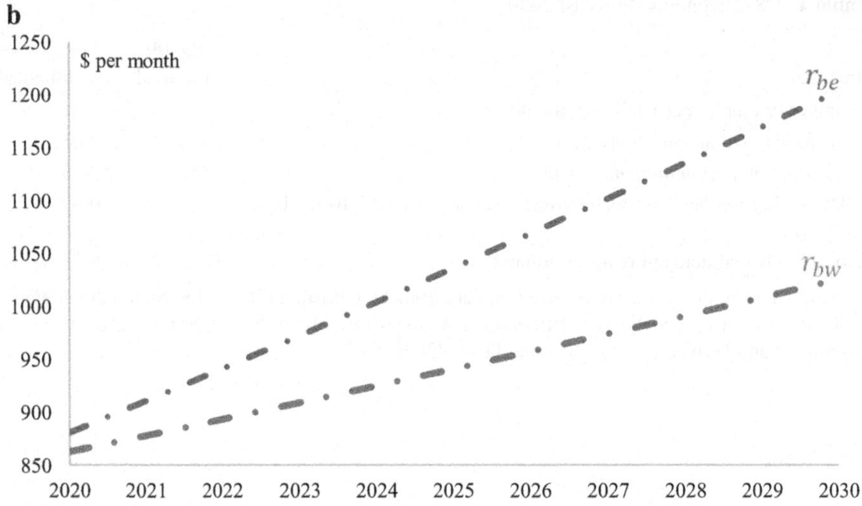

Fig. 5b Dynamics of basic income r_b (r_{be}, r_{bw}—number of monthly payments in the empirical and hypothetical scenarios). Source: Authors' creation

4.2 *Analysis of the Results*

Verification of the production function (1), carried out on the example of the US economy, shows that the model works well. This can be seen in Fig. 1, where the calculated and actual values of GDP almost coincide. The correspondence of model values to real ones is confirmed by high-quality assessments and statistical significance of the parameters (see Tables 1 and 2). Thus, the proposed modification of the simplest production function based on economic development modern ideas—taking into account human capital and increasing returns generated by high-tech science-intensive sectors of the economy—is adequately realistic and can be used in practice.

One of the key points is the accurate assessment of the parameters of the physical and human capital accumulation models (15–17) for making forecasts for the first half of the twenty-first century. Using the obtained statistically significant estimates (Table 3), factors K and H are simulated close to real values. The proposed capital models correspond to the ideas of Piketty and Stiglitz and can be used both to determine the average annual growth rate of potential GDP (in our calculations, it is 2.15%) and in related studies of the future dynamics of the capital resources of the economy.

Of greatest interest for analysis are the calculation results for two scenarios—hypothetical and empirical. As can be seen from Fig. 3a, in the case of a hypothetical scenario, the potential number of jobs is lower than the empirical option (on average, 2.9% per year). Moreover, judging by Fig. 3b, in the hypothetical scenario, there is a sharper decrease in the number of jobs occupied by people (–5.89%), compared with the empirical scenario (–0.49%). In the empirical scenario, despite technological substitution, there is even a slight increase in the number of jobs occupied by people in the first half of the forecast period (2020–2025).

At the same time, the average difference in forecast GDP values for the considered scenarios is equivalent to the difference in the potential number of jobs (2.9%), and the average growth rates are 1.6% and 1.1% for empirical and hypothetical options, respectively. Figure 4b indicates that the wage growth under the hypothetical scenario partially offsets the negative impact of declining employment on real demand for goods and services—the average discrepancy between Y_{rde} and Y_{rdw} curves is 1.1%.

The difference in approaches to the nominal wage determination between the 2 scenarios is also manifested at the level of UBI calculations. The calculations confirm the conclusion that there is a smaller gap between real demand and supply under the hypothetical scenario—the amount of funds needed to restore demand is on average 18.19% of the projected GDP for the empirical scenario and 17.01% for the hypothetical one. This fact affects the value of the UBI. According to our calculations for 10 years, in the hypothetical scenario, it is enough to increase the initial UBI ($860 / month per person) by about $160. While in the empirical scenario, a higher initial level of UBI ($880 / month per person) is required, alongside annual increases of the amount of payments to a level of $1200 / month in 2030.

In general, the forecasts obtained correspond to the hypotheses about the impact of digital transformation on the economy and new stylized facts. Acceleration of technological progress, automation, and robotization have a negative impact on the labor factor. Under these conditions, the dynamics of economic development indicators (GDP, real demand, and number of jobs) are inversely proportional to the change in the real wage rate. On the other hand, an increase in wages has a positive effect on smoothing inequality and reduces the required UBI value.

4.3 Discussion

It is necessary to compare the modeled results with the currently available estimates. According to forecasts of the US Congressional Budget Office (2020), the US potential real GDP by the end of 2030 will be 23.3 trillion dollars. That differs 1.7% from the values obtained using our model. An alternative estimate proposed by the OECD (2020) is 21.9 trillion dollars, which practically coincides with our empirical scenario projection. Hence, taking into account various scenarios of wage rate dynamics allows us to form a space of adequate estimates of future GDP.

On the other hand, according to the calculations of the US Department of Labor, Bureau of Labor Statistics (2019), the number of jobs in the US economy by 2028 will be 169.4 million, which is 6% higher than our forecast for the same year. In our opinion, this discrepancy once again emphasizes the complexity of the digital transformation process and the importance of finding tools to describe it.

Information and knowledge have become the main resources of the modern economy. The particularity of these resources lies in the fact that they are the result of human intellectual activity and information activities of the society. In this regard, the areas of production associated with the generation, transmission, processing, and use of information are becoming increasingly important in modern economic systems. This raises the question of using the concept of "intellectual capital" instead of human capital in future models of economic dynamics. The concept of intellectual capital (Edvinsson & Malone, 1997) is wider and deeper than the concept of human capital and includes information as an independent production resource.

In the scenarios of wage changes, both empirical and hypothetical, the forecasts about the decrease in the number of jobs due to automation and robotization of production, and, therefore, the prospect of a decrease in demand for goods and services, are confirmed. According to the model, in both scenarios, a gradual decrease in employment because of crowding out of human labor by intelligent machines can lead to a drop in real demand in the next decade. The identified problem poses a potential threat to the economic well-being of the USA. In this regard, as one of the solutions, the introduction of the UBI is proposed in order to create a balance between supply and demand. Estimating the level of UBI using our model, we got an initial value of $860–880 per month per person in 2020 and forecast values for 2030. Calculations within the framework of our model have shown that annual costs per person should be approximately 10–12 thousand dollars. This amount is close to what is currently voiced in a research environment, for example, in Kearney and Mogstad (2019). These calculations show that, depending on the selected UBI scenario, federal budget spending will range from $1.2 to $2.49 trillion (i.e., from 5.85% to 12.15% of GDP). This is significantly higher than the current payments for various social programs of the federal government (about $ 1 trillion). Nevertheless, as shown by the actions of the US administration to support the population in the context of the COVID-19 pandemic, macroeconomic instruments can be used to maintain consumer demand (Fabian & Sink, 2020). The model we have proposed is the simplest and, for special cases, may require a more accurate mechanism for tuning the UBI parameters.

5 Conclusion

In this work, we proposed a set of economic growth models, built in accordance with the new stylized facts of economic development formulated by J. Stiglitz and T. Piketty, and taking into account the endogenous nature of the formation of physical and human capital shares in national income, and technological progress.

The practical significance of the presented models lies in the wide possibilities of their application in predicting the dynamics of the potential number of jobs, taking into account technological substitution under various scenarios of real wage formation. In addition, with the help of models, we estimate the corresponding GDP volume and the level of decline in aggregate consumer demand caused by the reduction in the number of jobs occupied by people and the increasing role of robots in the economy.

Verification of our developed models with existing US statistics indicates their high accuracy, compliance of the calculated values with actual ones and low approximation error. In the considered scenarios of wage changes—empirical and hypothetical, the forecasts of economists of a decrease in the number of jobs due to automation and robotization of production, and, as a consequence, the prospect of a decrease in demand for goods and services, are confirmed. Based on this, we also presented the simplest model for determining the UBI, which provides a balance of real demand and supply in the economy.

Our proposed set of mathematical models is a useful decision-making tool in the areas of economic and social policy to ensure the stable development of the state.

Recommendations for further development of models can be divided into three groups. Firstly, a further complication is possible, for example, by introducing additional factors and parameters when calculating the UBI. Secondly, models should be verified on the statistics of other countries in order to identify possible shortcomings of the presented economic and mathematical apparatus, as well as to formulate recommendations for managing various national economies. Thirdly, a separate direction for the study is finding the optimal scenario for the formation of real wages for given criteria.

Acknowledgments The paper was prepared as part of the RFBR grant No. 20-010-00279 "An integrated system for assessing and forecasting the labor market at the stage of transition to a digital economy in developed and developing countries."

References

Acemoglu, D., & Restrepo, P. (2017). *Robots and jobs: Evidence from US Labor markets.* NBER Working Papers, No. 23285. National Bureau of Economic Research, Inc. https://doi.org/10.3386/w23285

Akaev, A. A., & Sadovnichy, V. A. (2018). Mathematical models for calculating the development dynamics in the era of digital economy. *Doklady Mathematics, 98*(2), 526–531. https://doi.org/10.1134/S106456241806011X

Arnold, D., Arntz, M., Gregory, T., Steffes, S., & Zierahn, U. (2016). *Herausforderungen der Digitalisierung für die Zukunft der Arbeitswelt.* ZEW policy brief, No. 8/2016. Zentrum für Europäische Wirtschaftsforschung (ZEW), Mannheim.

Arntz, M., Gregory, T., & Zierahn, U. T. (2016). *The risk of automation for jobs in OECD countries: A comparative analysis.* OECD Social, Employment and Migration Working Papers, No. 189. Paris: OECD Publishing. https://doi.org/10.1787/5jlz9h56dvq7-en

Arthur, W. B. (1996). Increasing returns and the new world of business. *Harvard Business Review, 74*(4), 100–109.

Atkinson, R. D., & Wu, J. J. (2017). *False alarmism: Technological disruption and the U.S. Labor Market, 1850–2015.* Business History. https://doi.org/10.2139/ssrn.3066052

Autor, D. H. (2015). Why are there still so many jobs? The history and future of workplace automation. *Journal of Economic Perspectives, 29*(3), 3–30.

Autor, D. H., & Dorn, D. (2013). The growth of low-skill service jobs and the polarization of the US labor market. *The American Economic Review, 103*(5), 1553–1597. https://doi.org/10.1257/aer.103.5.1553

Bainbridge, W. S., & Roko, M. C. (2006). *Managing Nano-Bio-Info-Cogno innovations: Converging technologies in society*. Springer.

Barro, R. J., & Sala-i-Martin, X. I. (2003). *Economic growth* (2nd ed.). The MIT Press.

Berg, A., Buffie, E. F., & Zanna, L. (2018). *Should we fear the Robot revolution? (The correct answer is yes)*. International Monetary Fund (IMF) Research Paper Series, No. 18/116. https://doi.org/10.1016/J.JMONECO.2018.05.014

Blanchard, O. (2016). *Macroeconomics* (7th ed.). MIT Press.

Brynjolfsson, E., & McAfee, A. (2014). *The second machine age: Work, progress, and prosperity in a time of brilliant technologies*. WW Norton & Company.

Carbonero, F., Ernst, E., & Weber, E. (2018). *Robots worldwide: The impact of automation on employment and trade* (ILO Working Papers, No. 36).

Chiacchio, F., Petropoulos, G., & Pichler, D. (2018). *The impact of industrial robots on EU Employment and Wages: A local labour market approach* (Bruegel Working Paper Issue 02/18).

Christian, M. S. (2017). Net investment and stocks of human capital in the United States, 1975–2013. *International Productivity Monitor, Centre for the Study of Living Standards, 33*, 128–149.

De Wispelaere, J., & Haagh, L. (2019). Welfare states: Opportunities and constraint. *Social Policy and Society, 18*(2), 237–242. https://doi.org/10.1017/S1474746418000489

Dengler, K., & Matthes, B. (2018). The impacts of digital transformation on the labour market: Substitution potentials of occupations in Germany. *Technological Forecasting and Social Change, 137*, 304–316. https://doi.org/10.1016/J.TECHFORE.2018.09.024

Easterly, W., & Levine, R. (2019). It's not factor accumulation: Stylized facts and growth models. *The World Bank Economic Review, 15*(2), 177–219. https://doi.org/10.2139/ssrn.269108

Edvinsson, L., & Malone, M. S. (1997). *Intellectual capital: Realizing your company's true value by finding its hidden roots*. Haper Collins.

Fabian, J., & Sink, J. (2020). *Trump signs $2 Trillion Virus Bill, largest ever U.S. Stimulus*. Bloomberg. https://www.bloomberg.com/news/articles/2020-03-27/trump-signs-2-trillion-virus-bill-largest-ever-u-s-stimulus

Ford, M. (2015). *Rise of the Robots: Technology and the threat of a jobless future*. Basic Books.

Frey, C. B., & Osborne, M. A. (2017). The future of employment: How susceptible are jobs to computerisation? *Technological Forecasting and Social Change, 114*, 254–280. https://doi.org/10.1016/j.techfore.2016.08.019

Gotev, G. (2016). *Swiss reject guaranteed basic income plan after 'Robot Debate'*. EURACTIV Media Network. https://www.euractiv.com/section/social-europe-jobs/news/swiss-reject-guaranteed-basic-income-plan-after-robot-debate/

Hoynes, H. W., & Rothstein, J. (2019). Universal basic income in the US and advanced countries. *Annual Review of Economics, 11*(1), 929–958. https://doi.org/10.1146/annurev-economics-080218-030237

International Federation of Robotics. (2019). *US Robot Density now more than double that of China*. IFR. https://ifr.org/ifr-press-releases/news/us-robot-density-now-more-than-double-that-of-china-ifr-says

Kaldor, N. (1961). Capital accumulation and economic growth. In D. C. Hague (Ed.), *The theory of capital* (International Economic Association Series) (pp. 177–222). Palgrave Macmillan.

Kearney, M. S., & Mogstad, M. (2019). *Universal Basic Income (UBI) as a policy response to current challenges*. (Report). Aspen Institute.

Korinek, A., & Stiglitz, J. E. (2017). *Artificial intelligence and its implications for income distribution and unemployment*. NBER Working Papers, No. 24174. National Bureau of Economic Research, Inc.. https://doi.org/10.7916/d8-8xt9-4v75

Kurzenev, V., & Matveenko, V. (2018). *Economic growth*. Piter.

Lee, S. (2018). Attitudes toward universal basic income and welfare state in Europe: A research note. *Basic Income Studies, 13*, 1–9. https://doi.org/10.1515/BIS-2018-0002

Leipziger, D., & Dodev, V. (2016). *Disruptive technologies and their implications for economic policy: Some preliminary observations* (Working Papers 2016–13). The George Washington University, Institute for International Economic Policy.

Mankiw, N. G., Romer, D., & Weil, D. N. (1992). A contribution to the empirics of economics growth. *Quarterly Journal of Economics, 107*(2), 407–437. https://doi.org/10.2307/2118477

McKinsey Global Institute. (2017). *A future that works: Automation, employment, and productivity*. McKinsey&Company. https://www.mckinsey.com/~/media/McKinsey/Featured%20Insights/Digital%20Disruption/Harnessing%20automation%20for%20a%20future%20that%20works/MGI-A-future-that-works_Full-report.pdf

Nedelkoska, L., & Quintini, G. (2018). *Automation, skill use and training*. OECD Social, Employment and Migration Working Papers, No. 202. Paris: OECD Publishing.. https://doi.org/10.1787/2e2f4eea-en.

OECD. (2017). *OECD Employment Outlook 2017*. Paris: OECD Publishing. https://doi.org/10.1787/empl_outlook-2017-en

OECD. (2020). *Real GDP long-term forecast (indicator)*. https://doi.org/10.1787/d927bc18-en

Piketty, T. (2014). *Capital in the twenty-first century*. The Belknap Press of Harvard University Press.

Pouliakas, K. (2018). *Determinants of automation risk in the EU labour market: A skills-needs approach*. IZA Discussion Papers, No. 11829. Institute of Labor Economics (IZA).

Roco, M. C. (2011). The long view of nanotechnology development: The National Nanotechnology Initiative at 10 years. *Journal of Nanoparticle Research, 13*, 427–445. https://doi.org/10.1007/s11051-010-0192-z

Stiglitz, J. E. (2012). *The price of inequality: How today's divided society endangers our future*. WW Norton & Company.

Stiglitz, J. E. (2016). New theoretical perspectives on the distribution of income and wealth among individuals. In K. Basu & J. E. Stiglitz (Eds.), *Inequality and growth: Patterns and policy* (International Economic Association Series) (pp. 1–71). Palgrave Macmillan.

U.S. Bureau of Economic Analysis. (2020a). *Population*. FRED, Federal Reserve Bank of St. Louis. https://fred.stlouisfed.org/series/POPTHM

U.S. Bureau of Economic Analysis, Fixed Assets Accounts Tables (2020b). *Table 1.2. Chain-Type Quantity Indexes for net stock of fixed assets and consumer durable goods*. https://apps.bea.gov/iTable/iTable.cfm?ReqID=10&step=2

U.S. Bureau of Economic Analysis, National Income and Product Accounts. (2020c). *Table 1.1.6. Real Gross Domestic Product, Chained Dollars*. https://apps.bea.gov/iTable/iTable.cfm?reqid=19&step=2#reqid=19&step=2&isuri=1&1921=survey

U.S. Bureau of Economic Analysis, National Income and Product Accounts. (2020d). *Table 6.5. Full-Time Equivalent Employees by Industry*. https://apps.bea.gov/iTable/iTable.cfm?reqid=19&step=2#reqid=19&step=2&isuri=1&1921=survey

U.S. Congressional Budget Office. (2020). *Real potential gross domestic product*. FRED, Federal Reserve Bank of St. Louis. https://fred.stlouisfed.org/series/GDPPOT

U.S. Department of Labor, Bureau of Labor Statistics. (2019). *Employment projections—2018–2028*. https://www.bls.gov/news.release/pdf/ecopro.pdf

University of Groningen and University of California. (2020). *Total factor productivity at Constant National Prices for United States*. FRED, Federal Reserve Bank of St. Louis. https://fred.stlouisfed.org/series/RTFPNAUSA632NRUG

Valero, J. (2019). *Finnish finance minister: 'Case closed' for Universal Basic Income*. EURACTIV Media Network. https://www.euractiv.com/section/economy-jobs/interview/finnish-finance-minister-case-closed-for-universal-basic-income/
Van Duijn, J. J. (2006). *The long wave in economic life* (1st ed.). Routledge.
Vermeulen, B., Kesselhut, J., Pyka, A., & Saviotti, P. P. (2018). The impact of automation on employment: Just the usual structural change? *Sustainability, 10*, 1661–1688. https://doi.org/10.3390/SU10051661
Wolfgang, D., Findeisen, S., Suedekum, J., & Woessner, N. (2018). *Adjusting to robots: Worker-level evidence* (Opportunity and Inclusive Growth Institute Working Papers, No. 13). Federal Reserve Bank of Minneapolis. https://doi.org/10.21034/iwp.13

The Dualistic Nature of Technological Convergence and Human Resources

Askar Akaev, Andrei Rudskoy, and Laszlo Ungvari

Abstract The convergence of technologies significantly changes both the patterns of production and the very nature of socio-economic systems. The need for constant knowledge updating and the continuity of the education process are becoming one of the key factors in achieving social harmony in society. However, uneven economic and technological development poses certain threats to both employment and production systems that create economic benefits in the form of goods or services. The paper shows the dualistic nature of the advance of technology and formation of human capital, when constantly and rapidly updating technologies may contribute to the ousting of mainly middle-skilled employees from the labor market. A mean of overcoming this situation is the extensive training of engineering personnel and qualified specialists capable of working in the environment of man–machine intelligent systems. Examples include the authors' projections on the distribution of employees of various skill levels in the US economy in the 2030s.

Keywords Convergence of technologies · Human resources · Skill level and distribution of employees

---

A. Akaev (✉)
Institute for Mathematical Research of Complex Systems, Lomonosov Moscow State University, Moscow, Russia

A. Rudskoy
Peter the Great Saint Petersburg Polytechnic University, Saint Petersburg, Russia
e-mail: rector@spstu.ru

L. Ungvari
Development in Relations of Industrial and Education Management GmbH, Wildau, Germany
e-mail: ungvari@driem-international.com

A. Rudskoi et al. (eds.), *Digital Transformation and the World Economy*, Studies on Entrepreneurship, Structural Change and Industrial Dynamics,
https://doi.org/10.1007/978-3-030-89832-8_6

1 Introduction

Technological progress (TP) has always been accompanied by the automation of human labor for certain professions, but at the same time, it has generated new activities by creating new jobs. Thus, on the one hand, machines replaced people, displacing them from performing certain tasks, and on the other hand, they complemented people in a more productive solution of other tasks, increasing the demand for human labor in other activities and possibly elsewhere. In the twentieth century, the complementing feature of the machines was much stronger than the substitutional one, so more new jobs were always created than were destroyed by technological substitution. However, after the 1980s, with the onset of the information age, as D. Acemoglu and P. Restrepo have discovered (Acemoglu & Restrepo, 2017), the substitutional force of technological progress outstripped the complementary one and, as a result, the demand for labor started to decline throughout the economy. In the first half of the twenty-first century, the same process will take place due to powerful clusters of converged NBIC technologies, as well as digital technologies and platforms. Due to their inherent property of mutual convergence, NBIC technologies generate a significant synergistic effect that may significantly increase the total factor productivity (TFP), i.e., accelerate technical progress. The same refers to the digital technology cluster. ICTs themselves are very encouraging as they greatly facilitate the process of creating innovations by facilitating the flow of ideas (Glaeser, 2014). TP, on the other hand, takes place most naturally and spreads unhindered at the presence of inclusive political and economic institutions. The latter are currently expanding and deepening in developed countries; they are also being formed in developing countries, narrowing the space of extractive institutions (Acemoglu, 2014).

D. Susskind shows very convincingly that technological unemployment, which originated in the information age, will only grow in the digital age (Susskind, 2020). Technological unemployment was more of a frictional nature in the past, i.e., a person could not take advantage of available jobs for a number of reasons, such as inconsistencies in skills or residence, as well as status discrepancies. According to D. Susskind, structural, technological unemployment will prevail in the future due to the widespread use of intelligent machines (IM) when there are simply not enough jobs for all people ready to work (Susskind, 2020, Ch.7). Moreover, medium-skilled jobs will be the first to disappear. It turned out that middle-skilled workers solve routine tasks that are easy to automate with intelligent machines (IM). Any routine work, including routine intellectual work, may now be automated by robots or computers with elements of artificial intelligence (AI), while such automation is becoming ever cheaper.

In the 1980s, automation was carried out mainly through the introduction of robotics and it replaced low-skilled labor above all, increasing the demand for highly skilled and highly paid labor; but then, with the introduction of IM, its influence on the labor market changed dramatically, and the demand for cheap, but non-routine labor that was difficult to automate or that was unprofitable from an economic point of view started to grow as well. As a result, employment has begun to concentrate in both the most and the least paid segments of the labor force, and the number of middle-paid jobs has begun to decrease rapidly. This phenomenon was called "workforce polarization" (Brynjolfsson & McAfee, 2014), and it has caused great concerns among economists, as it led to an increase in income inequality in society. Today, as predicted, the wash-out of various occupations requiring medium qualifications has accelerated in developed countries as a result of the substitution of the respective jobs by IM (Acemoglu, 2014). Thus, technological unemployment will primarily affect middle-skilled workers, encouraging them to improve their skills.

Technological unemployment will proceed against the background of demographic factors. There are three important conclusions from the UN's projections of the world's population growth: firstly, the world's population will continue to grow for a long period of time, and then it will stabilize; secondly, the population will keep aging in the developed and advanced countries; thirdly, our planet can easily accept this increased population, and there is no reason to worry about any acute resource shortages or conflicts associated with overpopulation (Acemoglu, 2014; Deaton, 2014; Glaeser, 2014; Roth, 2014). The development of labor-saving technologies may well solve the problem of labor shortages due to the aging population. There was no scarcity of natural resources in the twentieth century, labor was a limited economic resource, and technical progress was aimed at creating predominantly labor-saving technologies. As a result, for example, agriculture and industry have achieved such high levels of productivity that only 2–3% and 10–15% of workers in developed countries work nowadays in these basic sectors of the economy, respectively. Recently, even in developing countries, there has been a decline in agricultural employment and its expansion in the services sector. In the twenty-first century, the agricultural sector and industrial production will continue to shrink, giving way to the service sector (Solow, 2014).

Further development of labor-saving technologies may have a very positive effect on the socio-economic development of industrialized countries, as well as such advanced countries as China, where population aging is combined with the intensive development of robotics and IM. Population aging in developed countries no longer means that economic growth there will stop due to a shrinking labor force. They may now be successfully replaced by advanced robots and intelligent computers with AI elements. The strength of developed countries is their high level of human capital development, which may become the basis for economic growth even with a shrinking population. In fact, the development and production of IMs require a range of scientific knowledge and relevant labor skills, as well as the high-tech infrastructure available in developed countries. As a consequence of the above factors, labor immigration to the developed countries from the developing ones is no longer a prerequisite for their economic growth.

2 NBIC Technologies as an Example of Technological Convergence

The active process of technological convergence, which started in the late twentieth and early twenty-first century, means not only the mutual influence but also the interpenetration of technologies, when the boundaries between individual technologies are erased, leading to the final results within the framework of interdisciplinary research and development at the intersection of various fields of science and technology. Currently, technological convergence is particularly evident at the junction of NBIC technologies.

The concept of converging technologies was developed by experts from a number of EU and G8 countries in the early twenty-fisrt century. The concept was based on the principle of a "synergistic combination of four scientific and technological fields" developing with exceptional dynamism. These are (1) nanoscience and nanotechnology; (2) biotechnology and biomedicine, including genetic engineering; (3) information technology, including the latest computer and communication technologies; and (4) cognitive sciences that incorporate neuroscience and cognitive technologies. These areas have received the term NBIC technologies or NBIC convergence, which are generally accepted and used in world practice.

In addition to the process of technological convergence, an equally important synergistic process is underway. Synergetics is a scientific direction that studies the phenomena of self-organization, representing the theory of describing processes accompanied by a reciprocal, "cooperative effect." Instead of the concept of "synergy," the "synergetic effect" term is sometimes used, which characterizes the increase in the efficiency of activities as a result of integration and convergence of technologies. It is the synergy of NBIC technologies that will have a dramatic impact on the twenty-first century economy.

Distinctive features of NBIC convergence are:

- Intensive interaction between these specified scientific and technological areas
- Significant synergistic effect
- Qualitative growth of technological capabilities of individual and social development of a person

A synergistic effect caused by a very intensive interaction and mutual influence of new basic technologies, their cooperative action or, in other words, caused by NBIC convergence, may be so strong that its contribution to the increase in the aggregate productivity of factors will become decisive and the economic growth rates in developed countries may approach the record values of 4–5% again.

The world around us will change rapidly and dramatically with the widespread use of digital technologies and robotics. Unfortunately, these changes bring not only extraordinary new opportunities but great risks as well. In this regard, active creative work is required to develop effective social innovations in order to painlessly overcome the negative consequences of the new age of intelligent automation of production and management. As for the threat of technological unemployment and technological shift in the demand for labor towards high qualifications, these challenges should rely on "massive high-quality education" (Susskind, 2020). Today, this is truly the best response to the looming threat of technological unemployment for the middle class.

3 Formation of Human Resource in the Context of Convergence of Technologies

Technological progress in the twentieth century generally encouraged advanced training, which made the labor of educated employees more valuable. Nowadays, education is still one of the best investments in the future for young people (Susskind, 2020). Prominent experts believe that it is necessary to invest in quality education at all levels (Deaton, 2014), and it is important to revive the priority of such subjects as mathematics, science, and engineering specialties (Dixit, 2014). An age of competition between qualified professionals and machines in the face of an advanced robot or intelligent computer is coming. For example, the competition between low-paid labor and robotics in the production of electronic devices is best known. Modern gadgets and computers may be produced by both humans and robots. Therefore, they are produced in China, where low-paid labor is still very common. But only robots will be able to produce ICTs based on nanochips and biochips. Therefore, the education system should train people in the future to perform only those tasks in which IM will complement them rather than replace them. This is one of the directions of modernizing the current education system.

Requirements for engineering education are determined by the economic model of the state, the structure of its real economy and the long-term economic development strategy. All these might be easily illustrated by the example of Finland, a small but developed European country (Dahlman et al., 2006). With the outburst of the information revolution (in 1980s), Finnish society has been dynamically transformed towards an information society. Intensive investments have been made in mechanical engineering and science education, and this has been a success. The Finnish economy has undergone fundamental changes in the 1990s. There has been a revolutionary shift from capital-intensive and hierarchical sectors of the economy to the economy based on innovation and knowledge to an information society. Finland has become one of the most developed information societies in the world. It is considered that the fruitful activities and flexibility of Finnish engineering education have become one of the most important factors in making the transition of Finland to the knowledge economy. In turn, the modern Finnish economy is forming the informational focus of engineering education. It is mainly aimed at training highly qualified mechanical engineers capable of creating capital goods for the production of ICT (information and communication technologies) devices, as well as electronic engineers and software engineers for development and commercialization of ICT goods and services.

The world is entering a new age now—the age of the 4th Industrial Revolution, the age of the digital economy. Industry 4.0 will back the digital economy with the highest level of manufacturing automation, using intelligent computer machines and robots with elements of artificial intelligence (AI) capable of interacting with humans, learning and improving in production and management processes. The digital economy is able to meet the challenge of moving from mass production of standard goods and services to creating high-quality goods and services that meet individual needs and preferences. Industry 4.0 is essentially a flexible, digitally controlled programmable production that can be immediately adapted to manufacturing new products.

Hence, the new epoch makes demands on the knowledge and skills of employees in the digital age. Currently, advanced countries have not yet witnessed a true digital modernization of their education systems, despite a significant increase in training specialists in STEM areas that are most in demand in the digital economy. So, what are the key labor features for people in the age of the digital economy? Firstly, information and knowledge are becoming the main economic resources. The specificity of these resources is that they are the result of human intellectual activity. Therefore, in the age of the digital economy, it would be appropriate to speak about the strategy of intellectual capital formation (Edvinson & Malone, 1997). Human capital is defined as an employee's productive capacity. Intellectual capital is broader than the human one, and it includes creative skills and skills in using the information as a self-sustaining production factor, along with traditional factors such as labor and capital. It is the intellectual capital that will be the key determinant of efficiency in the digital economy.

Secondly, most employees in the digital economy will have to deal with maintenance and control of intelligent machines, i.e., computers, robots, and additive 3D printing devices with elements of artificial intelligence, the language of which is the language of digital technology. Therefore, they will require new skills and competencies, namely digital skills and competencies. The majority of university graduates still have a grossly inadequate level of digital skills and competencies. This also includes skills and abilities for analysis and processing of digital data and digital information, the so-called "computer analytics" of data and of "big data" in particular. Therefore, training in all traditional professions requires additional training in abilities and skills to work with digital data and digital technologies.

Thirdly, since the innovations of the Fourth Industrial Revolution predominantly emerge in the interdisciplinary field through the convergence of technologies, there is a need for dissemination of interdisciplinary education and research programs. The latter should now become the norm for most professions. The booming nanobiotechnology and genetic engineering industries are good examples of this. The ability to effectively interact with intelligent machines will be of particular importance for employees. Research shows that it is the symbiosis of a highly skilled human and a friendly intelligent robot that will be the most productive workforce in the digital economy. Moreover, a skillful and friendly partnership with intelligent machines will enable trained people to overcome their own natural limitations, both physical and mental.

Fourthly, given the exponential growth of digital technologies, which is a new phenomenon, special attention needs to be paid to the ability of employees to adapt to new working conditions constantly and to assimilate new skills and new technologies. Hence the requirement that continuous education throughout working life and adaptation to rapid technological changes become a need for every person, as they say, their "state of mind." The education system should be integrated into the consciousness of every person with a well-known folk wisdom "Live and learn" as an imperative.

The main features of the digital economy listed above lead directly to the basic requirements for the specialists of the future:

1. Deep fundamental knowledge in mathematics, information theory and natural sciences.
2. Ability to simulate complex processes on a computer and set up digital experiments using mathematical models.
3. Ability to innovate and think systemically.
4. Ability to work in an interdisciplinary team.
5. Willingness to continuous education, to periodically change the professional field.

Fundamental knowledge has always been more in demand in the periods of transition from one industrial revolution to another, from one technical and economic paradigm to another. This is the period we are going through nowadays. Most of the innovative products, including such unique ones as airliners and automobiles, are already being designed, modeled, and tested for their strength and performance entirely using software tools (3D CAD and PLM systems) on supercomputers. Interdisciplinary knowledge and skills allow an employee to acquire knowledge from different areas, combine and concentrate it for a successful solution of a specific practical problem.

Automation of production and management with intelligent machines will rapidly free people from routine mental activities and lead to a dramatic increase in the demand for highly skilled employees with digital skills and competencies. Such personnel were previously trained, so-called by a person, but now their training should be made in large numbers. Indeed, the well-known McKinsey Global Institute, based in the USA, investigated this issue and came to the conclusion that there is a rapid increase in demand for highly skilled jobs in the developed world today, requiring the use and support of computer (digital) technologies, development of mathematical models and software, and maintenance of robotics. McKinsey claims that high-tech companies around the world are experiencing a shortage of 40 million specialists with higher education in STEM fields (mathematics, programming, research, engineering, and high technology) (MGI, 2015).

In today's environment, knowledge-intensive industries represent the production base and the most important source of income for industrialized countries:

- Knowledge-intensive technologies and industries are now the main drivers of economic development, both domestically and globally; this applies to both products and services.
- Common features of knowledge-intensive industries that determine their role in the economy as a whole are growth rates two–three times higher than the growth rates in other sectors of the economy; a large share of added value in the final product; increased salary of employees; high innovation potential, serving not only this particular industry but other sectors of the economy as well, generating a "chain reaction" of innovations in the national and global economy.

Innovations in engineering and technology are currently mostly formed on an interdisciplinary basis as a result of the knowledge transfer from one area to another and their mutual influence. In the last decade, it has been common to highlight the need to develop special "competences" for the specialists, focused on the ability to apply them in practice, in real business, when creating new competitive products. As a result, a new quality of engineering education is achieved, providing a set of competencies, including fundamental and technical knowledge, the ability to analyze and solve problems using an interdisciplinary approach, and mastery of project management methods. The interdisciplinary learning approach allows one to teach students to independently "obtain" and classify knowledge from different areas, concentrate it for a specific task to be solved.

Engineering education, in particular, will play a central role in our future society based on knowledge and innovative technologies. Therefore, engineering education should be modernized, taking into account new trends in the development of society, requirements of the environment and atmosphere, as well as the strategic goals of the state. Engineers of the twenty-first century need to demonstrate good fundamental and applied scientific knowledge along with advanced general skills, such as the ability to acquire knowledge on their own, so that they could cope with a rapidly growing amount of new knowledge. The engineers of the future should be able to adapt to the changing emphasis in scientific fields such as information technology and bioengineering. It is also important to have interdisciplinary knowledge and communication skills, as well as a lifelong learning desire.

It is well known that it is not possible to provide engineering students with all the knowledge they may need in their professional practice. Professional skills often become obsolete so quickly that engineering education fails to achieve its goal if it prevents graduates from continually renewing their knowledge and skills. Teaching how to learn, and especially how to relearn, is becoming an increasingly important task. Lifelong continuous education should become a necessity for an engineer. A positive attitude towards learning and a desire to learn are key characteristics of the twenty-first century engineer, and these attitudes should be developed in engineering education. According to Rosstat, the participation of Russia's population in continuous education was 24.8% in 2008. Generally, this figure is much higher in countries with high innovation activity, i.e., it is 37.6% in the UK; 41.9% in Germany; 77.3% in Finland!

Continuity and interdisciplinarity should become important structural factors of engineering education. Interdisciplinary research helps engineers cope with the changing social, economic, and political environments that are interconnected with technology and its development. Thus, interdisciplinary research, especially in humanities and economics, should be an integral part of engineering education. The use of information and communication technologies to support the process of learning may lead to significant interdisciplinary research results.

Engineers as creators of new complex technologies cannot be narrow specialists. Multi-skilled engineers will be more and more in demand in the future. Engineers of the twenty-first century should be fluent in information and computer technologies. They need to have a deeper understanding of environmental issues, not only in terms of environmental damage already caused but also in predicting the impact of the engineering activities at present.

Engineering students prefer an active learning method. An engineering education program should include the widespread use of ICT, since it has become a widespread technology and is used in almost all sectors of the modern economy. Problem-based learning is preferable, so students should be encouraged to participate in teaching the subject. "Contextual learning," when the motivation for knowledge assimilation is achieved by building relationships between specific knowledge and its application, is one of the promising methods used in innovative engineering education. This method is quite effective, as the aspect of the application is critically important for students.

Thus, implementing new principles of education, especially in terms of engineers training, objectively will pave the way for the situation when not physical or financial capital will be the main production factor in the digital economy, but intellectual capital and human resources. It is the shortage of competent, highly qualified personnel rather than the availability of physical capital that may be a deterring constraint for the development of the digital economy. Therefore, developing and implementing a strategy for the formation of intellectual human capital for the coming digital age will be of paramount importance.

4 Technological Convergence and Job Substitution

Industrial production at the industrial stage of economic development was characterized by a gradual process of replacing living labor with materialized one. Therefore, the general trend of developing real production is to reduce labor intensity and increase products capital intensity at the same time. This process will only accelerate in the digital economy, and we will also observe a growth trend in knowledge intensity in addition. Manufacturing attracts large amounts of fixed investment when it becomes more knowledge-intensive, and, conversely, extended renewal of fixed assets is an important factor in the development of R&D. And the latter will increase the demand for research professionals. Consequently, knowledge intensity and capital intensity are interrelated processes in the course of digital transformation.

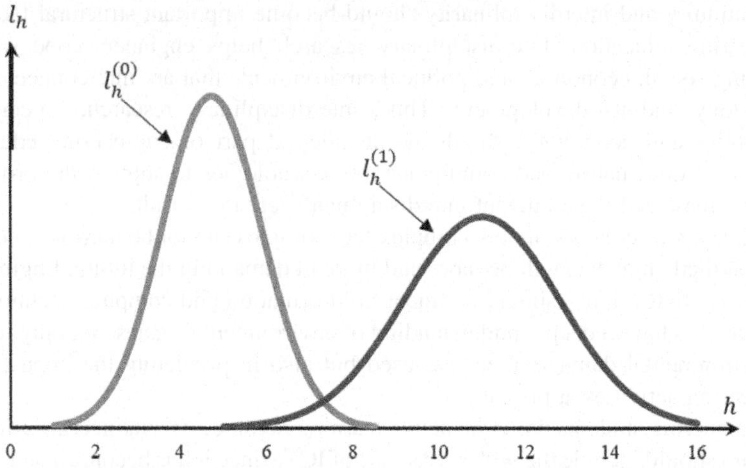

Fig. 1 Labor force supply distribution curves by skill levels in the 2020s $\left(l_h^{(0)}\right)$ and 2030s $\left(l_h^{(1)}\right)$. Source: Authors' creation

We have provided a detailed description of the mathematical models for assessing labor substitutions in the digital transformation of the economy in our earlier studies (Akaev et al., 2021). In the development of our proposed models, we obtained a more accurate assessment for the polarization of labor in the 2030s by constructing a forecast of distributing the relative labor force by skill level for the 2020s and 2030s for the American economy (Fig. 1).

We have constructed a distribution curve describing the probability of technological substitution of the labor force for the early 2030s using the predictive values of the distribution characteristics for the relative labor force by a skill level (see Fig. 2).

Model calculations have shown that the distribution of efficient labor force in the economy after the completion of digital transformation in the 2030s takes the form of a two-humped curve shown in Fig. 3.

Further, the model calculations allowed us to obtain the percentage of effective employees of low, medium, and high qualifications, which are placed in Table 1 in the "revised values" column.

As may be seen from this table, the initial assessments and revised values differ slightly from each other, which indicates the reliability of the initial assessment.

5 Conclusion

The convergence of technologies, primarily in the form of digital technologies, will permeate all spheres of society, since they are general-purpose technologies. Virtually all industries of the modern economy will see a decline in the need for human

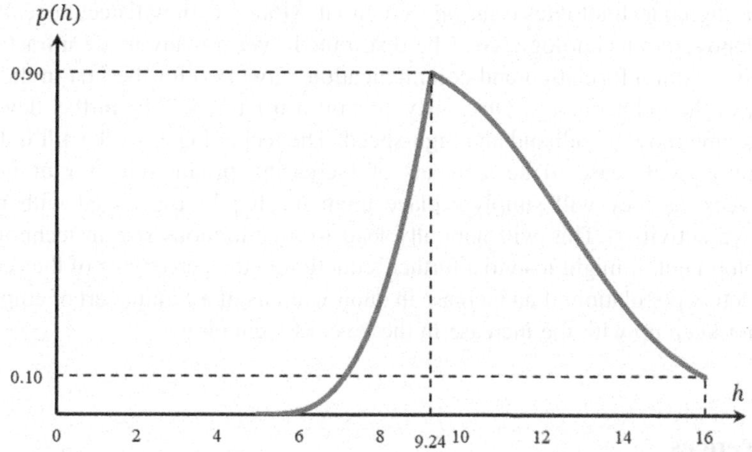

Fig. 2 Predictive curve of the probabilities for technological labor force substitution for the 2030s. Source: Authors' creation

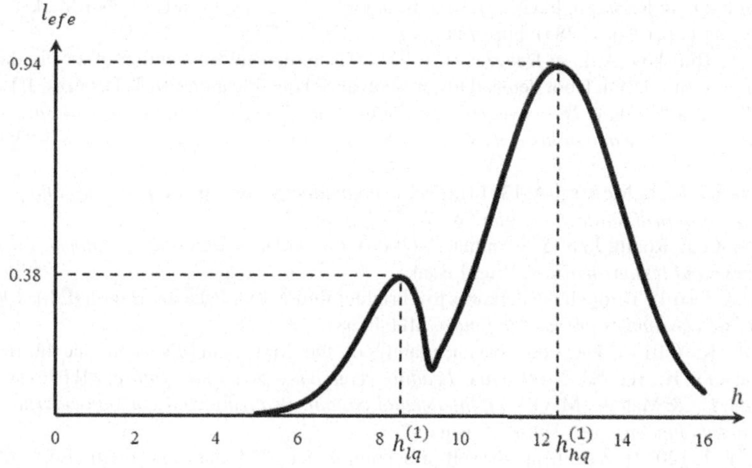

Fig. 3 Distribution curve of the efficient labor force employed in the digital economy in the 2030s. Source: Authors' creation

Table 1 Percentage of low-, medium-, and high-skilled employees before and after digital transformation (%)

Before digital transformation		$l_{ef}^{(l)} = 10.5\%$	$l_{ef}^{(m)} = 72.4\%$	$l_{ef}^{(h)} = 17.2\%$
After digital transformation	Initial assessment	$l_{efe0}^{(l)} = 14.0\%$	$l_{efe0}^{(m)} = 55.9\%$	$l_{efe0}^{(h)} = 30.1\%$
	Revised values	$l_{efe1}^{(l)} = 16.4\%$	$l_{efe1}^{(m)} = 54.3\%$	$l_{efe1}^{(h)} = 29.3\%$

labor as digital technologies is introduced into it. Moreover, it will decline really fast, since innovative technologies will be distributed over a ready-made infrastructure (namely digital information and communication networks) for the first in the entire history of the industrial age. Obviously, this infrastructure will be further developed and become more broadband and high-speed. The technologies of the 4th Industrial Revolution will cease to be a means of increasing productivity for millions of employees, as they will simply replace them in all jobs associated with routine cognitive activities. This will naturally lead to a continuous rise in technological unemployment. It might lead to a further reduction in the percentage of the economically active population, if an increase in qualifications of a certain part of employees does not keep up with the increase in the level of technology.

References

Acemoglu, D. (2014). The world our grandchildren will inherit. In I. Palacios-Huerta (Ed.), *100 years: Leading economists predict the future*. MIT Press.

Acemoglu, D., & Restrepo, P. (2017). Robots and jobs: Evidence from US Labor Markets (NBER Working Paper No. 23285). https://doi.org/10.3386/w23285

Akaev, A., Rudskoy, A. I., & Devezas, T. (2021). Technological substitution of jobs in the digital economy and shift in labor demand towards advanced qualifications. In T. Devezas, J. Leitão, & A. Sarygulov (Eds.), *The economics of digital transformation. Studies on entrepreneurship, structural change and industrial dynamics*. Springer. https://doi.org/10.1007/978-3-030-59959-1_6

Brynjolfsson, E., & McAfee, A. (2014). *The second machine age: Work, progress, and prosperity in a time of brilliant technologies*. W. W. Norton & Co..

Dahlman, C. J., Routti, J., & Ylä-Anttila, P. (2006). *Finland as a knowledge economy: Elements of success and lessons learned*. World Bank.

Deaton, A. (2014). Through the darkness to a brighter future. In I. Palacios-Huerta (Ed.), *100 years: Leading economists predict the future*. MIT Press.

Dixit, A. K. (2014). The cone of uncertainty of the 21st century's economic hurricane. In I. Palacios-Huerta (Ed.), *100 years: Leading economists predict the future*. MIT Press.

Edvinson, L., & Malone, M. (1997). *Intellectual capital. Realizing your company is true value by finding its hidden roots*. Harper Business.

Glaeser, E. L. (2014). Wealth and the self-protection society. In I. Palacios-Huerta (Ed.), *100 years: Leading economists predict the future*. MIT Press.

McKinsey Global Institute. (2015). Global growth: Can productivity save the day in an aging world?

Roth, A. E. (2014). In 100 years. In I. Palacios-Huerta (Ed.), *100 years: Leading economists predict the future*. MIT Press.

Solow, R. (2014). Thoughts on how things can go further. In I. Palacios-Huerta (Ed.), *100 years: Leading economists predict the future*. MIT Press.

Susskind, D. (2020). *A world without work: Technology, automation, and how we should respond*. Metropolitan Books.

Education System and Labor Market in the Context of Digital Transformation

Askar Akaev, Alexander Petryakov, Reiff-Stephan Jorg, and Laszlo Ungvari

Abstract Modern economic systems are characterized by great flexibility and ever-changing demands in relation to labor skill level. The need for constant knowledge renewal and continuity of the education process are becoming key factors in ensuring sustainability in the labor market. The chapter analyzes current trends in professional training found in different OECD countries and Russia and evaluates the adjustment level of higher education systems to new technological challenges. It is shown that despite dynamic changes in the education sector, it remains largely geared toward training professionals to staff the "Third Industrial Revolution." A structural shift from training medium-skilled professionals to training high-skilled professionals, including those in STEM (Science, Technologies, Engineering, and Mathematics) fields, will become a pivotal moment in education development. The countries that will succeed in coping with this structural challenge within a short period of time will gain considerable competitive advantages in international markets for high-tech goods and services.

Keywords Education system · Labor market · Labor skill level

A. Akaev
Institute for Mathematical Research of Complex Systems, Lomonosov Moscow State University, Moscow, Russia

A. Petryakov (✉)
Saint Petersburg State University of Economics, Saint-Petersburg, Russia

R.-S. Jorg
Technical University of Applied Sciences Wildau, Wildau, Germany
e-mail: jrs@th-wildau.de

L. Ungvari
Development in Relations of Industrial and Education Management GmbH, Wildau, Germany
e-mail: ungvari@driem-international.com

A. Rudskoi et al. (eds.), *Digital Transformation and the World Economy*, Studies on Entrepreneurship, Structural Change and Industrial Dynamics,
https://doi.org/10.1007/978-3-030-89832-8_7

1 Introduction

In the twentieth century, market systems, especially those in highly developed countries, progressively implemented mechanization and automation of manual labor, by developing predominantly labor-saving technologies. This resulted in a declining share of low-skill occupations in manufacturing, which was offset by a growing share of better-paid jobs for college-educated middle-class workers. This process, however, halted in the 1970s. In the wake of the economic crises of the 1970s and 1980s, demand for labor started polarizing. Data on the American economy from 1970 to 2010 indicates that the employment share of high-skilled workers increased from 23.4% to 39.4%, whereas the share in medium- and low-skill occupations declined from 40.5% to 31.6% and from 36% to 29%, respectively (Katz & Margo, 2014). The same trends were typical of 17 OECD member countries. Recent research has revealed that in the period from 1995 to 2015, the share of high-skill jobs increased from 29% to 37%, the share of medium-skill jobs declined from 49% to 40% and the share of low-skill jobs grew only marginally from 21% to 23% (OECD, 2017).

With the onset of the NBIC technological revolution, when the technologies of the Fourth Industrial Revolution and the Industrial Ethernet have become a practical reality and allowed fully automated make-to-order production and delivery, the trend toward actively pushing people out from the sphere of production and even services have materialized as well. Digital technologies are intensely labor-saving, which makes their use in the labor market "toxic." Digital computer technologies automated routine tasks from the very start. Robots have replaced workers on assembly lines. Large-scale digitalization, computerization, and robotization will accelerate the process of technological replacement of labor with capital within the next few decades. While thus far automation has been pushing people out from the mundane sphere of manual work and services, as of now, it will be pushing them out from the field of intellectual work by replacing routine mental workers, i.e., medium-skilled professionals who are mostly middle-class employees.

This means that the Fourth Industrial Revolution along with the complete automation of production and accelerated productivity and GDP growth may have some negative social consequences, primarily in the form of a drastic reduction in middle-skill occupations for the middle class and a further increase in income inequality in society. This is especially notable due to the empirical fact that the growth of economic inequality accelerated in almost every country after the first decade of the 2000s.

Since an increased demand for skilled labor is a major feature of the digital economy, one is to expect a new stage in labor market evolution caused by the transition to a high-tech and research-intensive digital economy, which implies that high-skilled labor will be concentrated in the branches relying on expertise in STEM (Science, Technologies, Engineering, and Mathematics). It follows that enhanced STEM literacy will ensure that any professional remains in high demand in the market for high-skilled labor.

STEM education is a new model integrating natural science and engineering. It relies on the convergent approach: mathematics, physics, chemistry, and biology are taught not discretely but in close relation to each other to tackle existing engineering and technology challenges. Such an approach directs a professional to regard the challenges at hand in a holistic way rather than in the context of a particular field of science or technology. Another cornerstone of STEM education is project-based research and training. This format combines a graduation project with an internship at a technology company where students can work on a complex technology project as part of a team and thereby develop "flexible" skills. As a result, graduates gain valuable on-the-job experience in their professional field.

Presently, STEM professionals are the most sought-after employees in the global labor market. The US Bureau of Labor Statistics forecasts that demand for STEM specialists will exceed that for professionals in other fields by 76% over the next decade. The US market alone will require approximately 10 million employees, and the personnel shortage will remain great even despite further accelerated training. Meanwhile, the average annual salary in STEM occupations stands at $ 86,980, which is more than double the $ 39,810 for other professions or trades in the country. Russia currently needs over 200,000 employees with STEM degrees, and by 2025 the shortage will grow to 300,000 employees.

2 Qualifications, Education, and Wage Level

The relationship between the remuneration for work and the level of educational attainment and qualifications (skills) has been one of the key issues in all economic formations. Historical data indicates that from the fourteenth to the nineteenth century, i.e., up to the end of the Industrial Revolution, the skill premium for craftsmen, especially carpenters, in Great Britain was 1.5 higher than that for laborers in construction (Roser & Nagdy, 2020). Separate studies on the same subject in relation to the development of the capitalist economy in the twentieth century have also revealed that the wage gap never closed even though it had its variations and temporary increases due to the peculiarities of national economies. For instance, data on the US economy shows that educational and occupational wage differentials were exceptionally high at the beginning of the twentieth century and then decreased in several stages over the next eight decades. However, starting in the early 1980s, the labor market premium to skill rose sharply, and by 2005 the college wage premium was back at its 1915 level (Goldin & Katz, 2007). In view of its particular importance, this issue of the American economy is closely examined in a number of scientific papers which acknowledge that there is a growing polarization in wages in the present-day US economy and part of it is due to differences in educational attainment: remuneration for work is proportional to the level of education (Acemoglu & Restrepo, 2017; Autor, 2014; Blau & Kahn, 2005).

The same issue is relevant for a lot of European countries. There are countries in Europe with both high skill inequality and high wage inequality (Italy and

Germany), and others with both low skill inequality and low wage inequality (Scandinavian countries), there are also countries with high skill inequality but low wage inequality (France), although, generally, workers with higher skills have wages that are 60% higher than those of low-skilled workers (Broecke, 2016). Extensive research undertaken by the Organization of Economic Cooperation and Development (OECD) (OECD, 2011; OECD, 2015; Paccagnella, 2015) shows that there is evidence at the inter-country level that, as a rule, countries which are better at meeting the demand for skills also have lower wage inequality. Yet, from 33% to 57% of wage inequality in OECD countries is attributed to differentials in skill levels. University graduates earn on average 1.57 times more than high school graduates (OECD, 2019).

Research conducted under the auspices of the International Labour Organization (ILO) and involving developed as well as developing economies uncovers some inter-country differences: in European countries, wage distribution is skill-related, that is, the bottom seven deciles are made up of employees with secondary education whereas the upper three deciles include a higher share of workers with university degrees. In the Russian Federation, a similar distribution is quite surprising: deciles three to ten appear to be dominated by university graduates (ILO, 2017).

Despite a variety of established views on the interrelation of levels of educational attainment, qualification, and wages, there prevails an opinion that long-term trends attest to a close relationship among them. Occasional mismatches mostly occur because technological changes transform the level and distribution of demand for workforce that is partly overcome by labor reallocation. The latter implies that employees have to comply with new requirements for educational attainment and qualification.

3 Interrelations between Technological Change and Level of Qualification

Economic development, especially in the last two centuries, has been driven, in large part, by advancements in science and education. Their tight interconnection provided the material-producing sectors and later the service sector with new technologies and materials, which enabled rapid transformations in economic and social spheres. Yet, as world experience indicates, the interrelations between technical progress and employment have always been intricate and nuanced. At the company level, innovative technologies have most commonly resulted in job cuts. At the level of individual sectors and the national economy as a whole, this adverse effect has been alleviated through institutional factors (such as state intervention or spatial shifts) or market mechanisms (internal labor migration, establishing new companies, etc.). Economic literature boasts of many works describing mechanisms for the interaction of innovative technologies and employment, of which some recent ones are worthy of notable mention (Arntz et al., 2016; Autor & Salomons, 2018; Bessen, 2018; Graetz & Michaels, 2018; Pellegrino et al., 2015).

One of the first pioneer studies published in 2003 pointed out that production and clerical medium-skill jobs are characterized by highly intensive activities that can be accomplished by following explicit rules (so-called "routine tasks") and relatively easily replaced with computer programs (Autor et al., 2003). Rapid advancement that began in the field of information and communication technologies in the early 1980s accelerated the automation of such routine tasks, enabling the start of people replacement in many medium-skill occupations, such as accounting, record-keeping, and batch production. This resulted in a significant reduction in the relative economy-wide demand for common medium-skill occupations. However, there is still a substantial layer of nonstandard manual cognitive tasks in the economy that are not yet easily accomplished by machines or software (e.g., driving a car or cleaning an office).

These trends induced in the labor market by technological factors took place against the backdrop of a significantly increased educational attainment level of those employed in the economy. For instance, the share of the employed in the US economy with a secondary education in 1985 amounted to 73.9% against 24.5% in 1940 and subsequently increased to 89.8% in 2018 (US Department of Education, 2020). Concurrently, European and American economies witnessed a growing wage gap between high- and medium-skilled workers (i.e., those with secondary education and those with tertiary education): in 2008, earnings of the average college graduate in the USA exceeded those of the average high school graduate by 97% while in the early 1980s this gap amounted to only 15–20% (Acemoglu & Autor, 2011). Due to a fall in occupations specializing in routine tasks medium-skilled professionals were washed out from the labor market and reallocated into two zones, that is, into the zone of high-skill and high-wage labor and into the zone of low-skill and low-wage labor. This new social phenomenon has come to be called the "employment polarization" (Autor & Dorn, 2013).

In the 1980s, about one in three Americans was employed in a routine occupation; currently, the figure stands at one in four. Also, since 1991, employment in routine occupations has been failing to recover from recessions even though it did turn around during the recessions of the 1970s and 1980s (Siu & Jaimovich, 2012). The polarization process accelerated after the 2000s. This was facilitated by emerging computer technologies with AI elements which already started replacing people in the spheres that require performing advanced cognitive activities, such as rendering financial or legal aid services, education, and healthcare. A number of breakthrough technologies enabled a new technological leap. There was a rapid advancement of NBIC technologies (Roko, 2011). The new technologies of the Fourth Industrial Revolution along with Industry 4.0 became a practical reality (Kagermann et al., 2013; Schwab, 2016; Schwab & Davis, 2018). Meanwhile, the Industrial Internet, a digital platform that ensures effective Internet-based interactions among objects of industrial production, is becoming the underlying infrastructure for Industry 4.0 (Greengard, 2015). The rise of intelligent robots means they will be widely used in most social and economic spheres of life (Ford, 2015). Also, there has appeared a multifunctional digital information technology designed to reliably record various assets and operations with them, that is, Blockchain technology (Swan, 2015).

All these technologies in the aggregate constitute a new, digital infrastructure capable of transforming the whole economic landscape. This new stage in technological development will involve a loss of many traditional professions. Most low-skill jobs in the service sector will remain available to people for the sole reason that it will be economically unviable to substitute them with expensive intelligent machines. It is, therefore, to be expected that a considerable share of medium-skilled employees may be eligible for low-wage positions in the service industries. To avoid such a scenario and to maintain demand for middle-class medium-skilled workers, significant adjustments should be made to practices in professional education and training so as to ensure that new requirements for employees match up with their level of professional educational attainment.

4 Modern Professional Education and the Labor Market

In developed countries, the modern system of education and professional training was established after the Second World War. It primarily catered to the needs of the middle class that at that time provided the basis for the economic and political stability in developed capitalist societies, and mostly trained professionals with medium and upper-medium skills. In very general terms, this system included the following levels of education and qualifications. The lowest educational qualifications are provided by primary education (4 years of study), which offers minimal body of knowledge and basic training in reading, writing, and arithmetic. The next level of education is lower secondary education (typically, 9 years of study). These two levels of education prepare workers for unskilled or low-skill jobs. Upper secondary education provides general secondary or vocational training (typically, 10–12 years of study). Combined with two-year college programs and four-year bachelor's programs, these three levels of education account for training professionals with medium and upper-medium skills. It can thus be seen that 12–16 years of training is enough to attain a qualification level and enter the middle class by income level.

The next upper levels of education, master's and doctoral, aim at training highly qualified professionals, and their training takes from 18 to 20 years. The Soviet system of education was quite similar to the described above: it took 10–12 years to train medium-skilled professionals and 16–20 years to prepare high-skilled ones. Below, there is a dynamics of the share of the US population over 25 years old with a bachelor's degree or higher, over the period 1940–2018. As seen from Fig. 1, the proportion of high-skilled workers was growing at a slower rate than that of medium-skilled workers. By 2018, the share of the latter amounted to 89.8% and that of the former to 34.5%. So, it can be concluded that the American system of education was primarily geared toward the education and professional training of medium-skilled workers. And it is precisely this social group that formed the basis of the American

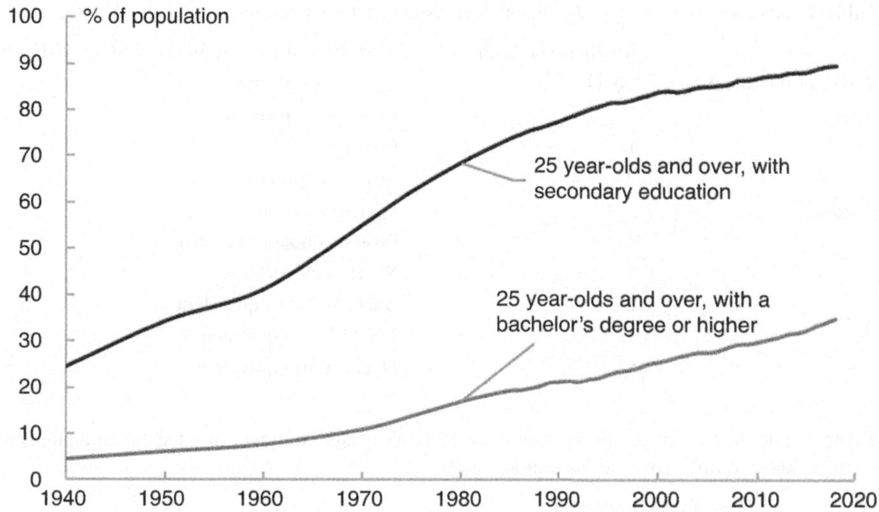

Fig. 1 Dynamics of educational attainment in the USA. Source: US Census Bureau (1940–2015)) Current Population Survey

Table 1 Educational attainment of 25–64 year olds (% of total population)

	Secondary education			Tertiary education		
Countries	2010	2015	2016	2010	2015	2016
USA	89.0	88.4	90.1	41.7	44.6	45.7
Germany	85.8	86.8	86.5	26.6	27.6	28.3
Russia	92.8	93.7	94.0	50.4	52.4	53.1
OECD average	75.0	77.6	78.8	30.6	34.7	35.8

middle class. But, as was shown earlier, the explosive growth of the information and communication technology sector, which started in the 1980s, initiated the trend toward replacing people in medium-skill occupations with means of automation, robotization, and software products.

Table 1 represents data on the educational attainment of 25–64 year olds across different countries, including Russia (OECD, 2019). The table singles out two levels of education: secondary (10–12 years of study) and tertiary, encompassing bachelor's (two- and four-year programs), master's, and doctoral.

As seen from the table, the employment rate of tertiary-educated adults in Russia is very high—almost twice that in Germany. This raises a legitimate question as to the closeness of relations between education systems and the rapidly changing demands of the modern labor market in terms of skills and professional training of new employees.

According to the International Standard Classification of Education (UNESCO, 2012), the OECD and UNESCO identify nine levels of education (UNESCO, 2017).

Table 2 Levels of educational attainment according to international education standards

	International Standard Classification of Education (UNESCO, 2012)	
Level of qualification	Level	Verbal description
Low	0	Incomplete primary
	1	Primary
	2	Lower secondary
Medium	3	Upper secondary
	4	Post-secondary non-tertiary
	5	Short-cycle tertiary
	6	Bachelor's or equivalent
High	7	Master's or equivalent
	8	Doctoral or equivalent

Table 3 Distribution of the population over 25 years of age, by level of educational attainment corresponding to different qualification levels (%)

	Levels of qualification				
	Low			High	
Country	Total	Including unskilled adults (levels 0–1)	Medium	Total	Including doctoral or equivalent
Australia	18.1	4.4	73.5	8.4	1.2
Canada	8.4	2.2	81.4	10.3	–
France	20.6	6.8	67.1	12.3	0.9
Germany	13.3	3.7	73.6	13.1	1.4
Italy	38.3	5.7	46.9	14.9	0.5
Japan	–	–	100.0	–	–
South Korea	11.8	4.2	83.0	4.7	–
UK	20.7	0.2	66.1	13.2	1.4
USA	9.2	3.3	77.7	13.1	2.0
China	75.5	28.2	24.0	0.4	–
Russia	4.8	0.5	65.6	29.6	0.3

Table 2 contains descriptions for every level and their equivalents in the Russian system of education standards.

We used this classification to systematize data on levels of educational attainment in different countries as in 2017–2018 (Table 3). Table 3 indicates that the distribution of labor supply by the level of educational attainment is approximately the same in such countries as the USA (the share of low qualifications ≅9.2%; the share of medium qualifications ≅77.7%; the share of high qualifications ≅13.1%), Germany (13.3%; 73.6%; 13.1%), the UK (20.7%; 66.1%; 13.2%), and France (20.6%; 67.1%; 12.3%). In some countries, due to a quite abnormally high proportion of workers with medium levels of qualification (81.4% in Canada, 83.5% in South Korea, and a whopping 100% in Japan), the patterns of distribution are different.

Table 4 Dynamics of the share of the employed population with medium and high levels of qualification, 1990–2018 (%)

	Medium		High	
Country	1990	2018	1990	2018
Canada	49.6	81.4	–	7.1
France	48.3	67.1	–	12.3
South Korea	48.4	83.0	–	4.7
Sweden	55.4	65.8	–	19.7
USA	77.6	89.8	10.1	13.1

Yet, if one looks closely at the share of the employed with a medium level of educational attainment over the last 25 years (see Table 4), it becomes evident that this process was not evenly distributed.

It is particularly notable that the share of the employed with a high level of qualification in the USA has increased insignificantly over the last 30 years. As for the share of the employed with a medium level of qualification, it has notably almost doubled in Canada and South Korea. Sweden, a country traditionally known for its high social standards, demonstrates consistency in the field of training medium-skilled professionals. A high share of workers with a medium level of qualification may indirectly indicate that the system of education in these countries is largely geared toward training professionals for the traditional rather than digital economy. A marked feature of Tables 3 and 4 is that they show the distribution of labor by the levels of qualification established in the labor market.

In the digital age, market demand for highly qualified workers will be growing for a whole variety of reasons. Firstly, digital technologies are expected to generate a considerable number of new jobs in such spheres as big data analytics, AI training and management, development of intelligent computing technologies and software, training, maintenance, and management of intelligent robots. Secondly, diffusion of new technologies always produces an indirect effect by creating new occupations in related industries. Jobs in these emerging industries will require deep and versatile math and engineering expertise and work skills that can only be attained by completing graduate and postgraduate studies. For instance, high-tech sector currently employs 2.9 million people in the USA (1.9% of all the employed) and 2.4% of all the labor force in Germany. McKinsey Global Institute predicts that an increase in spending on technology will generate, within the global economy, a demand for 20–46 million additional, mostly highly skilled, workers by 2030, and half of them will be needed in such countries as China, Germany, India, the Netherlands, and the USA. It is also expected that by then work activities taking up around 30% of the time spent in all occupations will be automated (Manyika et al., 2017). The US Department of Labor projects that by 2024 new jobs will be created in the following STEM fields: ICT (+76%), Mathematics (+7%), Science (+6%), Engineering (+11%) (US BLS, 2014).

Secondly, the world today is going through another stage in labor market evolution caused by the transition to a high-tech and research-intensive economy. At present, research- and knowledge-intensive industries are generally divided into two subcategories: leading-edge technologies with a threshold of 9% of internal

R&D expenditure on sales; and high-level technologies with a threshold of 3% (Gehrke et al., 2012). It should be pointed out that nearly all the technologies forming a new, digital economy are advanced. This is mostly due to the fact that these technologies are associated with knowledge generation based on human capital investments (Gehrke et al., 2012). So, expectations are raised as to some exponential growth in spending on science and education. It should also be taken into account that the R&D sector employs "rare production factors," that is, highly trained professionals, researchers, and scientists. It follows that the growing knowledge intensity of the digital economy also increases demand for highly qualified professionals from the STEM sector.

At the EU level, STEM core fields of study include life science; physical science; computing; mathematics and statistics; engineering and engineering trades; manufacturing and processing. As for professional occupations, core STEM occupations are science and engineering professionals; ICT professionals; science, engineering, and ICT associate professionals (technicians). STEM professionals encompass a wide range of knowledge-intensive occupations, including scientists (i.e., physicists, mathematicians, and biologists), engineers, and architects. There were 6.6 million employed in these occupations in the EU28 in 2013. They comprised 17% of all professionals and 3% of the total employment. STEM technicians encompass technical occupations connected with research and technology, including technicians in physics, life science, engineering, supervisors, and process control technicians in industry, ship, aircraft, and ICT technicians. In 2013, there were 9.7 million employed in this group in the EU28. They comprised 27% of all technicians and 5% of the total employment (DTI, 2015).

Consider the dynamics of the share on STEM graduates in selected OECD countries over the period 2010–2017 (OECD, 2018). See Tables 5a and 5b.

First off, it is important to point out that leading countries (Germany, South Korea, and the UK) apparently prioritize STEM studies, approximately one-third of bachelor's graduates earn their degrees in STEM subjects. Germany and Sweden have approximately the same proportions among master's graduates. The share of doctoral graduates in STEM disciplines approaches 50% across all the selected countries and amounts to a whopping 62.4% in France. These trends in training highly qualified professionals are congruent with labor market demands. In EU countries, the STEM employment rate has been growing steadily since 2000. In 2013, the number of STEM employees was 13% higher than in 2000. It is also projected that employment in STEM occupations will increase by 12.1% by 2025. In 2013, around 3 million of the 15 million STEM professionals employed in EU28 countries worked in high-tech industries. A higher labor market demand for STEM occupations translates into higher wages in the field: the average wage premium for STEM professionals amounts to 19% (DTI, 2015).

Traditional European STEM disciplines are very close to those encompassed within the US field of Science and Engineering. Data provided by the National Science Board, which keeps track of vocational training in S&E, and the National Center of Education Statistics allowed for tracing the dynamics of US graduates with high qualifications over the period 2000–2015 (NCES, 2018; NSB, 2018).

Table 5a Dynamics of the share of STEM graduates in selected OECD countries (%)

	Germany	France		Sweden	
Field of study	2017	2010	2017	2010	2017
Bachelor's degree					
Natural sciences, mathematics, and statistics	6.0	11.4	10.1	2.1	3.7
ICT	5.0	4.2	3.0	2.0	4.1
Engineering	23.9	9.0	8.3	9.6	11.3
Total	34.9	24.6	21.4	13.7	19.1
Master's degree					
Natural sciences, mathematics, and statistics	11.6	8.3	7.8	5.6	4.6
ICT	4.4	4.0	3.5	2.2	2.0
Engineering	19.4	17.5	15.6	24.1	24.1
Total	35.4	29.8	26.9	31.9	30.7
Doctoral degree					
Natural sciences, mathematics, and statistics	29.1	42.1	42.8	–	20.3
ICT	3.4	5.2	5.4	–	5.2
Engineering	13.2	12.4	14.2	–	24.9
Total	45.7	59.7	62.4	–	50.4

Table 5b Dynamics of the share of STEM graduates in selected OECD countries (%)

	South Korea		Canada		UK	
Field of study	2010	2017	2010	2017	2010	2017
Bachelor's degree						
Natural sciences, mathematics, and statistics	7.6	5.9	10.4	9.8	–	17.0
ICT	2.4	4.8	1.9	2.3	–	4.1
Engineering	23.6	21.0	8.8	8.9	–	8.2
Total	33.6	31.7	21.1	21.0	–	29.3
Master's degree						
Natural sciences, mathematics, and statistics	5.5	5.2	10.5	6.5	–	8.3
ICT	0.7	3.0	2.1	3.4	–	2.8
Engineering	16.9	15.2	9.4	12.7	–	9.7
Total	23.1	23.4	22.0	22.6	–	20.8
Doctoral degree						
Natural sciences, mathematics, and statistics	11.3	13.3	31.3	26.2	25.0	29.1
ICT	1.1	3.3	4.0	3.5	4.5	3.9
Engineering	22.7	24.4	20.0	21.4	14.8	14.7
Total	35.1	41.0	55.3	51.1	44.3	47.7

Let us consider two US trends. First, there has been a considerable growth in the number of S&E graduates: in the course of 15 years, it increased 1.7 times and exceeded 1 million people in 2015. Second, S&E graduates constitute nearly 30% of the total number of all graduates and 34% of the bachelor's graduates. It is also important to point out that the US system of education keeps a strong focus on training professionals with medium qualifications, namely, graduates with two-year

Table 6 Comparative dynamics of US graduates with medium and high qualifications, including the S&E, (thousand people)

Qualification level	2000 S&E	2015 S&E	Total	Share, %
Associate's in S&E (2 years)	38.0	91.0	1014.3	23.0
Associate's in S&E technologies (2 years)	83.7	144.0		
Bachelor's	398.3	649.2	1894.9	34.0
Master's	96.0	180.9	758.9	23.0
Doctorate	28.0	39.2	178.5	21.0
Total	644.0	1104.3	3846.6	28.0

associate's degrees. Data in Tables 5a, 5b and 6 indicate that Western education systems training STEM professionals with medium and high qualifications adjust to the changing needs of the labor market and can, to a significant degree, meet economic demand for professionals much needed in the emerging digital economy.

5 Modern System of Education in Russia

The dissolution of the USSR forced the Russian system of education to go through a difficult period of transformation and adjustment to new economic conditions. There can be no doubt that the country's educational potential inherited from the socialist system was largely lost. The task of establishing a new system of professional training is fraught with many challenges, most notably related to ensuring the quality of graduate training and the compliance of their qualifications with labor market needs. Table 7 cites data from the Rosstat on the number of graduates 2006–2018 with different qualification levels, whereas Table 8 shows the distribution of graduates by the level of qualification: medium, high, and very high (Russia in Figures, 2012, 2018, 2019).

First of all, most conspicuous is the fact that the number of graduates with secondary complete general education has halved and the number of blue- and white-collar workers has shrunk to a quarter over the last 15 years. All this combined has reduced the share of medium-skilled graduates from 70% to 58%. Overall, this trend can be seen as positive since the share of highly skilled professionals has concurrently risen from 28% to 41%. However, these qualitative changes were accompanied by a decline in the absolute number of highly qualified professionals, especially compared to 2011, by more than a third. It is also prominent that the share of graduates with very high qualifications, that is, postgraduates and doctorates, has fallen dramatically—by half. Data from the Russian Ministry of Education made it possible to analyze the dynamics of percentage distribution among highly qualified professionals who attained bachelor's, specialist's, or master's degrees in 2013–2018 (MSHE, 2019). The results of this analysis are shown in Table 9.

Table 7 Dynamics of graduate output from Russian educational and research institutions (thousand people)

Type of graduates	2006	2011	2016	2017	2018
Students with a Certificate of Basic General Education	1944.1	1354.1	1198.3	1234.3	1283.0
Students with a Certificate of Secondary Complete General Education	1466.0	1466.0	647.8	635.2	621.2
Graduates of training programs for skilled workers, office workers	703	581	368	199	194
Graduates of training programs for mid-level specialists	684	572	446	469	507
Graduates with bachelor's, specialist's and master's degrees	1151	1468	1161.1	969.5	933.2
Postgraduates (people)	33,561	33,763	25,992	18,069	17,729
Postgraduates with a publicly defended dissertation (people)	10,650	9611	3730	2320	2198
Doctoral graduates (people)	1383	1321	1346	253	330
Doctoral graduates with a publicly defended dissertation (people)	450	382	151	65	82

Table 8 Distribution of graduates from Russian educational and research institutions by the level of qualification

Level of qualification	2006	2011	2018
Medium	70.0	63.0	58.0
High	28.0	35.0	41.0
Postgraduates and doctorates	2.0	2.0	1.0
Total	100	100	100

Table 9 Percentage of graduates from Russian institutions of higher education by level of qualification (%)

Level of qualification	2013	2014	2015	2016	2017	2018
Bachelor's degree	9.3	17.5	45.3	65.7	75.6	70.8
Specialist's degree	86.3	76.4	48.7	27.2	10.2	11.0
Master's degree	4.4	6.1	6.0	7.1	14.2	18.2
Total	100	100	100	100	100	100

As seen from Table 9, there has been a sharp increase in the relative share of bachelor's degrees, which are awarded today to every seventh graduate from a higher education program. The share of master's degrees has grown more than fourfold while the share of specialist's degrees has reduced more than sevenfold over the same time period.

The percentage of graduates by occupation and field of study is also of certain interest. As noted before, core STEM occupations are set to play a key role in many sectors of the emerging digital economy. The dynamics of graduate output by STEM occupation in regard to bachelor's, specialist's, and master's degrees is presented in

Table 10 Dynamics of graduate output from Russian institutions of higher education (including STEM fields) by level of qualification

	2013			2015			2018		
		including STEM			including STEM			including STEM	
Level of qualification	All	ppl	%	All	ppl	%	All	ppl	%
Bachelor's degree	120,172	16,426	13.0	589,754	124,822	21.0	660,950	144,125	21.0
Specialist's degree	1,114,277	94,168	8.0	633,316	63,535	10.0	101,766	25,068	24.0
Master's degree	56,521	19,802	35.0	77,401	26,391	34.0	170,437	57,841	33.0
Total	1,290,970	130,396	10.0	1,226,156	142,708	11.0	933,153	227,034	24.0

Table 11 Postgraduate and doctorate output by STEM field of study in Russia

	Postgraduates			Doctorates		
Fields of study	2011	2016	2017	2011	2016	2017
All	33,082	25,992	10,612	1321	1346	253
Physics and Mathematics	1910	1677	907	87	111	14
Chemistry	806	658	428	50	49	4
Engineering	7547	7286	3079	345	366	50
Earth Science	1111	1050	336	46	47	5
Agriculture	1074	954	381	37	40	13
Biology	1750	1437	763	45	42	9
STEM fields, total	14,198	13,062	5894	610	655	95
STEM graduate share	42.0%	50.0%	55.0%	46.0%	48.0%	37.0%

Table 12 Comparative table of output of STEM graduates with bachelor's, master's, and doctoral degrees in Russia and the USA

	Russia, 2018			USA, 2015		
		including STEM			including S&E	
Levels of qualification	All	ppl	%	All	ppl	%
Bachelor's program	660,950	144,125	21.0	1,849,900	649,200	34.0
Master's and Specialist's programs	272,203	82,909	30.0	758,900	180,900	23.0
Doctoral program	15,795	6197	39.0	178,500	39,200	21.0
Total	948,948	233,231	24.0	3,846,600	1,104,300	28.0

Table 10. Table 11 contains similar data but in regard to postgraduates and doctorates (Russia in Figures, 2012, 2018, 2019).

As seen from Tables 10 and 11, there has been a significant increase in the share of STEM bachelor's and specialist's degrees over the last 6 years. The proportion of STEM master's degrees remains stable at 33% and that of postgraduate and doctoral degrees has barely changed over the last ten years and is generally around 50%. Conversely, there has been a decline in the total number of STEM high-skilled graduates: there are now three times fewer postgraduate degrees and almost five times fewer doctoral degrees awarded in the STEM field. This is an extremely alarming symptom indicative of an emerging development trend discordant to current global trends. For comparison purposes, Table 12 shows the total output of graduates, including those in STEM fields, in Russia and the USA in 2018 and 2015, respectively.

As seen from Table 12, the education systems of both countries devote great attention to the training of professionals for STEM-based industries and occupations. Interestingly, the USA has the highest relative proportion of STEM professionals among bachelor's graduates (34%) and the lowest among doctoral graduates (21%). In Russia, on the contrary, 30–40% of graduates with master's, postgraduate and doctoral degrees specialize in STEM. However, the overall output of STEM graduates in the USA is quite impressive and exceeds 1.1 million people a year, which is

Table 13 Distribution of the employed by level of educational attainment

Level of educational attainment	2008	2011	2015	2016	2017	2018
Employed in the economy, total	100	100	100	100	100	100
With higher education	27.9	29.5	33.0	33.5	34.2	34.2
With secondary vocational education, including:	47.5	46.4	45.0	45.1	44.8	45.0
– On training programs for mid-level specialists	28.2	26.9	25.8	25.9	25.6	25.5
– On training programs for skilled workers (office workers)	19.3	19.5	19.2	19.2	19.2	19.5
With secondary complete general education	20.1	19.7	18.4	18.1	17.4	17.2
With basic general education	4.1	3.9	3.4	3.2	3.4	3.4
With no schooling	0.4	0.5	0.2	0.1	0.2	0.2

five times more than that in Russia. This is a strong incentive to start thinking about the direction in which the Russian system of education should make a breakthrough.

Tables 9–11 contain data on the dynamics and percentage distribution of graduates from Russian educational and research institutions. These figures reflect the structure of the supply of highly qualified professionals in the labor market. But it is also necessary to consider the percentage distribution of the employed by level of educational attainment. This data is shown in Table 13.

Comparison of data from Tables 9–11 reveals a discrepancy in qualification levels between the percentage distribution of graduate output and the current structure of the labor market. The education system produces more high-skilled graduates than the labor market can employ. This may explain why 9% of 2010–2015 graduates with master's degrees and about 15% of those with bachelor's degrees are unemployed (MoL, 2016). One of the contributing factors to this situation can be a discrepancy in qualification levels between the percentage distribution of graduate output (i.e., supply) and the economic demand of the labor market.

6 Levels of Qualification, Industry, and Regions

As can be seen, the issue of discrepancy between the level of qualification attained by the bulk of graduates with a higher education degree and market expectations is complex. It involves closely intertwined technological factors, the ever-changing behaviors of firms and companies, labor migration, and regional factors. Indeed, as it was already mentioned above, periodic mismatches between supply and economic demand for skilled workforce can be reduced through labor reallocation, which raises an important practical question: Can regions with no high-tech industries benefit from such technologies? If yes, then in what way?

One of the latest studies of data covering 15 EU countries (Austria, Belgium, Denmark, Spain, Finland, France, Germany, Greece, Ireland, Italy, Luxemburg, the Netherlands, Portugal, Sweden, and the UK) and also including Australia, Japan, South Korea, and the USA over the period 1970–2017 yielded a number of interesting and applicable results (Autor & Salomons, 2017). The value of the study also lies in its analysis of development dynamics for 32 industries.

Most notably, the study draws two conclusions about the effect of productivity on employment:

- Productivity growth resulting from technological progress has produced positive effects at the national economy level on aggregate employment growth over the last 35 years in all countries studied.
- These positive employment effects have been distributed across all groups of workers unevenly.

An uneven distribution of these effects can be due to a change in the relative demand for skills within industries, which upsets the established balance among differently skilled workers, and to sectoral reallocations stemming from unbalanced productivity growth across industries that spur changes in aggregate labor demand by skill group. To substantiate this statement, the authors refer to some calculations, whose results indicate that a 10% productivity gain in high-tech services, and in health and education, raises economy-wide employment by 0.7–0.9%. The external effects of productivity growth in low-tech services are roughly twice as great as in any other sector, and estimated at 1.7%. This effect may stem from the fact that low-tech services are the largest sector in all five major economies studied, encompassing 30–40% of employment (Autor & Salomons, 2017, pp. 29–30, 41–42). Consequently, it is at the intersection of industries and regions where the greatest effects for regional development may be achieved.

7 Conclusion

1. The conducted analysis has revealed that the supply of professionals generated by the modern education system by level of their qualification mostly meets the demand of a Third Industrial Revolution economy (1950–2010), although rapidly advancing technologies of the Fourth Industrial Revolution persistently shift demand for labor toward high-skilled professionals.
2. The digital economy, high-tech and research-intensive, is bound to need increased expenditure on education and R&D. Most of all, it will require experts and researchers from such STEM fields as R&D, high-tech, engineering, and mathematics for digital technologies and AI.
3. Leading industrially advanced countries have significantly bolstered training for medium- and high-skilled STEM professionals (i.e., in bachelor's, master's, and doctoral programs) in accordance with the demands of the emerging digital economy by taking advantage of state support and private funds.
4. In the future, broadening training for STEM professionals may be economically constrained, among other things, by online global recruitment platforms and affiliates of high-tech companies bringing in retired employees to execute contracts. Such global online platforms as Upwork and Kaggle can potentially attract

over 4 million top-level professionals to solve tasks associated with STEM occupations.

5. A complex approach conjugating both established qualification levels of the employed in the industries and the technological development level of the region itself appears to be the most promising avenue to take when planning regional development. Given the external effects of productivity growth in high-tech services, there are always opportunities for development in low-tech services which account for 30–40% of the total employment even in the most developed countries.

References

Acemoglu, D., & Autor, D. H. (2011). Skills, tasks and technologies: Implications for employment and earnings. *Handbook of Labor Economics, 4B*, 1043–1171.
Acemoglu, D., & Restrepo, P. (2017). Robots and jobs: Evidence from US Labor Markets (NBER Working Paper No. 23285). https://doi.org/10.3386/w23285
Arntz, M., Gregory, T., & Zierahn, U. (2016). The risk of automation for jobs in OECD countries: A comparative analysis (OECD Social, Employment and Migration Working Papers 189).
Autor, D., & Salomons, A. (2017). Robocalypse now—Does productivity growth threaten employment? Paper prepared for the ECB Forum on Central Banking.
Autor, D. H. (2014). Skills, education, and the rise of earnings inequality among the other 99 percent. *Science, 344*(6186), 843–851.
Autor, D. H., & Dorn, D. (2013). The growth of low-skill service jobs and the polarization of the US labor market. *The American Economic Review, 103*(5), 1553–1597.
Autor, D. H., Levy, F., & Murnane, R. (2003). The skill content of recent technological change: An empirical exploration. *Quarterly Journal of Economics, 118*(4), 1279–1333.
Autor, D. H., & Salomons, A. (2018). Is automation labor share-displacing? Productivity growth, employment, and the labor share (NBER Working Paper No. 24871).
Bessen, J. E. (2018). Automation and jobs: When technology boosts employment (Boston Univ. School of Law, Law and Economics Research Paper No. 17-09).
Blau, F. D., & Kahn, L. M. (2005). Do cognitive test scores explain higher U.S. wage inequality? *The Review of Economics and Statistics, 87*(1), 184–193.
Broecke, S. (2016). Do skills matter for wage inequality? IZA World of Labor, vol. 232. https://doi.org/10.15185/izawol.232
Danish Technological Institute (DTI). (2015). Does the EU need more STEM graduates? https://op.europa.eu/en/publication-detail/-/publication/60500ed6-cbd5-11e5-a4b5-01aa75ed71a1
Ford, M. (2015). *The rise of the robots: Technology and the threat of a jobless future*. Basic Books.
Gehrke, B., Frietsch, R., & Rammer, C. (2012). *Re-definition of research-intensive industries and goods*. Commission of Experts for Research and Innovation.
Goldin, C., & Katz, L. F. (2007). The race between education and technology: The evolution of U.S. educational wage differentials, 1890 to 2005 (NBER Working Paper 12984).
Graetz, G., & Michaels, G. (2018). Robots at work. *Review of Economics and Statistics, 100*(5), 753–768.
Greengard, S. (2015). *The internet of things*. MIT Press.
ILO. (2017). Wage inequality in the workplace. (Global Wage Report 2016/17).
Kagermann, H., Wahlster, W., & Helbig, J. (2013). *Recommendations for implementing the strategic initiative INDUSTRIE 4.0—Securing the Future of German Manufacturing Industry (Final Report of the Industrie 4.0 Working Group)*. Acatech: National Academy of Science and Engineering.

Katz, L. F., & Margo, R. A. (2014). Technical change and the relative demand for skilled labor: The United States in historical perspective. In L. Boustan, C. Frydman, & R. A. Margo (Eds.), *Human capital in history*. University of Chicago Press and NBER. https://doi.org/10.7208/chicago/9780226163925.003.0002

Manyika, J., et al. (2017). *A future that works: Automation, employment, and productivity*. McKinsey Global Institute.

Ministry of Labor of the Russian Federation (MoL) (2016). Analysis of the position of graduates with higher and secondary education in the labor market in Russia. http://spravochnik.rosmintrud.ru/storage/app/media/Analiz%20polojeniya%20vepucknikov_VNII%20tpuda.pdf

Ministry of Science and Higher Education of the Russian Federation (MSHE). (2019). https://minobrnauki.gov.ru/

National Center for Education Statistics (NCES). (2018). Digest for education statistics. https://nces.ed.gov/programs/digest/

National Science Board (NSB). (2018). 'Science & Engineering Indicators. https://www.nsf.gov/statistics/2018/nsb20181/report

OECD. (2011). *Divided we stand: Why inequality keeps rising*. OECD Publishing.

OECD. (2015). Skills and wage inequality. OECD Employment Outlook 2015. Paris: OECD Publishing.

OECD. (2017). *OECD Employment Outlook 2017*. OECD Publishing. https://doi.org/10.1787/empl_outlook-2017-en

OECD. (2018). Distribution of graduates and entrants by Field. https://stats.oecd.org/Index.aspx?datasetcode=EAG_GRAD_ENTR_FIELD

OECD. (2019). *Education at a glance 2019: OECD indicators*. OECD Publishing. https://doi.org/10.1787/f8d7880d-en

Paccagnella, M. (2015). Skills and wage inequality: Evidence from PIAAC (OECD Education Working Papers, No. 114). https://doi.org/10.1787/5js4xfgl4ks0-en

Pellegrino, G., Piva, M., & Vivarelli, M. (2015). How do new entrepreneurs Innovate? *Economia e Politica Industriale, 42*(3), 323–341.

Roko, M. C. (2011). The long view of nanotechnology development: The national nanotechnology initiative at 10 years. *Journal of Nanoparticle Research, 13*, 427–445.

Roser, M., & Nagdy, M. (2020). *Returns to education*. Our World in Data. https://ourworldindata.org/returns-to-education

Russia in Figures. (2012). Brief Statistical Book. M: ROSSTAT. https://gks.ru/bgd/regl/b12_11/Main.htm

Russia in Figures. (2018). Brief statistical collection. M: ROSSTAT. https://gks.ru/bgd/regl/b18_11/Main.htm

Russia in Figures. (2019). Brief statistical book. M: ROSSTAT. https://gks.ru/bgd/regl/b19_11/Main.htm

Schwab, K. (2016). *The fourth industrial revolution*. Crown Business.

Schwab, K., & Davis, N. (2018). *Shaping the future of the fourth industrial revolution: A guide to building a better world*. Portfolio Penguin.

Siu, H., & Jaimovich, N. (2012). Jobless recoveries and the disappearance of routine occupations (NBER Working Paper No. 18334).

Swan, M. (2015). *Blockchain: Blueprint for a new economy*. O'Reilly Media.

U.S. Department of Education. (2020). National Center for Education Statistics. https://nces.ed.gov/fastfacts/display.asp?id=27

UNESCO. (2017). Institute for statistics, Educational attainment—Share of population by educational attainment. http://data.uis.unesco.org/index.aspx?queryid=168

UNESCO. (2012). *Institute for statistics. International Standard Classification of Education ISCED 2011*. http://uis.unesco.org/sites/default/files/documents/international-standard-classification-of-education-isced-2011-en.pdf

US BLS. (2014). Employment Projection 2014. www.bls.gov/emp/ep_table_102.htm

US Census Bureau. (1940–2015). Current Population Survey.

Structural Change in Developed Economies in the Digital Age

Askar Sarygulov, Alexander Petryakov, Bulat Khusainov, and Zoltan Zeman

Abstract The economic development of OECD countries in the past 50 years has been marked by a decline in the share of manufacturing and an increase in the share of the service sector in their national economies. This structural imbalance was one of the causes of the 2008–2009 crisis. Empirical data analysis for the leading OECD countries shows that the decline in the share of people employed in manufacturing has practically stabilized by 2020, while production volumes continue to grow. Information and communication technologies, which have already become general purpose technology, play an important role in this development trend. Based on the new role of ICT the work proposes a five-sector model of the economy (instead of a three-sector model), as it best reflects the technological trends of modern development. In particular, it is proposed to single out a separate sector related to human resources, which includes education, health care, social services and science. Another sector should be manufacturing, construction, transport, and mining, the development of which will largely depend on the use of ICT.

Keywords Structure of the economy · ICT · Employment · Five-sector model

A. Sarygulov · A. Petryakov (✉)
Saint Petersburg State University of Economics, Saint-Petersburg, Russia
e-mail: dept.cfr@unecon.ru

B. Khusainov
Economic Research Institute JSC, Nur-Sultan, Kazakhstan

Z. Zeman
Szent Istvan University, Godollo, Hungary
e-mail: zeman.zoltan@gtk.szie.hu

A. Rudskoi et al. (eds.), *Digital Transformation and the World Economy*, Studies on Entrepreneurship, Structural Change and Industrial Dynamics,
https://doi.org/10.1007/978-3-030-89832-8_8

1 Introduction

Economic practice periodically encounters such fundamental phenomena as crises. For example, the US economy only in the post-war years (1945–2013) experienced 11 crises of varying duration. The most destructive in nature were the crises in the mid-1970s and the last crisis (2008–2009), when the recession phase was exacerbated by the structural imbalance of the economic system as a whole. It should be noted, however, that the longest growth interval of the American economy in the twentieth century was between 1991 and 2001, 10 years precisely. This development sustainability was largely due to the technological factor—the boom in information and communication technologies contributed to the financial markets development, ensured an increase in labor productivity and creation of new jobs. However, the ensuing IT technology crisis raised the question of the reasons for the sharp decline and the nature of the new wave of development.

The arsenal of economic theory accumulated over the years is not always able to provide formulas for overcoming such depressions, since the ever-changing business environment requires certain adaptation of existing theories to changed conditions. In real economies, it has proved extremely difficult to draw a clear line between monotonous growth and development discontinuity, since both structural changes and wave processes are inscribed in the living tissue of the economy. Since the mechanism of self-sustaining economic dynamics lies within the structure of the economy, then it (structure) should be considered as an endogenous factor of the development. At the same time, cyclical processes are dualistic in their impact on the economic system. The problem of ensuring long-term economic growth comes down to the need to maintain appropriate structural changes taking into account the emerging cyclical processes. In this regard, the achievement of structural balance and its conjugation with development cycles will significantly reduce the loss of economic systems. These losses will be less, the more precisely the effects of microeconomic fluctuations on macroeconomic changes are determined.

The development of economic systems is uneven. Among the sufficiently large number of factors determining this uneven development, it is necessary to single out the key ones. Crisis 2008–2009 was caused by a number of reasons, but one of the main ones was deep structural imbalances in the economies of the most developed economies of Western Europe and the USA. This crisis has shown that to rely only on the "invisible hand of the market" is extremely dangerous, since structural changes that have taken shape at the microeconomic level for years can at a certain time "shoot" large macroeconomic imbalances, which take time and substantial financial resources to overcome. Resources to "remedy" structural imbalances are usually requested from the state, and this is a lot of evidence in the latest crisis. This naturally raises the question of whether the state is able to economically affect the creation of an economic structure that can contribute to economic growth. Today, in the structure of the GDP of the developed countries of the world, about 97% is in services and industry, and only 3% is in agriculture and the industries that directly serve it. As the share of agriculture is not expected to decline further, improvements in the quality of the macroeconomic structure can only be achieved through a change in the ratio between services and industry.

The current economic systems in Western countries are based on an orientation towards market mechanisms, where private companies and their daily activities largely predetermine development trends. Technology, innovation, and management systems prefer, become decisive in the formation of the technological and sectoral structure of the economy. At the same time, changing structures can influence both positively and negatively the rate of economic development. In modern economic literature, there are two main reasons for the emergence of structural shifts—the uneven development of technical progress and the heterogeneous nature of consumption. At first, it really looks like this. However, there are deeper root causes that relate to the nature of innovation and its potential to change the type of production, consumer behavior and economic environment. This is due to the fact that not all innovation can become part of real economic systems, and in this context, a special role is assigned to basic innovation and a convoy of innovation that can radically change the technological and economic environment. In addition, the ability of an economy to perceive technical inventions and turn them into innovation directly depends on the prevailing structure of the economy.

2 Structure and Its Role in the Economic Development

The most recent crisis (2008–2009) was predetermined not only by financial "bubbles," but also by the allometric nature of sectoral development, when disproportionately high shares in national economies were in some sectors (finance, services), and the share of other sectors (primarily processing) declined dramatically.

The dominant feature of modern economic research is a strict distinction between macro- and microeconomic research. In reality, these two systems function together, mutually influence each other, and only their joint interaction determines the trends and fluctuations of the entire system as a whole. In a long chain of economic processes, it is necessary to find such a key link that most naturally connects both levels of the economy. As the results of individual studies show (Akaev et al., 2011, 2013; Akaev & Hirooka, 2009; Rumyantseva, 2003; Sarygulov, 2011), the structure of economic systems can act as such a connecting link. Since the dynamics of structural changes is predetermined by the economic activity of the economic agents themselves, the key factors of these changes are the entrepreneurial demand for new ideas and the speed of their development, or, on the contrary, their complete absence. In the first case, there will be new industries emerging and developing; in the second—stagnation and withering away.

A systemic study of structural changes in the economy, primarily as a factor influencing economic growth, dates back to the mid-1930s (Clark, 1957). In order to determine the conditions for economic progress, C. Clark proposed a simplified (highly aggregated) structure of the economic system, when the main sectors of the economy, where all the elements of national wealth are created, were combined into three main groups, depending on the nature and main purpose of their products.

Subsequent studies of the economic structure were carried out by S. Kuznets, who took the classification and grouping proposed by C. Clark as a basis for such an analysis, somewhat clarifying and supplementing it, after which it acquired the following form: a) Group A (Agriculture): agriculture, forestry, fishing, and hunting; b) Group I (Industry): mining and processing industries, construction, transport and communications, energy, gas, water supply; c) Group S (Service): trade, insurance, finance, real estate, government, including defense and other services (Kuznets, 1971).

A distinctive feature of S. Kuznets's approach is close attention to fixed capital as a source of economic growth. This gave impetus to the creation of a leading sector theory. Kuznets's concept of a leading sector has two aspects. On the one hand, the sectoral structure of the economy can be broken down into two large sectors: the manufacturing sector and the agricultural and mining sector. On the other hand, a sector can be understood as a group of technologically and organizationally interrelated industries. The life cycle of any such group of industries is a reflection of the life cycle of certain technological innovation and the technological mode of production based on them. Production and price trends in the leading sector concept reflect the life cycle of a basic technological innovation, which develops in accordance with the law of logistics and the law of diminishing returns. Subsequently, many economists turned to this theory when analyzing structural changes (Quatraro, 2009).

V. Leontief, as the founder of the input-output model, significantly pushed the boundaries of the possible use of the models he proposed (Leontief, 1941, 1953). With these studies, he initiated the widespread use of matrix models for the study of horizontally integrated structures. In 1970, A. Carter completed work (Carter, 1970), which analyzed not only economic, but also technological changes in the American economy over the period from 1939 to 1963.

Industry shifts in the Indian economy for 1950–2000 were investigated using input-output models (Dasgupta & Chakrobarty, 2005). Based on the aggregation of 72 industries into a three-sector model (high-intensity raw materials, high-intensity technological, high-intensity "capital-labor"), the interrelationships and mutual influence of sectoral structural shifts are assessed. Matrix models also form the basis for studying structural changes in the Chinese energy sector (Kahrl & Roland-Horst, 2009), assessing the diffusion process of new technologies (nuclear power) based on logistics functions and their relationship with technological coefficients in the input-output matrix for the Chinese economy. This class of models is also widely used to study the processes of structural transformation in economies of various types (Kei-Mu & Zhang, 2010), to analyze the relationship between the rates of technological progress and the level of savings of the population for a two-sector economy (Laitner, 2000). UNIDO studies of structural and sectoral changes in the economies of five Southeast Asian countries (Indonesia, Republic of Korea, Malaysia, Philippines, Thailand) for 1975–2000 were also based on input-output balance models (UNIDO, 2010).

Another important vector of research on structural change was the work of L. Pasinetti (1981) on the relationship between vertically integrated structural change and economic growth. His fruitful ideas gave impetus to extensive research in such areas as the state of the labor market and the relationship between unemployment and inflation (Kurose, 2013) and the construction of a new class of models that take into account industrial and technological development (Arena & Porta, 2012; Oda, 1999). Among other studies on the relationship between cycles, growth, and structural change, it is necessary to highlight the work (Punzo, 2001), which is based on the results of the Summer School in Siena in 1998.

3 Some Empirical Facts

Over the past two decades, China and India have been world leaders in economic development. In this regard, certain interests arouse by trends in the structure of those employed in the economies of these countries. The processes of changing the employed structure in the Chinese economy, as evidenced by various studies, are rather contradictory and have obvious national characteristics. In Evans and Stavetieg (2008), it is noted that, despite the high growth rates of the national economy over the past 40 years, the structure of employment is a picture that is not subject to such radical changes as the Chinese economy as a whole. The authors of the study, drawing historical parallels in the industrial development of Great Britain, South Korea and China, note a significant difference in the rate of change in the structure of employment. The UK has achieved 80% of employment in the service sector over more than 200 years (1800–2000), with less than 15% in manufacturing and less than 1% in agriculture. In the case of South Korea, the structural change has progressed at a faster pace—over 40 years, the share of employment in agriculture has dropped from 70% to 7%, and in the service sector has increased from 20 to 70%. In the Chinese economy, the peak of the employment share in the industry fell in the mid-1990s (15%), after which it began to fall, and the share of those employed in agriculture over the past 50 years has decreased from 90 to 55%, with not very impressive growth in employment in the service sector—from 5 to 20%. The data of other researchers confirm this picture of the structure of the employed (Lo, 2007). The development of the Indian economy over the past 20 years, although not at such an impressive pace, is of particular interest in relation to the dynamics of the employment structure. An important feature of the dynamics of the structure of employed in the Indian economy was noted in (Papola, 2012). First of all, this is the inverse relationship between the GDP growth rate and the growth rate of employed in sectors of the economy: this was most clearly manifested in 2005–2010, when the GDP growth rate was more than 9%, and the employment growth rate was only 0.22%. For comparison, in 1973–1983, these indicators were at the level of 4.7 and 2.4%, respectively, and in 1994–2004—6.5 and 1.8%. The structure of the employed population living in rural areas deserves special attention. If in the early 1990s 78% of the employed were associated with the processing of agricultural products, then by 2010 their share decreased to 68%, and at the same time, the share of those employed in such sectors as construction, industry, and services increased to 32%. As for the structure of the employed as a whole, the dynamics of the process is very inertial: the share of those employed in agriculture over 40 years (1972–2010) decreased from 74 to 51%, the share of those employed in industry increased over the same period from 11 to 22%, and in the service sector—from 15 to 27%. The inertial nature of the change in the structure of employed in the Indian economy, as in the case of China, is due to the low mobility of the labor force and the very high absolute number of people employed in the economy (about 500 million people in the Indian economy and more than 800 million people in the Chinese economy). In the context of the impossibility of providing a job for all labor resources, the dynamics of structural changes is significantly slowing down, and a still high proportion of employed people are forced to live in rural areas, either adapting to the seasonal nature of the job, or moving to the informal sector of the economy.

In the work (Moody et al., 1996), it is noted that qualitative changes in industrialized economies were manifested, first of all, in a sharp increase in the share of those employed in the service sector throughout the second half of the twentieth century. According to their research, the share of employment in the service sector increased between 1958 and 1992 in the US economy from 47.7 to 61.4%, while the share of those employed in the manufacturing industry declined from 25 to 15.2%. Similar trends were observed in other industrialized countries, but the growth in the share of employment in the service sector was not always accompanied by a faster growth rate of the productivity of the service sector compared to the growth rate of GDP. Analyzing in more detail the reasons for such processes on the example of the American economy, the authors come to the conclusion that the reasons lie in the uneven rates of development of various types of services: the highest growth rates were observed in "technologically intensive industries"—telecommunications, transport, wholesale, and retail trade, while in healthcare, car repair, and in the provision of legal and other types of services, productivity even fell, which meant their inability and unwillingness to use the information and communication technologies that had already appeared by that time (Opt.cit. p. 15). As for the countries of the European Union, as evidenced by the results of studies (Sepp et al., 2009), for the period 2000–2005, the service sector was also dominant—it accounted for almost 70% of all employed in the economy, and the share of industry—20%, while the share of those employed in agriculture did not exceed 5%. It should be noted that other studies indicate slightly different, higher, indicators for the service sector in 2012 for countries such as France (78%) and EU-17 (74.5%) (Bocean, 2013).

Our analysis of the dynamics of the sectoral structure of GDP of the most developed OECD member countries for the period 1970–2010 (USA, Canada, Japan, Korea, Finland, Italy, Sweden, Austria, Spain, Germany, France, Belgium, Denmark, Norway, Netherlands) (OECD, 2021) showed that some industries were marked by a pronounced tendency to reduce their shares in GDP (this, first of all, agriculture), others—on the contrary, a steady upward trend (for example, the

Table 1 Dynamics of the sectoral composition of GDP (%)

Industries	1970	1980	2010
Agriculture, Fishing, and Hunting	9.7	6.4	1.6
Mining	1.5	2.0	1.3
Utilities	2.1	2.5	2.6
Construction	7.2	7.4	5.9
Wholesale, Retail, Hotels, and Restaurants	14.5	15.1	13.3
Transport, Storage, and Communication	7.6	7.7	5.1
Finance, Insurance, Property, and Business service	14.3	15.8	25.7
Service: public, private, social	17.8	18.8	22.8
Manufacturing	25.4	24.4	17.0

finance sector). At the same time, there are sectors shares in GDP of which are subject to insignificant fluctuations throughout the entire study period (we conditionally called them "traditional" industries—trade, construction, transport, electricity, gas, and water supply, mining). Table 1 shows the dynamics of the share average values of all sectors of GDP for the studied sample for this period.

The data given in Table 1 allow us to make several general comments that are of fundamental importance for understanding the essence of structural changes at the macroeconomic level.

First, the period under consideration (1970–2010) was marked by qualitative changes for the world economy, primarily in the nature of the use of accumulated knowledge, when the transition to a knowledge economy from the economy of production processes and resources began.

Second, the value of production resources, especially energy, has significantly increased, and, as a result, the search for new effective technology of a mass nature has begun, which would solve not only the problems of resource conservation but also the protection of the natural environment.

Third, the emergence of the knowledge economy has led to the development of knowledge-intensive sectors and human capital as important factors in increasing the efficiency of the economy as a whole.

Fourth. Economic development took place against the backdrop of turbulent political processes associated with the collapse of the statist principles of state and economy building and the development of globalization processes, primarily in the sector of informatics and telecommunications.

Fifth. An increasing proportion of economic benefits are now created by knowledge and information, which are also a valuable economic resource and require the development of digital technologies for collecting, storing, and processing. Information has become an object of everyday economic activity and has become a commodity and products of digital production.

Another conclusion, based on the analysis of data for the same sample of countries, refers to the "traditional" industries—trade, construction, transport, electricity, gas, and water supply, mining, which constitute the "infrastructure" component of development. Consider the data in Table 2.

Table 2 Traditional industries sector structure (%)

Year	I	II	III	I	II	III	I	II	III
	Canada			Finland			Sweden		
1970	48.0	11.7	40.3	62.7	2.8	34.5	58.7	2.8	38.5
1980	44.3	20.4	35.3	58.0	1.8	40.2	58.6	1.6	39.8
1990	47.3	12.0	40.7	59.2	1.2	39.6	58.8	1.3	30.9
2000	42.9	17.9	39.2	60.7	0.7	38.6	54.2	1.1	44.7
2003	44.4	14.8	40.8	60.1	0.9	39.0	56.0	0.7	43.3
	Japan			Korea			USA		
1970	53.2	2.5	44.3	41.1	5.3	53.6	43.4	4.4	52.2
1980	54.5	1.5	44.0	52.7	5.5	41.8	41.1	9.7	49.2
1990	59.3	0.6	40.1	58.9	2.3	38.8	43.3	5.0	51.7
2000	56.1	0.3	43.6	60.8	1.3	37.9	43.1	4.1	52.8
2003	55.8	0.3	43.9	65.1	1.0	33.9	43.2	4.1	52.7

I—infrastructure (utilities, transport, and communication, construction); II—mining; III—trade

First of all, we note that infrastructure industries are dominant in the traditional sector of the economy of four countries—Sweden, Finland, Japan and Korea, and they account for 52.1–65.1% of this sector. In the case of the American and Canadian economies, the infrastructural component takes a smaller share—about 43% in the case of the USA; this figure is slightly higher for Canada (about 45%). Trade clearly dominates the sector structure for the USA (about 52%) and is the second most important for the Canadian economy.

Let us note the fundamentally important tendencies of a social and institutional nature, which had the most significant impact on the development of infrastructure industries in all the countries under consideration.

1. From 1980 to 2003, social spending has increased substantially in virtually all OECD countries, from 16 to 21% of GDP (OECD, 2007). The main reasons for this were the increased costs of health care and pensions. This trend will continue in the future, since one more item will be added to these cost items—the need to finance all types of education.
2. The growth in social spending was accompanied by a reduction in government spending on infrastructure projects: the share of government spending in total capital investment for these purposes fell from 9.5% in 1990 to 7.0% in 2005 (OECD, 2007).
3. In the OECD countries, a large-scale program of privatization of infrastructure facilities began in 1980, because of which assets worth more than one trillion dollars were privatized, and about two-thirds were transport, telecommunication and electricity, gas and water supply facilities (OECD, 2007).
4. The last third of the twentieth century, despite the economic crises, was a time of stable and progressive economic development, when the rates of economic growth and labor productivity were the highest in the twentieth century.

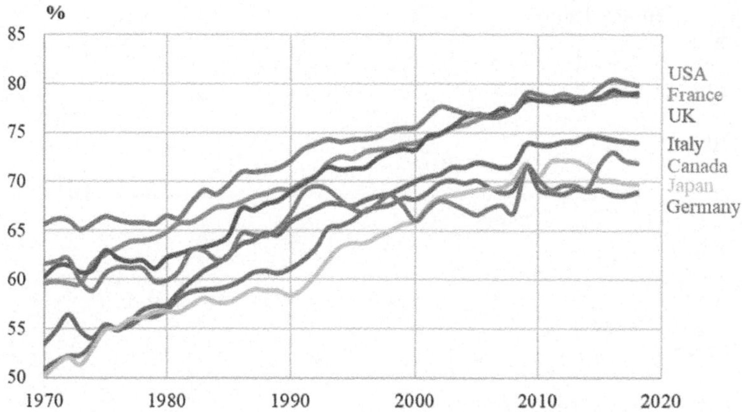

Fig. 1 Share of services in GDP (G-7 countries 1970–2017). Source: Authors' creation based on data from https://data.oecd.org/natincome/value-added-by-activity.htm

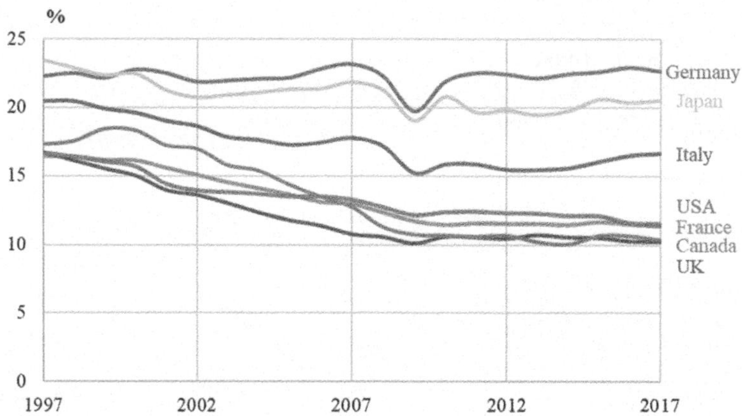

Fig. 2 Share of manufacturing in GDP (G-7 countries 1997–2017). Source: Authors' creation based on data from https://data.oecd.org/natincome/value-added-by-activity.htm

Our analysis of updated statistics for the G-7 countries for 1970–2017 shows that the previously identified trends in sectoral development continue: the share of the service sector in GDP is growing, and the share of the industrial sector in the economies of these countries is decreasing (Figs. 1 and 2).

The manufacturing industry was a key sector of the economy of the leading countries of the world in the twentieth century. However, as can be seen in Fig. 2, over the past 20 years, its share in the benefit of GDP of the most developed countries has only been decreasing. A distinctive feature of this process was the absolute reduction in the number of people employed in the sector with a simultaneous increase in the production volumes themselves. These trends have been particularly pronounced since 2000 in selected G-7 countries, with the exception of the UK, as can be seen in Figs. 3–6.

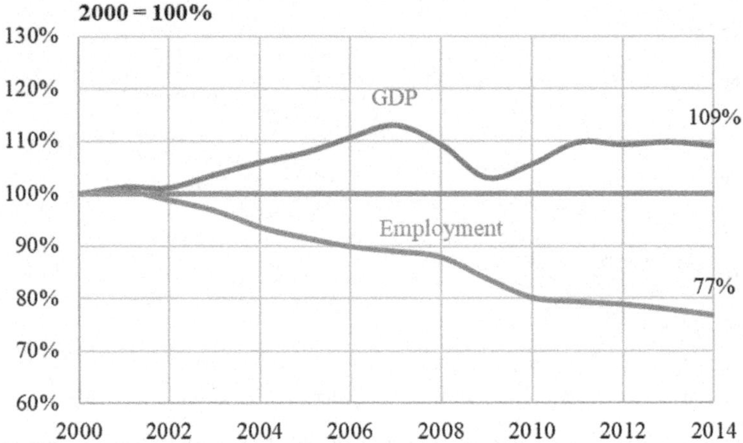

Fig. 3 Employment and value added of the manufacturing industry in France. Source: Authors' creation

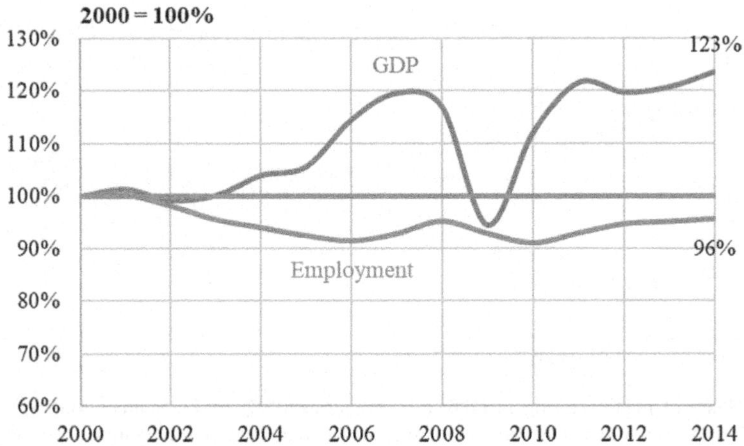

Fig. 4 Employment and value added of the manufacturing industry in Germany. Source: Authors' creation

As for the downward trend in the share of the manufacturing industry in GDP, back in the late 1990s, publications appeared where the question of the real deindustrialization of the highly developed economies was raised. Specialists from the International Monetary Fund (Rowthorn & Ramaswamy, 1997) have proposed their own interpretation of this process. In their opinion, the process of deindustrialization does not bring alarming trends for economic growth and is caused by higher rates of productivity in the industry compared to the service sector. However, the crisis of 2008–2009 indicates that the processes of real deindustrialization had a negative impact on the stability of, for example, the American economy. The sharply

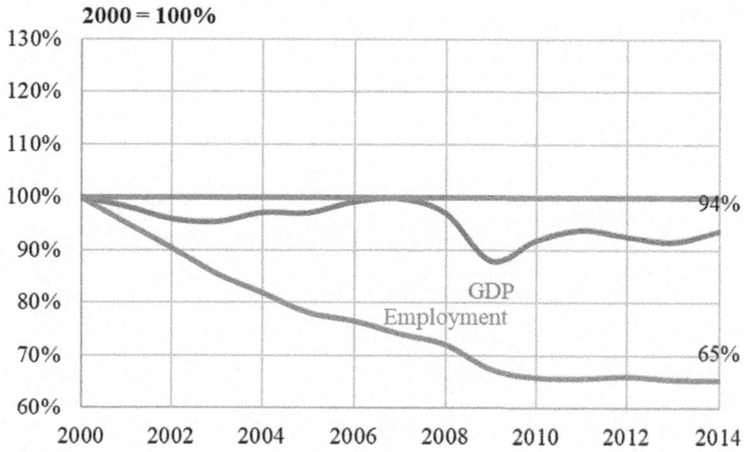

Fig. 5 Employment and value added of the manufacturing industry in the UK. Source: Authors' creation

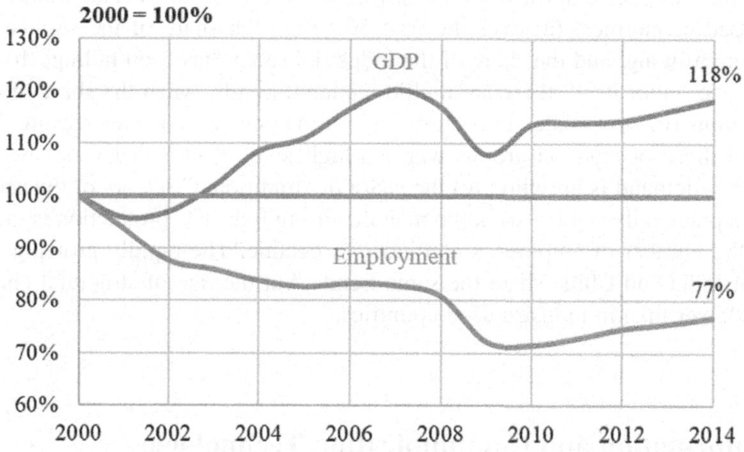

Fig. 6 Employment and value added of the manufacturing industry in the USA. Source: Authors' creation

increased unemployment rates in almost all OECD countries in the crisis early years indicated that there is a structural imbalance and significant disparities in the structure of employment.

Our in-depth analysis of the structure of employed in the American economy for the period 2003–2016, however, shows that within the Services sector itself, various trends are observed, as evidenced by Fig. 7. For example, the share of those employed in trade, administrative, and office personnel are falling, but the share of those employed in management is growing. A separate line shows a downtrend in the share of people employed in manufacturing and intra-industrial transport.

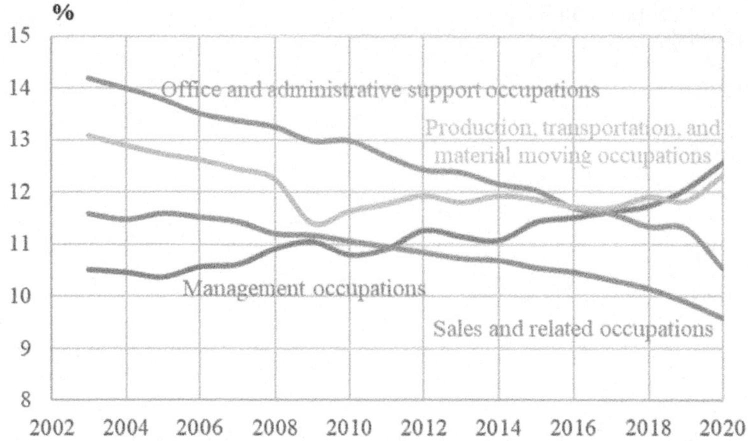

Fig. 7 Dynamics of the share of employed by certain occupation groups in the US economy (2003–2020). Source: Authors' creation based on data from https://www.bls.gov/cps/tables.htm

As we can see, empirical data confirm the presence of several trends in the developed economies: (a) over the past 50 years, the share of the service sector has been growing, and the share of the industrial sector has been falling; (b) within the service sector itself, there are multidirectional trends, when the share of certain occupations (mainly related to performing routine operations) is decreasing, but the share of those occupation groups where a high level of knowledge or low-skilled labor is in demand is growing; (c) the share of "traditional" sectors of the economy remains practically stable; (d) in the manufacturing industry, production is growing, while the number of employees continues to decline. The rapidly growing economies of India and China share the same trends, but the rate of structural change is much slower than in industrialized countries.

4 Information and Communication Technologies and the Structure of the Economy

The changes described above in the structure of national economies were largely associated with technological changes, and in the last 20 years—with the rapid development of information and communication technologies (ICT). ICTs today play the same role in economic development as the steam engine and electricity did in their time. Currently, the NBIC sector is growing rapidly (Bainbridge & Roco, 2006; Roco, 2011). The technologies of Industry 4.0 have become a practical reality (Schwab, 2016; Schwab & Davis, 2018) and Industry 4.0 itself (Kagermann et al., 2013). At the same time, the industrial Internet is becoming the basic infrastructure of Industry 4.0 (Greengard, 2015), a digital platform that ensures effective interaction of all industrial production facilities based on the Internet. With the advent of

Table 3 Dynamics of the number of employed by aggregated sectors (× 10^3)

Employment	USA		UK		Canada	
	2000	2017	2000	2018	2000	2017
Total	129,739	142,549	28,549	33,307	14,760	18,417
Agriculture	461	471	371	404	346	366
Manufacturing, Construction, Transport, Mining	33,498	30,259	5652	5096	3268	3488
Separate: Human Recourse—Science, Health, Education, Social service	21,741	29,752	6204	9264	3225	4851
Separate Service infrastructure: Utilities; Wholesale, Retail, Hotels, and restaurants; Finance, Insurance, Property, and Business service; Service public, private	74,039	82,067	16,322	18,543	7921	9712
Service total	95,780	111,819	22,526	27,807	11,146	14,563

Sources: https://www.bls.gov/oes/tables.htm; https://www.gov.uk/government/publications/; http://www5.statcan.gc.ca/cansim/

intelligent robots, it will be widely used in most spheres of public life and the economy (Ford, 2015). At the same time, Blockchain, a multifunctional digital information technology, appeared, designed for reliable accounting of assets and their transactions (Swan, 2015).

At the same time, digital technologies have an intensive labor-saving property, which makes their use "toxic" for the labor market. Digital computing has automated many routine tasks from the very beginning. Robots replaced workers in mass production conveyors. If until now automation has pushed people out of the sphere of routine physical labor and services, now it will push them out of the sphere of mental labor, replacing specialists with average qualifications.

In this regard, a reasonable question arises that the traditional three-sectoral model for describing the structure of the economy does not fully reflect the changes that occurred in the last 50 years, primarily of a technological nature. The service sector, which today in developed countries accounts for up to 80% of GDP, needs a more accurate description and separation from it, first of all, those industries that are associated with the formation and support of human capital. It is possible that instead of a three-sector economy (Agriculture, Industry, and Service) with a grouping of industries proposed by C. Clark and generalized by S. Kuznets, today we should consider a five-sector one, highlighting two new sectors. First of all, this is a sector that forms and uses human capital and consists of the following sectors—education, health care and R&D. This sector will play an ever-increasing role in the future. We also believe that the share of manufacturing has already reached its lowest point and has practically stabilized. In this regard, it is fair to assert about a new sector, which, in addition to the manufacturing industry, would include the sectors of the industrial infrastructure: mining, construction, and transport. Below in Tables 3 and 4 show

Table 4 Employment structure by aggregated sectors (%)

Employment	USA		UK		Canada	
	2000	2017	2000	2018	2000	2017
Total	100	100	100	100	100	100
Agriculture	0.004	0.003	0.013	0.012	0.023	0.02
Manufacturing, Construction, Transport, Mining	25.82	21.23	19.80	15.30	22.14	18.94
Separate Service infrastructure: Utilities; Wholesale, Retail, Hotels, and restaurants; Finance, Insurance, Property, and Business service; Service public, private	57.416	57.897	58.457	56.878	55.98	54.70
Separate: Human Resourse—Science, Health, Education, Social service	16.76	20.87	21.73	27.81	21.85	26.34
Service total	74.176	78.767	80.187	84.688	77.83	81.04

Calculation by authors based on sources: https://www.bls.gov/oes/tables.htm; https://www.gov.uk/government/publications/; http://www5.statcan.gc.ca/cansim/.

data on the number of employees and the structure of employment for the case of a five-sector economy for countries such as the USA, Canada, and the UK.

5 Conclusion

Globalization processes in the world economy have significantly changed not only the nature of trade economic relations between countries, but also became a powerful catalyst for the free movement of capital and labor between countries. The modern sectoral and technological structure of industrialized economies had developed because of almost forty years of post-war development; when, in conditions of political competition with socialist countries, these countries were forced to take into account the social component of development, providing great opportunities for the population in the field of education and health care. The natural result of this development was the formation of a qualitatively new level of human capital, and, as a consequence, the rapid development of the service sector and the diversification of the main sectors of the economy. These processes were significantly accelerated due to the rapid development of information and computer technologies in the 1990s. Thus, by the beginning of the twenty-first century, the most developed countries of the world (primarily the OECD member states) had such an economic structure where industries related to the provision of various types of services (from household to financial and state) became dominant, while the share of manufacturing industries dropped sharply. The proposed five-sector structure of the economy, we believe, more accurately reflects new trends in technological development, especially those associated with the emergence of learning machines with elements of artificial intelligence and the formation of a qualitatively new human resource capable of effective communication and control in new human–machine systems.

Acknowledgments This paper was prepared as part of the RFBR grant No. 20-010-00279 "An integrated system for assessing and forecasting the labor market at the stage of transition to a digital economy in developed and developing countries."

References

Akaev, A. A., & Hirooka, M. (2009). A mathematical model for long-term forecasting of the dynamics of innovative economic activity. *Doklady Mathematics, 79*(2), 275–279.

Akaev, A. A., Rumyantseva, S. Y., Sarygulov, A. I., & Sokolov, V. N. (2011). *Economic cycles and economic growth*. Polytechnic University Press.

Akaev, A. A., Sarygulov, A. I., & Sokolov, V. N. (2013). *Structural changes in developed and developing economies*. Polytechnic University Press.

Arena, R., & Porta, P. L. (2012). *Structural dynamics and economic growth*. Cambridge University Press.

Bainbridge, W. S., & Roco, M. C. (2006). *Managing Nano-Bio-Info-Cogno innovations/converging technologies in society*. Springer.

Bocean, C. G. (2013). Trends in human resources structure. *Management & Marketing, XI*(2), 255–264.

Carter, A. P. (1970). *Structural change in the american economy*. Harvard University Press.

Clark, C. (1957). *The conditions of economic progress*. Macmillan & Co LTD. N.Y. St. Martin's Press.

Dasgupta, P., & Chakrobarty, D. (2005). The structure of the Indian economy. In Fifteenth International Input-Output Conference. Renmin University in Beijing, China.

Evans, P., & Stavetieg, S. (2008). The changing structure of employment in contemporary China. In *Creating wealth and poverty in post-socialist China*. Stanford University Press.

Ford, M. (2015). *The rise of the robots*. Basic Books.

Greengard, S. (2015). *The internet of things*. MIT Press Essential Knowledge Series.

http://www.oecd.org/statisticdata/ ошибка в ссылке

http://www5.statcan.gc.ca/cansim/ ссылка на офиц. сайт

https://www.bls.gov/cps/tables.htm не работает ссылка

https://www.gov.uk/government/publications/ ссылка на офиц. сайт

Kagermann, H., Wahlster, W., & Helbig, J. (2013). *Recommendations for implementing the strategic initiative INDUSTRIE 4.0*. Frankfurt-Main. http://www.acatech.de/fileadmin/user_upload/Baumstruktur_nach_Website/Acarech/root/de/Material_fael_Sonderseiten/Industrie_4.0/Final_report_Industrie_4.0_accessible.pdf

Kahrl, F., & Roland-Horst, D. (2009). Growth and structural change in China's energy economy. *Energy, 34*(7), 894–903.

Kei-Mu, Yi, & Zhang, J. (2010). Structural Chang in an open economy (Working paper 595). Ann Arbor: University of Michigan.

Kurose, K. (2013). The importance of demand structure in economic growth: An analysis based on pasinetti's structural dynamics. In 15th Conference of the Association for Heterodox Economics London Metropolitan University.

Kuznets, S. (1971). *Economic growth of nations: Total output and production structure*. Cambridge, MA.

Laitner, J. (2000). Structural change and economic growth. *Review of Economic Studies, 67*(232), 545–561.

Leontief, W. W. (1941). *The structure of the American economy, 1919–1929*. Harvard University Press.

Leontief, W. W. (1953). *Studies in the structure of the American economy*. Oxford University Press.

Lo, D. (2007). China's economic growth and labor employment—Structural change, Institutional Evolution and Policy Issues. https://www.networkideas.org/ideasact/jun07/Beijing_Workshop_07/Dic_Lo.pdf

Moody, G., Cooke, S., Young, K., & Henry, D. (1996). Service industries and economic performance. In *Industrial Organization 9603003*. University Library of Munich.

Oda, S. H. (1999). *The analysis and simulation of non-proportionally growing economies with changing technology: A generalisation of Pasinetti's vertical hyper-integration.* http://www.cc.kyoto-su.ac.jp/~oda/PDF_files/Oda1999a.pdf

OECD. (2007). Infrastructure to 2030. vol. 2. Paris: Mapping Policy for Electricity, Water and Transport.

OECD. (2021). Value added by activity (indicator). https://doi.org/10.1787/a8b2bd2b-en.

Papola, T. S. (2012). *Growth and structure of employment in India. Long-term and post-reform performance and the emerging challenge*. Institute for Studies in Industrial Development.

Pasinetti, L. L. (1981). *Structural change and economic growth*. Cambridge University Press.

Punzo, L. F. (Ed.). (2001). *Cycles, growth and structural change. Theories and empirical evidence*. Routledge.

Quatraro, F. (2009). Innovation, structural change and productivity growth evidence from Italian regions, 1980–2003. *Cambridge Journal of Economics, 33*, 1001–1022.

Roco, M. C. (2011). The long view of nanotechnology development: The National Nanotechnology, Institute at 10 years. *Journal of Nanoparticle Research, 12*, 427–445.

Rowthorn, R., & Ramaswamy, R. (1997). *Deindustrialization—Its causes and implications*. IMF.

Rumyantseva, S. Y. (2003). *Long-term waves in economics: Multifactor analysis*. Saint-Petersburg State University Press.

Sarygulov, A. I. (2011). *The structural dynamics of macroeconomic systems*. Polytechnic University Press.

Schwab, K. (2016). *The fourth industrial revolution*. World Economic Forum.

Schwab, K., & Davis, N. (2018). *Shaping the future of the fourth industrial revolution: A guide to building a better world*. Portfolio Penguin.

Sepp, J., Kaldaru, H., & Eerma, D. (2009). Comparative analysis of employment sectoral structure in European Union countries. *International Review of Business Research Papers, 5*(2), 76–88.

Swan, M. M. (2015). *Blockchain: Blueprint for a new economy*. O'Reilly.

UNIDO. (2010). *Structural change and sectoral growth in selected East Asian countries*. UNIDO.

Theory and Practice of Territories Spatial Development Based on the Smart City Concept

Timur Ablyazov and Nauryz Baizakov

Abstract Spatial development of territories in the digital economy is a relevant area of research since the introduction of digital technologies has become an integral trend of urban development what happened from the beginning of the twenty-first century to ensure a comfortable and safe living environment. Theoretical approaches to the spatial development of territories and the definition of theSmart City concept have been analyzed in this study. The authors also justify the relevance of Smart City strategy development and implementation as the most important stage in territory spatial development and discuss the practical experience of the spatial development of territories of the world and Russia based on the Smart City concept. The existing programs for the spatial development of territories are described; digital technologies, which are tools for implementing Smart City strategies, are examined, and projects planning and implementing approaches on spatial development of territories based on the Smart City concept are analyzed in work as well. The authors identified problems in the sphere of spatial development and proposed a scheme for managing smart city spatial development as a result of this study.

Keywords Smart City · Spatial development · Strategy · Digital technologies

1 Introduction

Spatial development of territories is one of the key tasks in the sphere of improving the human life environment, and at present, technological aspects of this process are gaining more and more importance. In the context of urbanization, as a result of

---

T. Ablyazov (✉)
Saint Petersburg State University of Architecture and Civil Engineering, Saint Petersburg, Russia

N. Baizakov
Economic Research Institute JSC, Nur-Sultan, Kazakhstan

A. Rudskoi et al. (eds.), *Digital Transformation and the World Economy*, Studies on Entrepreneurship, Structural Change and Industrial Dynamics,
https://doi.org/10.1007/978-3-030-89832-8_9

which 68% of the population will live in cities by 2050 (this indicator was only 30% in 1970, and already 56%—in 2019), the relevance of compliance of population life quality to infrastructural capacities of modern cities is becoming more significant (UN, 2018).

Basis for the spatial development of modern cities is the Smart City concept, which is a theoretical basis for comprehensive improvement of the entire set of spheres of life and activities of territory—from health care and education to urban planning (Vishnivetskaya & Alexandrova, 2019). A Smart City should be understood as a large-scale project of national importance that has a specific time frame and budget and covers all aspects of city's activities.

Such a project should have a goal and strategy to achieve it. In the case of Smart City, the goal is to optimize urban processes, increase resource management efficiency and improve the availability of services for the population (Aguilera et al., 2017). However, about 60% of Smart City initiatives are coming to an end at the project discussion stage; moreover, all the goals set at the initial stage are not achieved due to the implementation of every second project (Pivkina, 2019).

The key factor in the stagnation of Smart City projects is problems in the sphere of strategic planning of territory spatial development. The Smart City strategy should not be a kind of formally developed document, which is reviewed at the end of the reporting year with a statement of non-compliance. The strategy should be a daily used development benchmark, which indicates specific goals with the timing of their achievement; put forward tasks, activities, and indicators that allow to assess the implementation pace in each area of strategy. In general, topical issues of the spatial development of territories based on the Smart City concept have not been sufficiently studied, which in turn justifies the need of the research in this area. Purpose of this work is to analyze theoretical foundations of the spatial development of territories based on the Smart City concept, as well as to review the world practice of introducing this concept into city management.

Spatial development of territories based on the Smart City concept is a subject of research of many scientists, and the study of this issue is carried out in various directions. So, on the one hand, there is an opinion suggesting that spatial development requires the use of a nationwide approach, since this approach allows to provide efficient allocation of resources and obligations, and also, if necessary, it is a basis for supporting regions lagging behind in terms of development rates due to the possibility of redirecting resources, financial ones in particular (ABB & European House-Ambrosetti, 2012; Hodgkinson, 2011; Tranos & Gertner, 2012). On the other hand, most researchers of this issue believe that spatial development should be based on a strategy developed for a specific city, that is, adhere to a local approach that allows to:

- Consider the geographical features of territories (Bria, 2012; Coe et al., 2001; Nam & Pardo, 2011; Townsend et al., 2009).
- Objectively assess the competitiveness of cities, since this aspect directly depends on individual characteristics of the territory (Cosgrave & Tryfonas, 2012; Giffinger et al., 2010; Giffinger & Gudrun, 2010).

- Set achievable goals for territory development, taking into account local problems and advantages of the city (Caragliu & del Bo, 2012).

In addition, similar cities can share spatial development experiences and transform their strategies (Bria, 2012; Tranos & Gertner, 2012).

Also, the spatial development of territories differs depending on whether it is a newly established city or already has an infrastructure. A number of researchers believe that development of a smart city started at greenfield that allows to introduce a maximum possible number of new technologies without adapting the existing infrastructure (Bélissent, 2010; Pentikousis et al., 2011; Washburn & Sindhu, 2010). A. Townsend, A. S.-K. Pang, R. Weddle also believe that spatial development of a smart city in a new territory provides ample opportunities for studying various schemes for project implementation (Cosgrave & Tryfonas, 2012), since there are very few cities that are not affected by traditional processes of territory functioning. However, spatial development of new territories is associated with substantial amounts of funding; it requires the involvement of residents, which together can slow down the implementation pace of planned activities and lead to the closure of projects (Alawadhi et al., 2012; Lind, 2012; Mortensen et al., 2012; Ratti & Townsend, 2011).

Most scientists study the issues of the spatial development of existing cities as they already have stakeholders who can be involved in the implementation of activities both financially and in terms of considering views (for example, city residents, business entities), and start the project immediately (Bakici et al., 2012; Paskaleva, 2011; Schaffers et al., 2012; Schuurman et al., 2012; Vicini et al., 2012). Moreover, N. Walravens, A. Dornan believe that spatial development of existing cities can be financed through the introduction of paid services that will cover expenses, as well as implement further measures to transform the city (Garner & Dornan, 2011; Walravens, 2011). Nevertheless, the city spatial development with an already existing infrastructure is recognized by a number of researchers as a rather complex process, which is associated with a need to take into account the interests of many subjects of the living environment, urban systems shortcomings and impossibility of their adaptation to new functioning ways (Pentikousis et al., 2011; Ratti & Townsend, 2011). It is important to plan development strategically, prioritizing various goals and objectives in such conditions (Bélissent, 2010).

Also, scientists recognize the importance of studying interaction processes of cities with each other in such areas as resources, production, human recourses and technology, since it is impossible to consider spatial development of an individual city in the modern world without taking into account processes of mutual influence of adjacent territories on each other (Smirnova & Ponomareva, 2019). In addition, Russian researchers paid special attention to issues of the spatial development of the country's industrial regions (Akberdina, 2019), involvement of territories in foreign economic relations (Myslyakova et al., 2019). Spatial development in Russia is also often considered within the framework of a transit-oriented approach to territory development, which is expressed in an increase in the scope of construction of residential, commercial buildings, public spaces in accordance with the city transport routes (Koncheva & Zalesskiy, 2016).

The conducted literature review in the sphere of spatial development of territories based on the Smart City concept allows to conclude that each city has unique characteristics, which affect its transformation. Therefore, it is impossible to classify clearly certain measures for transforming a city to the effective one since it is necessary to take into account individual characteristics of the territory.

However, is there a general guideline for the spatial development of modern cities? To date, the Smart City concept is the most significant for the development of territories. This concept still does not have an unambiguous definition despite the study by many scientists. Initially, the increase in efficiency of resource flow management (energy, utilities, transport, financial, etc.) was recognized as the result of the introduction of smart city technologies. It was achieved through the use of modern digital technologies within various infrastructures of the city life necessities (United Nations Environment Programme, 2018). In recent years, the scientific community has pointed to the fact that the Smart City concept implies not only technologies, but is also intended to consider the needs of society (Albino et al., 2015), and should be based on human capital development to ensure the economy growth and well-being of citizens (Angelidou, 2017). The smart city is largely based on data analytics and the Internet of Things, which are being introduced into infrastructure, and are applicable even in traditional areas of the economy, for example, in construction (Ablyazov, 2019; Vishnivetskaya & Ablyazov, 2019).

Summarizing the various interpretations of smart cities, it can be said that the basis of a smart city is the use of digital technologies to transform all infrastructures of territory in order to increase efficiency and environmental friendliness of their functioning, as well as to increase the level of comfort and safety of lives of the population (Aldama-Nalda et al., 2012; Cosgrave et al., 2013; Mallapuram et al., 2017; Marsal-Llacuna et al., 2015). In addition, scientists point to the need to develop models for sustainable development of urban areas in the context of rapid development of technologies and acceleration of urbanization processes (Beatley, 2012; Didier et al., 2012), which is reflected in the emergence of a smart, sustainable city concept that combines social, economic, and environmental aspects of the territory development (Höjer & Wangel, 2014).

It is important to provide a theoretical basis that reflects the elements of a smart city fully due to the uniqueness of the spatial development of the territory. It is exactly the strategic planning of cities spatial development that is designed to provide an effective solution to economic, social, and environmental problems that increase inevitably with a rise of population density and load on all infrastructure of the territory (Rasoolimanesh et al., 2016). On the one hand, it is believed that the territory development strategy should cover such issues as decentralization of management, globalization, and sustainable development (de Graaf & Dewulf, 2010). On the other hand, more and more emphasis is being placed on the involvement of all parties concerned in the development and implementation of the city's strategy, which includes the development of various forms of partnership between the private and public sectors (Zhang, 2013).

Smart City development and implementation strategy are currently carried out due to the process of digital transformation of all spheres of life, which has not been studied sufficiently by the scientific community, since smart city technologies are just getting their distribution in the practice of improving territories.

2 Practice of Territory Spatial Development Based on the Smart City Concept

There has been a global growth of interest in smart city technologies since the beginning of the twenty-first century, despite the lack of a common understanding of the Smart City concept and clearly fixed directions for its implementation. (Catapult, 2017). Earlier, in 2011–2013, smart city strategies were aimed at intensifying economic development of territories, which is typical for Europe, Asia, and North America. On the other hand, African countries were more focused on solving a variety of social problems, which was reflected in the development of urban strategies. Following the strategies implementation, in 2014–2017, most Asian countries, having achieved an acceptable level of economic growth, began to pay more attention to social objectives and environmental preservation. At the same time, European countries are still more focused on solving economic problems, although measures to develop the social sphere and improve the environmental friendliness of life are also taking place there. Speaking about the countries of North America, it can be noted that their strategies have been focused on social issues over the last 5 years, without moving to the next level of development—improving environmental sustainability.

Research conducted by Roland Berger international consultancy found that 153 cities have smart city strategies as of 2019, with 41% of strategies in Europe, 27% in Asia, 24% in North America and only 8% accounted for Africa and South America (Roland Berger, 2019). Moreover, in comparison with 2017, only 18% of cities have not made changes to development strategy. A quarter of cities under study adapted their strategy to conditions of 2019, and 57% of cities. In the period 2017–2019 in particular, announced the smart city strategy for the first time (Roland Berger, 2019). Despite the fact that the territory development strategy is secured under the legislation by a document used by authorities, it is not always publicly available and may not even be published.

According to the Smart City Strategy Index (SCSI), in 2019, the leaders in Smart City concept implementation are Vienna, London, and St Albert (Canada), a detailed analysis of their development strategies is presented in Fig. 1.

Let us take a closer look at the development program of one of the largest cities in the world—London. Spatial development of London is based on the Smarter London Together Roadmap with five global goals highlighted in it (The Greater London Authority, 2021):

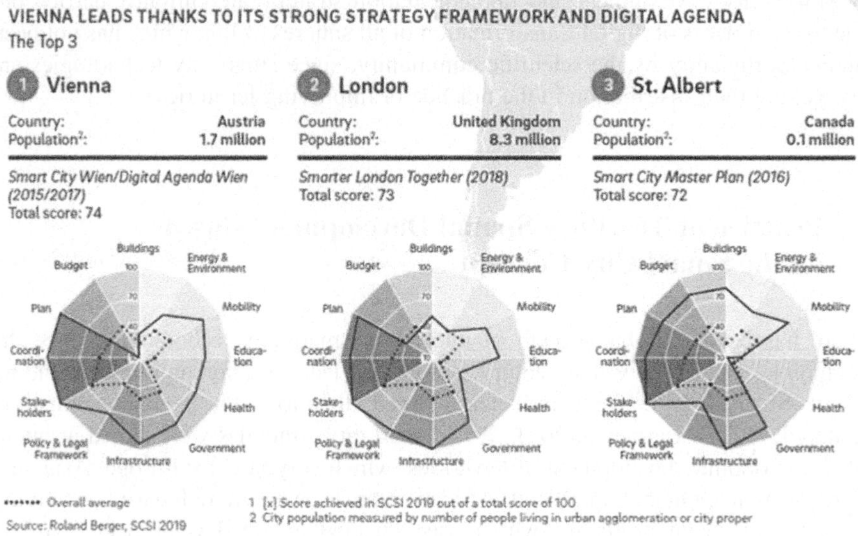

Fig. 1 Top 3 Smart City strategies in 2019 (Roland Berger, 2019)

1. An increase in the number of services developed with users participation, for which the Talk London interaction platform between the population and authorities was introduced; the Civic Innovation Challenge program to intensify private technological development (since 2018, solutions have already been developed in urban planning, crime reduction, logistics, and transport), crowdfunding online platform.
2. A high level of work with big data, which was expressed in the creation of the London Datastore with an interactive presentation of more than 700 data sets; The London Development Database in the sphere of development planning, as well as various services providing information on air quality, transport system, cultural objects, etc.
3. Increase the degree of urban systems interconnection to meet better the requirements of the digital economy (Connectivity Map and Sharing Cities).
4. Development of digital skills for different groups of populations (Digital Talent Programme, Digital Inclusion).
5. Improvement of city-wide cooperation for achievement of special development, which is expressed in projects such as London Office of Technology and Innovation (LOTI), GovTech for London, London Underground Assets Register (LUAR), Infrastructure Mapping Application (IMA).

In Asian countries, Singapore is the undisputed leader in spatial development based on the Smart City concept. In 2014, the Smart Nation Initiative was launched with a total implementation cost of US $ 1.73 billion (Thales, 2020). This strategy includes territory development in such areas as mobility increase, healthcare improvement, the practice of using mobile applications, support for entrepreneurship, skills development in working with digital technologies. These areas include projects related to open data, contactless payments, the Internet of Things, telemedicine, robots, unmanned vehicles, artificial intelligence and other most modern technologies.

In Russia, the Smart City concept is becoming more widespread. The digitalization index of urban economy IQ cities published by the Ministry of Construction of Russia in 2020 showed that Moscow, Yekaterinburg, Kazan, and St. Petersburg are the leaders among the largest cities in Russia (Minstroj Rossijskoj Federacii, 2019).

In Moscow, the Smart City-2030 Strategy (Oficial'nyj sajt Mera Moskvy, 2021), adopted in 2018, was a continuation of Digital Moscow programs that had been implemented since the early 2000s (computerization of management sphere), and Information City (automation of management, including the emergence of electronic services and multifunctional centers—MFC). The development of Moscow is carried out in six areas, namely in the urban environment, digital mobility, urban economy, safety and ecology, digital government, human and social capital. A distinctive feature of the Moscow Smart City Strategy is a principle of supporting domestic technologies, which is reflected in reasonable import substitution and targeted support of Russian manufacturers. It is expected that, as a result of the implementation of the Smart City 2030 Strategy, such innovations in human life environment as personalized medicine, use of artificial intelligence in management, electronic referendums on development of houses, districts and cities, spread of smart homes, unmanned vehicles, and robot assistants.

St. Petersburg is guided by the Economic and Social Development Strategy 2035 (Zakon Sankt-Peterburga, 2018), which emphasizes four directions of city development—smart population, smart living environment, smart management and smart economy (Komitet po ekonomicheskoj politike i strategicheskomu planirovaniyu Sankt-Peterburga, 2015). The regulatory legal acts almost do not contain direct reference of "smart," however, territory transformation consists in the process based on digital technologies.

Kazan also has a Development Strategy 2030, which plans to introduce technologies at the level of Moscow and St. Petersburg, as a result of which the city will become "a territory of health, convenient for the life of active, responsible, and creative citizens, open government and a safe environment" (SHakirov, 2021).

Yekaterinburg for 2018–2019 increased its rating by 37% in the Russian smart cities ranking (Torgovceva, 2021). The Smart City project here is based on five principles: human orientation; technological effectiveness of urban infrastructure; improvementof urban resource management quality; comfortable and safe environment; emphasis on economic efficiency, including the service component of the urban environment (Informatizaciya goroda Ekaterinburga, 2021).

Therefore, the use of the Smart City concept is a global trend in spatial development at the present stage of digital technologies development. Practice of territorial development shows that the presence of a strategy is one of the main factors in the successful implementation of city transformation projects.

Each territory has unique characteristics, which does not allow to adopt fully the development experience of other cities. However, it can be seen that the directions of the considered strategies are largely similar. Tools for implementation of various strategies and transforming approaches to spatial development are considered in the next part of this study, which can be used both to update existing urban development projects and to form a list of activities that have not been previously implemented in a given territory.

3 Digital Technologies as Tools for Implementing Territorial Development Strategies

Implementation of measures within the framework of strategies for territory development is directly related to the introduction of a digital technologies complex that qualitatively transforms approaches to the spatial development of cities. In accordance with the experts of International Data Corporation (USA, Framingham) (Rajan et al., 2016), smart city digital technologies should be divided into such groups as social, mobility, big data/analytics, cloud, which are collectively defined by abbreviation SMAC (Frank, 2012). According to the China-Britain Business Council, digital technologies should be defined as SMIC, namely social, mobile, internet, cloud (EU SME Centre, 2015). There are five technology groups in Canada (SMAAC)—social, mobile, applications, analytics and cloud (ICTC, 2016). In addition, Ernst & Young experts highlight technology of the Internet of Things, which they define globally as the Internet of Everything (Ernst & Young, 2015).

Concept of end-to-end technologies for a smart city is widespread in Russia including virtual, augmented and mixed reality, artificial intelligence, big data and predictive analytics, blockchain, 5G communication technologies, the Internet of Things, neurointerfaces, 3D modeling, scanning, and printing. A similar list of technologies is common for Moscow Development Strategy (Oficial'nyj sajt Mera Moskvy, 2021).

The main characteristic of digital technologies in a smart city is online functioning to update data continuously. These technologies include city-wide broadband connectivity, remote sensing (RS), global positioning system (GPS), geographical information systems (GIS), the Internet of Things (IoT), AI/ML elements (artificial intelligence and machine learning) (Intellias, 2020).

It is worth to note that big data and the Internet of Things play an important role in a smart city, allowing this data to be collected and transmitted to processing and analysis centers. To provide a city management based on big data, it is necessary to implement technologies such as cloud computing, RFID, wireless sensor networks (WSN), wireless communication platforms, 4G / 5G networks, network function virtualization (NFV) (Hashem et al., 2016).

It becomes possible to form digital platforms that allow to combine together all smart city technologies and visually present information to users as a result of the use of the above technologies (Ablyazov, 2021). In the sphere of territorial development planning, the most popular are platforms used to aggregate geo-data. There are open platforms such as OpenStreetMap and Mapillary, which allow users to update data about territory, as well as use them for research.

Platforms used in the distribution of property rights to real estate are widespread as well. For example, Civic Insight operates on the basis of the manufacturer of ESRI geographic information systems. There is a public cadastral map of Rosreestr in Russia, which is not an open platform but provides data online.

The ultimate goal of introducing data collection technologies is the formation of digital twins of cities. One of the leaders in this area is the Virtual Singapore program, within the framework of which a highly detailed model of the city has been created, providing data on buildings (area, materials, and location), statistics of the urban environment functioning in areas of transport, trade, medicine, and the state of the environment. Authorities, organizations, researchers, residents have access to the model, which contributes to effective analytics of city spatial development, making it possible to simulate the impact of innovations on the urban environment in advance.

Despite the importance of creating a holistic twin of the city, the most common technologies for modeling a separate sphere of the urban environment are often the transport system. Transformation is based on the concept of mobility-as-a-service (MaaS), which implies a transition to intelligent public transport systems (including car sharing) instead of using private transport. To introduce digital platforms within the framework of MaaS, it is necessary to spread 4G/5G communication technologies, smartphones, contactless payments, as well as the Internet of Things, with the help of which the transport schedule and routes will be updated (Paul Budde Communication Pty Ltd, 2016). Transition to MaaS Platforms is already observed in Helsinki, Paris, Eindhoven, Gothenburg, Montpellier, Vienna, Hanover, Las Vegas, Los Angeles, Denver, Singapore, and Barcelona (Fishman & Bornstein, 2017).

Therefore, the implementation of smart city strategies aimed at spatial development of territories requires the use of digital technologies that contribute to urban environment transformation. The key tool for implementing these strategies is big data and the Internet of Things technologies, the use of which makes it possible to form digital twins of cities. Various digital platforms and models serve as the basis for analyzing the urban environment and further improving spatial development strategies.

4 Approaches to Territory Spatial Development Based on the Smart City Concept

Formation of a strategy is a priority stage in the spatial development of territory based on the Smart City concept. Task of strategic planning of spatial development in a smart city is to develop a system of measures aimed at achieving long-term goals of the territory development in spheres of economics, management, health care,

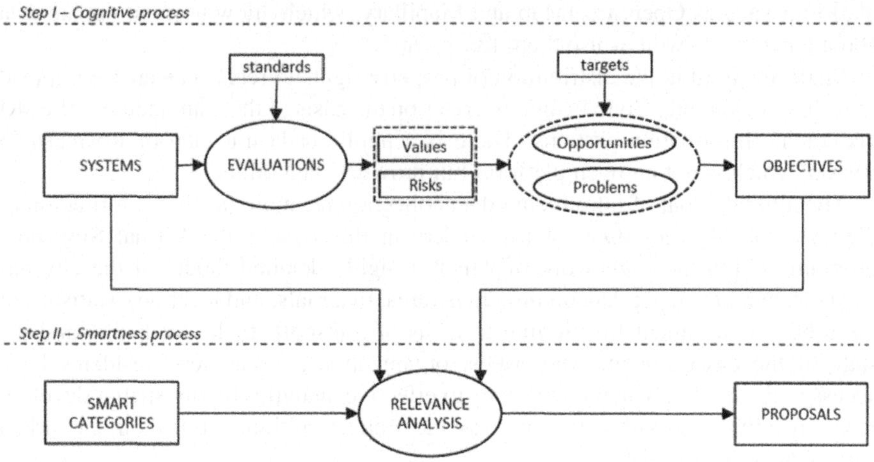

Fig. 2 Smart City strategy development model (Panuccio, 2019)

education, ecology, transport, housing and communal services, etc. Development of a smart city strategy takes place in 2 stages (Fig. 2).

The first stage (cognitive process) includes assessment of the existing urban systems, highlighting the risks and main advantages of their functioning, identification of problems and development opportunities on the basis of the existing standards and goals set, and as a result, development of goals that need to be included in the strategy. At the second stage (smartness process), existing systems and identified goals are analyzed in accordance with the smart city categories to formulate proposals for inclusion to the smart city strategy. Smart city categories are defined as natural resources (environment), transport (mobility), human capital (population), quality of life (living), governance and economy (Panuccio, 2019).

The considered model of a smart city strategy development can be implemented using two opposite approaches—top-down and a collaborative one (Catapult, 2017). In the first case, a specially created committee (agency, department, etc.) is engaged in development of the strategy, which allows to go through quickly all the planning stages if it is impossible to conduct a long negotiations on the strategy with all parties concerned. As a rule, the top-down approach is used in Asian countries (China, Indonesia, and South Korea). A collaborative approach, on the other hand, implies the involvement of as many experts, scientists, government officials, technology owners and citizens as possible in the strategy development process. This approach allows to consider the interests of all parties as fully as possible, but it requires a lot of time and resources to conduct such a negotiation. This strategy development format is more common in Europe and North America; particularly, it is actively used in Dublin and Toronto.

Once the strategy is developed and approved, it is necessary to implement digital technologies and manage a smart city. It is common to represent the process of smart city management in accordance with the levels of technology use, for example, as

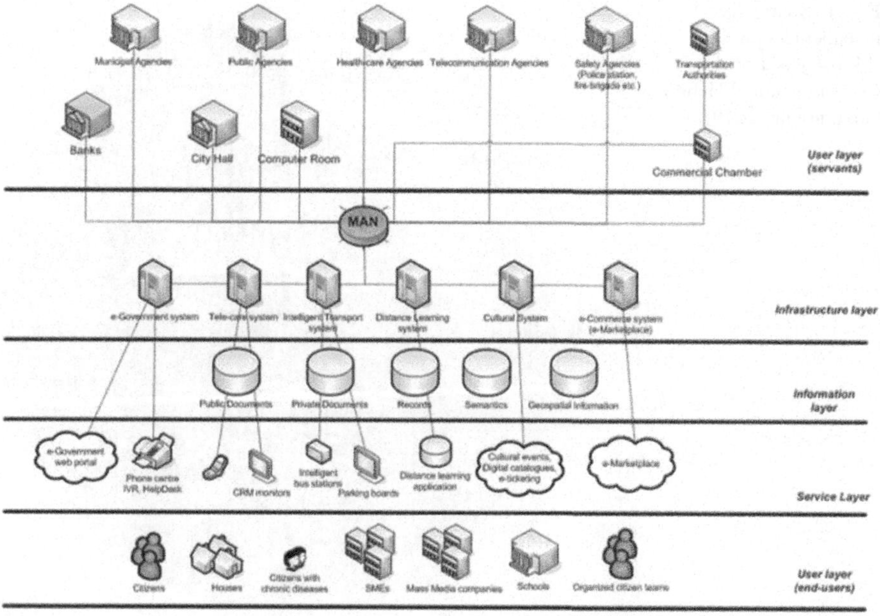

Fig. 3 Management levels in a smart city (Anthopoulos & Vakali, 2012)

shown in Fig. 3. A peculiar feature of this management scheme is the division of users into end consumers and user-workers, including representatives of government authorities, city services, financial and credit spheres. The main part of the management process is infrastructure, information, and service layers, which are filled with various digital technologies mentioned above.

In addition, a smart city management is based on answering such questions as "What goals do we want to achieve?" "How to achieve them?" and "What is the current state of the city?" A detailed scheme for smart city management according to these three phases is presented in Fig. 4. It is worth to note that the process is cyclic as technologies are constantly changing, and the priorities of spatial development are also subject to adjustment.

In Russia, the smart city management scheme, in particular in St. Petersburg, involves the allocation of four layers (Mityagin et al., 2019):

- Physical means of information interaction (sensors and other means of control, automated workstations, active elements of the urban environment, i.e., traffic lights, lanterns, etc.).
- Cross-industry functional elements (information resources, data storage and processing centers, means of ensuring information interaction).
- Sector-specific functional elements (transport, education, social support, economy, culture, housing, and communal services, energy and engineering support, ecology, landscaping, health care, physical culture and sports, tourism, territorial development, industrial policy and innovation, security, law and order).

Fig. 4 Smart city management phases (Ministry of Local Government and Hebron Governorate, 2019)

– Socio-technical functional elements (electronic services, open data portals, Internet of Things).

The authors believe that smart city management generally corresponds to the scheme presented in Fig. 5.

Smart city management implies the participation of all subjects of the urban environment; therefore, it is important to collect reviews of the population. Also, an interdisciplinary approach should be used as it makes it possible to determine the development priorities common for the city (Ablyazov, 2020). In addition, the required activities may be different for various districts of the city or types of infrastructure, while there are city-wide problems that cannot be solved without integrated development of the entire city territory. Potential solutions to city's problems are determined in order to achieve the identified development priorities, which shall necessarily be subject to expertise, upon completion of which a smart city development strategy will be drawn up. Further, implementation of the planned activities is carried out while simultaneously monitoring the achieved results. New problems of city's development, as well as new technologies, may be identified during the process of strategy implementation, which in turn will lead to an adjustment of the action plan according to a similar scheme.

It should be noted that spatial development based on the Smart City concept is associated with a number of issues. The main problem is the lack of awareness of the fact that each city is unique: excellent location, different management approaches, different concerned parties are involved. Therefore, strategies for the country capital,

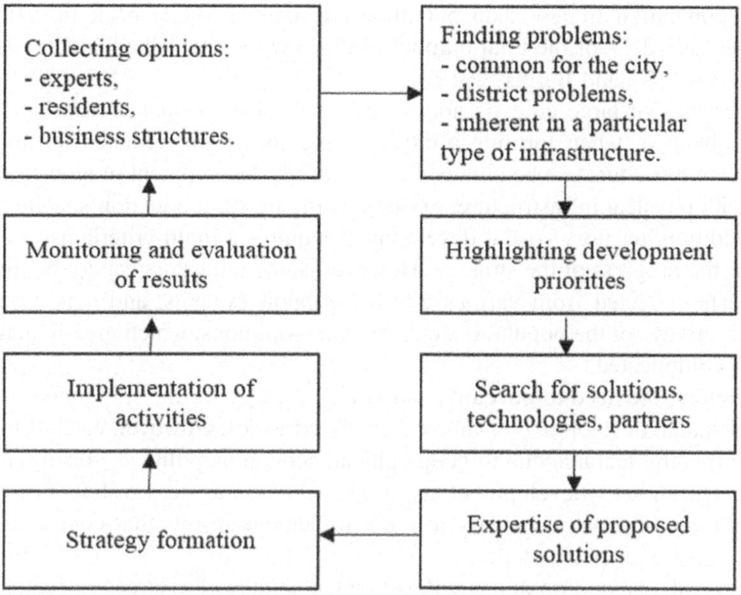

Fig. 5 Spatial development management scheme of a smart city (Source: authors' creation)

an industrial center and a city in the agricultural region should be developed using different indicators, although the main vectors of development are universal.

Implementation of projects in the sphere of a smart city is associated with a high degree of risk, since often the project result is not guaranteed due to the lack of experience in the introduction of certain new technologies on a city scale. Solution to this problem is the testing of new approaches within a small territory (for example, a district, house, transport route), but this approach extends the deadline for project implementation and requires additional costs. Consequently, cities that have not participated in digital transformation previously and have no experience in implementing modern digital systems can completely exit such projects due to the impossibility of making a high-risk decision in the context of insufficient funding for innovative development activities.

Lack of funding often leads to early completion of smart city projects (Diaconita et al., 2018; Hamalainen & Tyrvainen, 2016). This problem can be solved by a combination of different sources of funding, for example, in the framework of public-private partnerships. World experience shows that more than half (56%) of smart city projects are implemented with the attraction of both public and private investments, a third of projects (33%) are financed by the state, and only 11% are financed by private investors (Angelidou, 2015).

It is also important to distinguish large cities from small towns when elaborating a spatial development strategy. Foreign statistics have shown that strategies are initially developed for large cities, while small towns begin the process of digital transformation later. So, by 2019, 39% of smart city strategies accounted for cities with a population of less than 500 thousand people, while back in 2017, they involved only 20% of the total number of cities with a published strategy (Roland Berger, 2017; Roland Berger, 2019).

Experience of large cities is not always applicable to small territories, and the results obtained, when forming a city in a previously unpopulated territory, will differ from those that can be obtained as part of the development of already existing cities with physical infrastructure, existing traffic flows, production specifics, etc.

In addition, territory spatial development requires a multi-criteria assessment to monitor the progress of the strategy. However, some indicators cannot be measured using data collected from various city life support systems, and it is required to conduct surveys of the population, collect expert opinions, which greatly makes this process complicated.

Therefore, the need to develop a smart city strategy for the subsequent management of spatial development is inherent in all territories. However, each of them has its own specific features due to geographical, economic, political, social, and other factors. The strategy development and implementation processes should be adapted to conditions of a particular city in order to achieve results that contribute to the development of a specific territory.

In general, elaboration of a city development strategy has already become one of the traditional elements of territory management, but the assessment of its application effectiveness is often paid appropriate attention only in large cities, which is an urgent topic for further research.

5 Conclusion

Improvement of approaches to territories' spatial development is recognized as an important area of transformation of the urban environment in the context of urbanization and spread of digital technologies. Currently, a global trend in the sphere of territories spatial development is the use of the Smart City concept; strategy development is an essential element of the successful transformation of the living environment within the framework of this concept. Strategy allows to plan programs and projects necessary for a particular city, as well as monitor the degree of achievement of target indicators and adjusting implementation of measures due to the underperformance of strategic plan, changes in financing conditions, the emergence of more advanced technologies, etc.

Practice of spatial development of territories shows that the strategy elaboration process is becoming an integral stage in the implementation of the Smart City concept, since world experience shows that the presence of an officially enshrined plan for territory development leads to a more effective transformation of city infrastructures based on the rational implementation of digital technologies. The strategy implementation is influenced to a large extent by possibility of attracting public and private investments in such projects, the willingness of the authorities to stimulate innovative activity in the region, as well as by the project team's experience in introducing new technologies at the city level.

Technologies are changing extremely quickly in the course of transition to the sixth technology revolution, and it is important to always assess the existing situation on the basis of conditions of a particular city, its infrastructure, needs of the population and long-term development goals previously defined in the strategy. The authors believe that a smart city strategy should not only be formally developed but should also require implementation based on the collection of the best world practices and their adaptation to specific territories through the adoption of a set of state programs that ensure implementation of the goals specified in the strategy.

Acknowledgments the given article was developed with the financial support of the President of the Russian Federation (Grant No. MK-462.2020.6).

References

ABB & European House-Ambrosetti. (2012). *Smart cities in Italy: An opportunity in the spirit of the Renaissance for a new quality of life*. Caleidograf—Osnago (LC).

Ablyazov, T. (2020). Application of an interdisciplinary approach to the implementation of projects to create a comfortable environment for human life. *Journal of Environmental Treatment Techniques, 8*, 1136–1139.

Ablyazov, T. (2021). Application of digital platforms in the urban infrastructure development. Proceedings of the 3rd International Scientific and Practical Conference "Modern Management Trends and the Digital Economy: From Regional Development to Global Economic Growth".

Ablyazov, T. K. (2019). Digital information about the economic relations' subjects and objects collection algorithm'. Proceedings of the 33rd International Business Information Management Association.

Aguilera, U., Peña, O., Belmonte, O., & López-de-Ipiña, D. (2017). Citizen-centric data services for smarter cities. *Future Generation Computer Systems, 76*, 234–247.

Akberdina, V. V. (2019). *Ekonomika industrial'nyh regionov: strukturnaya i prostranstvennaya transformaciya*. Institut ekonomiki UrO RAN.

Alawadhi, S., Aldama-Nalda, A., Chourabi, H., Gil-Garcia, J., Leung, S., Mellouli, S., Nam, T., Pardo, T. A., Scholl, H. J., & Walker, S. (2012). *Building understanding of smart city initiatives*. Springer.

Albino, V., Berardi, U., & Dangelico, R. M. (2015). Smart cities: Definitions, dimensions, performance, and initiatives. *Journal of Urban Technology, 22*, 3–21.

Aldama-Nalda, A., Chourabi, H., Pardo, T., Gil-Garcia, J. R., Mellouli, S., Scholl, H. J., Alawadhi, S., Nam, T., & Walker, S. (2012). Smart cities and service integration initiatives in North American Cities: A status report. Proceedings of the 45th Hawaii International Conference on System Sciences.

Angelidou, M. (2015). Strategic planning for the development of smart cities (PhD thesis).

Angelidou, M. (2017). The role of smart characteristics in the plans of fifteen cities. *Journal of Urban Technology, 4*, 3–28.

Anthopoulos, L. G., & Vakali, A. (2012). Urban planning and smart cities: Interrelations and reciprocities. *Lecture Notes in Computer Science, 7281*, 178–189.

Bakici, T., Almirall, E., & Wareham, J. (2012). A smart city initiative: The case of Barcelona. *Journal of the Knowledge Economy. Special Issue: Smart Cities and the Future Internet in Europe, 4*, 135–148.

Beatley, T. (2012). *Sustainability in planning: The act and trajectory of a movement, and new directions for the twenty-first-century. Planning ideas that matter: Livability, territoriality, governance, and reflective practice*. Cambridge, MA: MIT Press.

Bélissent, J. (2010). *Getting clever about smart cities: New opportunities require new business models*. Forrester.

Bria, F. (2012). New governance models towards an open Internet ecosystem for smart connected European cities and regions. Open innovation, directorate-general for the information society and media, European Commission (pp. 62–71).

Caragliu, A., & del Bo, C. (2012). Smartness and European urban performance: Assessing the local impacts of smart urban attributes. *The European Journal of Social Science Research, 25*, 97–113.

Catapult. (2017). *Future cities Catapult Smart city strategies: A global review*. Retrieved May 10, 2021, from https://futurecities.catapult.org.uk/wp-content/uploads/2017/11/GRSCS-Final-Report.pdf

Coe, A., Paquet, G., & Roy, J. (2001). E-governance and smart communities: A social learning challenge. *Computers and Social Sciences Review, 19*, 80–93.

Cosgrave, E., Arbuthnot, K., & Tryfonas, T. (2013). Living labs, innovation districts and information marketplaces: A systems approach for smart cities. *Procedia Computer Science, 16*, 668–677.

Cosgrave, E., & Tryfonas, T. (2012). Exploring the relationship between smart city policy and implementation. Proceedings of the 1st International Conference on Smart Systems, Devices and Technologies.

de Graaf, R., & Dewulf, G. (2010). Applying the lessons of strategic urban planning learned in the developing world to the Netherlands: A case study of three industrial area development projects. *Habitat International, 34*, 471–477.

Diaconita, V., Bologa, A. R., & Bologa, R. (2018). Hadoop oriented smart cities architecture. *Sensors, 18*.

Didier, S., Morange, M., & Peyroux, E. (2012). The adaptive nature of neoliberalism at the local scale: Fifteen years of city improvement districts in Cape Town and Johannesburg. *Antipode, 45*, 121–139.

Ernst & Young. (2015). *Imagining the digital future. How digital themes are transforming companies across industries*.

EU SME Centre. (2015). *The ICT market in China*, China-Britain Business Council.

Fishman, T., & Bornstein, J. (2017). *The rise of mobility as a service: Reshaping how urbanites get around*. Deloitte.

Frank, M. (2012). *Don't Get SMACked: How social, mobile, analytics and cloud technologies are reshaping the enterprise*. Cognizant Future of Work.

Garner, C., & Dornan, A. (2011). How can knowledge cities become smart? Proceedings of the 4th Knowledge Cities World Summit.

Giffinger, R., & Gudrun, H. (2010). Smart cities ranking: An effective instrument for the positioning of cities? *ACE: Architecture City and Environment, 4*, 7–25.

Giffinger, R., Haindlmaier, G., & Kramar, H. (2010). The role of rankings in growing city competition. *Urban Research and Practice, 3*, 299–312.

Hamalainen, M., & Tyrvainen, P. (2016). A framework for IoT service experiment platforms in smart-city environments. Proceedings of the 2nd International Smart Cities Conference: Improving the Citizens Quality of Life.

Hashem, I. A. T., Chang, V., Anuar, N. B., Adewole, K., Yaqoob, I., Gani, A., Ahmed, E., & Chiroma, H. (2016). The role of big data in smart city. *International Journal of Information Management, 36*, 748–758.

Hodgkinson, S. (2011). *Is your city smart enough? Digitally enabled cities and societies will enhance economic, social, and environmental sustainability in the urban century*. OVUM.

Höjer, M., & Wangel, J. (2014). Smart sustainable cities: Definition and challenges. In *Advances in intelligent systems and computing* (Vol. 310). Springer.

ICTC. (2016). *Digital talent: road to 2020 and beyond. A national strategy to develop Canada's talent in a global digital economy*. Retrieved April 05, 2021, from https://www.ictc-ctic.ca/wp-content/uploads/2016/03/ICTC_DigitalTalent2020_ENGLISH_FINAL_March2016.pdf

Informatizaciya goroda Ekaterinburga. (2021). *Proekt 'Umnyj gorod'*. Retrieved May 14, 2021, from https://xn%2D%2D80aaucbcxhjuyt8a2j.xn%2D%2D80acgfbsl1azdqr.xn%2D%2Dp1ai/%D1%83%D0%BC%D0%BD%D1%8B%D0%B9_%D0%B3%D0%BE%D1%80%D0%BE%D0%B4

Intellias. (2020). *Digital urban planning today and tomorrow*. Retrieved May 05, 2021, from https://www.intellias.com/digital-urban-planning-today-and-tomorrow/

Komitet po ekonomicheskoj politike i strategicheskomu planirovaniyu Sankt-Peterburga. (2015). *Strategiya 2030 ekonomicheskogo i social'nogo razvitiya Sankt-Peterburga*. Retrieved May 13, 2021, from https://www.gov.spb.ru/static/writable/ckeditor/uploads/2016/02/25/Mini-RUS-05-05.pdf

Koncheva, E., & Zalesskiy, N. (2016). Spatial development of the largest Russian cities during the post-soviet period: orienting towards transit or maintaining soviet trends. Basic research program working papers, Series: Urban and Transportation Studies.

Lind, D. (2012). *Information and communications technologies creating livable, equitable, sustainable cities*. State of the world 2012: Moving toward sustainable prosperity. Island Press/Center for Resource Economics.

Mallapuram, N., Ngwum, F. Y., Lu, C., & Yu, W. (2017). Smart city: The state of the art, datasets, and evaluation platforms. Proceedings of the 16th International Conference on Computer and Information Science.

Marsal-Llacuna, M. L., Colomer-Llinàs, J., & Meléndez-Frigola, J. (2015). Lessons in urban monitoring taken from sustainable and livable cities to better address the Smart Cities initiative. *Technological Forecasting and Social Change, 90*, 611–622.

Ministry of Local Government and Hebron Governorate. (2019). *Spatial development strategic framework Hebron Governorate*. Retrieved March 09, 2021, from https://unhabitat.org/sites/default/files/2020/05/hebron_eng_1.pdf

Minstroj Rossijskoj Federacii. (2019). *Umnyj gorod: indeks IQ gorodov 2019*. Retrieved March 05, 2021, from https://minstroyrf.gov.ru/upload/iblock/ad5/Rezultat-IQ-2019-_polnaya_.pdf

Mityagin, S., Karsakov, A., Buhanovskij, A., & Vasil'ev, V. (2019). 'Umnyj Sankt-Peterburg': kompleksnyj podhod k vnedreniyu informacionnyh tekhnologij upravleniya megapolisom. *Vestnik elektroniki, 65*, 46–55.

Mortensen, J., Rohde, F. J., Kristiansen, K. R., Kanstrup-Clausen, M., & Lubanski, M. (2012). *Danish smart cities: Sustainable living in an urban world. An overview of Danish smart city competencies*. Copenhagen Capacity.

Myslyakova, Y. U. G., SHamova, E. A., & Tarasov, A. G. (2019). *Diversifikaciya eksporta kak odin iz prioritetov regional'nogo razvitiya. Strategicheskie napravleniya i prioritety regional'nogo razvitiya v usloviyah global'nyh vyzovov*. Ekaterinburg: UrO RAN.

Nam, T., & Pardo, T. (2011). Smart city as urban innovation: Focusing on management, policy, and context. Proceedings of the 5th International Conference on Theory and Practice of Electronic Governance.

Oficial'nyj sajt Mera Moskvy. (2021). *Moskva 'Umnyj gorod-2030'*. Retrived February 06, 2021, from https://2030.mos.ru/

Panuccio, P. (2019). Smart planning: From city to territorial system. *Sustainability, 11*.

Paskaleva, K. A. (2011). The smart city: A nexus for open innovation? *Intelligent Buildings International, 3*, 153–171

Paul Budde Communication Pty Ltd. (2016). *Global smart infrastructure—Smart city transformation 2016*. Retrived April 04, 2021, from https://www.budde.com.au/Research/2016-Global-Smart-Infrastructure-A-Smart-Approach-to-Smart-Cities-in-2016

Pentikousis, K., Zhu, D., & Wang, H. (2011). Network infrastructure at the crossroads: The emergence of smart cities. Proceedings of the 15th International Conference on Intelligence in Next Generation Networks.

Pivkina, N. Y. U. (2019). Umnye goroda kak novyj standart kachestva zhizni naseleniya. *Gumanitarnye nauki. Vestnik Finansovogo universiteta, 9*, 120–125.

Rajan, R., Black, P., Chinta, K., & Clarke, R. (2016). *Future cities: Time to smarten up*. IDC Analize the Future.

Rasoolimanesh, S. M., Badarulzaman, N., & Jaafar, M. (2016). 'City development strategy: Theoretical background, themes, and building blocks. *International Journal of Urban Sciences, 20*, 285–297.

Ratti, C., & Townsend, A. (2011). *'Harnessing residents' electronic devices will yield truly smart cities Scientific American*. Retrived May 19, 2021, from http://www.scientificamerican.com/article.cfm?id=the-social-nexus

Roland Berger. (2017). *Smart city, smart strategy*. Retrived April 25, 2021, from https://www.rolandberger.com/ru/Publications/The-rise-of-the-smart-city.html

Roland Berger. (2019). *The Smart City Breakaway*. Retrived April 26, 2021, from https://www.rolandberger.com/en/Publications/Smart-City-Strategy-Index-Vienna-and-London-leading-in-worldwide-ranking.html

Schaffers, H., Komninos, N., & Pallot, M. (2012). *Smart cities as innovation ecosystems, sustained by the future internet*. FIREBALL.

Schuurman, D., Baccarne, B., de Marez, L., & Mechant, P. (2012). Smart ideas for smart cities: Investigating crowdsourcing for generating and selecting ideas for ICT innovation in a city context. *Journal of Theoretical and Applied Electronic Commerce Research, 7*, 49–62.

SHakirov, I. S. (2021). *Strategiya social'no-ekonomicheskogo razvitiya g. Kazani do 2030 goda*. Retrived May 05, 2021, from http://crimea.gov.ru/content/uploads/files/OKMO_10_01/Kazan.pdf

Smirnova, O. P., & Ponomareva, A. O. (2019). Modelling interregional cooperation in the real sector of the Russian Economy. *Amazonia Investiga, 8*, 6–14.

Thales. (2020). *Singapore: The world's smartest city*. Retrived May 08, 2021, from https://www.thalesgroup.com/en/worldwide-digital-identity-and-security/iot/magazine/singapore-worlds-smartest-city

The Greater London Authority. (2021). *Smart London*. https://www.london.gov.uk/

Torgovceva, A. (2021). *Slabo umnyj: Smol'nyj "nemnozhko otoshyol" ot cifrovizacii gorodskoj sredy*. Retrived March 22, 2021, from https://www.dp.ru/a/2021/01/13/Slabo_umnij

Townsend, A., Pang, A. S.-K., & Weddle, R. (2009). *Future knowledge ecosystems: The next twenty years of technology-led economic development*. Institute for the Future.

Tranos, E., & Gertner, D. (2012). Smart networked cities? *The European Journal of Social Science Research, 25*, 175–190.

United Nations Environment Programme. (2018). *The weight of cities: Resource requirements of future urbanization*. Retrived March 05, 2021, from https://www.resourcepanel.org/reports/weight-cities

Vicini, S., Bellini, S., & Sanna, A. (2012). How to co-create internet of things-enabled services for smarter cities. Proceedings of the 1st International Conference on Smart Systems, Devices and Technologies.

Vishnivetskaya, A., & Alexandrova, E. (2019). "Smart city" concept. Implementation practice. *IOP Conference Series: Materials Science and Engineering*, vol. 497.

Vishnivetskaya, A. I., & Ablyazov, T. H. (2019). The digital transformation of subjects of investment and construction activities interaction mechanisms. *Advances in Economics, Business and Management Research, 105*, 169–173.

Walravens, N. (2011). The city as a platform. Proceedings of the 15th International Conference on intelligence in next generation networks.

Washburn, D., & Sindhu, U. (2010). *Helping CIOs understand 'Smart City' initiatives*. Forrester.

Zakon Sankt-Peterburga. (2018). *O Strategii social'no-ekonomicheskogo razvitiya Sankt-Peterburga na period do 2035 goda.* Retrived February 12, 2021, from http://docs.cntd.ru/document/551979680

Zhang, L. Y. (2013). City development strategies and the transition towards a green urban economy. *The Economy of Green Cities, 3*, 231–240.

Exo-intelligent Data-Driven Reconfigurable Computing Platform

Vladimir Zaborovskij, Alexander Antonov, and Igor Kaliaev

Abstract The key concept of the digital age is based on the Turing machine abstraction, which defines computational processes as the evolution of the states of a machine that performs a basic set of computational operations (BSCO) step by step. Based on Ludwig Boltzmann's statement that "available energy is the main object at stake in the struggle for the evolution of the world," the article discusses the possibility of creating a heterogeneous computing platform using specialized hardware to perform a basic set of operations that reduce costs energy for algorithm implementation. The platform being developed has a certain entropy potential in relation to possible options for hardware and software configurations of the computational structure and composition of the BSCO, which is formed using so-called basic computational equivalent (BCE), which can build on standard universal multicore processors (CPU), GPU accelerators or FPGA-based reconfigurable coprocessors. FPGA configuration files are organized into a specialized knowledge base that is constantly updated using machine learning techniques that are used to target computational platform reconfiguration and meet different requirements to algorithms implementation.

Keywords Computer technology · Artificial intelligence · Machine learning · Exo-intelligence · Cognitive functions

V. Zaborovskij (✉) · A. Antonov
Peter The Great St. Petersburg Polytechnic University, Saint-Petersburg, Russia

I. Kaliaev
South Federal University, Rostov-on-Don, Russia

A. Rudskoi et al. (eds.), *Digital Transformation and the World Economy*, Studies on Entrepreneurship, Structural Change and Industrial Dynamics,
https://doi.org/10.1007/978-3-030-89832-8_10

1 Introduction

For several decades, there has been a boom in the penetration of digital technologies, computer modeling and artificial intelligence in various areas of the economy, industry, natural, and social sciences.

Although the process of "digitalization" has a long history, its modern stage is associated with a relatively new problematic, which goes back to the mathematical abstraction of the so-called Turing Machines—a formal model of a finite automaton capable of reading and writing digital data into the cells of a moving tape, serving as a carrier information consisting of symbols of the final alphabet.

The number of states of such an automaton is also finite and expresses the complementarity relationship between the number of alphabet symbols using to define algorithm and the number of finite automaton states. It is shown in the theory of algorithms (Amdahl, 1967; Wigderson, 2019) that for any computable function, there is a corresponding Turing machine, but there is also a "universal" Turing machine (Amdahl, 1967; Wigderson, 2019), capable of simulating the operation of any other Turing machine designed to implement a specific algorithm.

However, modern computer systems are not created by synthesizing a finite automaton for specific algorithm, as suggested by A. Turing, but use a formally simpler method, when computational algorithms are created by a person and entered into a "universal" finite state machine in the form of some external data set. In practice, this calculation procedure is implemented using the so-called von Neumann's computer architecture, which clearly demonstrates the dual nature of the relationship "computation algorithm—hardware."

The long-term practice of using computers with such an architecture has made it possible to formulate various phenomenological rules for their use, such as Landauer's principle, Amdahl's law, Moore's law and others, which characterize both the properties of the algorithms themselves and the possibility of their use, including the ways how to accelerate of computing processes based on new electronic component base.

However, these "laws" consider a situation in which the results of a step-by-step set of basic operations are not reflected in any way on the program itself or the structure of the computer' hardware, in other words, the results of calculations are not reflected and does not affect the sequence, mechanisms, and energy costs associated with the implementation of the algorithm on a computer.

At the same time, any improvement of algorithms or optimization of operating modes of computers is possible only by attracting "external" but naturally restricted cognitive resources that is reflect person's intellect features and their clear ideas of the purpose of using specific algorithms.

As a result, Gottfried Leibniz's fundamental scientific principle of a sufficient reason or every process must have a cause, can in fact be applied to algorithms, computational structures, and the energy consumed to perform operations, but currently had no a significant impact on the evolution of modern computer technology although, according to Ludwig Boltzmann, one of the founders of thermodynamics, "available energy is the main object at stake in the struggle for the existence and evolution of the world." Recent studies show that the share of electricity generated in the world, which is spent on ensuring the operation of computer systems, is approaching 10% (Dongarra, 2019; Usman, 2018).

Therefore, the indicator of the energy-computational efficiency of computational processes, which actually determines the promising directions of the development of informatics and technologies, becomes critically important. Extreme values of this indicator can be achieved in various ways, starting from the space-time distribution of computing resources required to implement a specific algorithm, the use of specialized processors (GPU) or hardware reconfiguration of hardware components (FPGA), or using "intellectualization" of computing processes.

Obviously, that the bases of any intellectualization process are the phenomenon of understanding, in the context under consideration—understanding the relationship between the structure of the computer hardware, the features of the algorithm and the amount of energy spent on obtaining the final result with sufficient accuracy.

Considering certain limitations, the phenomenon of understanding, in principle, can be replaced by a "machine learning" procedure aimed at choosing such a structure of the computer system that, in accordance with choosing criteria provides a meaningful "computational" result. One of the natural choosing of hardware structure of computer can be based on criteria like of minimal energy consumption for some specific class of algorithms, minimum time computation or maximum speed up of algorithm.

It is also obvious that formally the processes of intellectualization are dual to the processes of algorithmicizing, and these processes themselves are very complex and have a multifaceted essence (Pais, 1991), which, within the framework of modern computer science, are usually divided into two classes—strong and weak artificial intelligence.

In the first case, they usually talk about the phenomenon of "understanding" information and endowing the obtained data with a certain intentional (aimed at a specific topic) content (Horst, 2021). In the second case, understanding as such is not required, and the solution of the problem comes down to organizing a process similar to syntactic inference, based on the rules of converting an input word into an output sequence in the form of a vector or digital code of some "entity," which with some probability is associated with input word of specific algorithm.

The such process of mapping can be called semantic "quantizing" of data flow into a set of concepts, or in other words, a homomorphic mapping of input data to a set of concepts that have a clear meaning associated with the goal-setting function that pure attribute' of natural human consciousness.

Obviously, that this task cannot be fully formalized, but to obtain a meaningful result, it is quite possible to form a set of specific exo-intellectual resources (Attig, 2011), which can be effectively used to calculate characteristic functions of some input/output data set or find statistically significant matches of data to their possible semantic content, which is determined taking into account the context of the problem being solved.

For a large number of practically interesting cases, increasing the level of intellectualization of computational processes requires a solution to the so-called inverse problems of the theory of algorithms, the regularization process of which is based on considering the context of their application. It should be noted that the organization of the feedback loop at the level of the structure of the computing system and characteristics of the external environment is currently widely used in the implementation of machine learning methods known as reinforcement learning (Antonov, Zaborovsky, & Polyanskiy, 2021). This teaching method is a special case of the "learning with a teacher" method when the teacher who has a direct impact on the neuromorphic structure is the external environment of the neural network.

Obviously, if the reaction of the environment is associated with some measurable physical indicators, for example, thermal energy released in the process of calculations, then the result of "learning" can also be a new structure of the computing platform that causes dissipation of thermal energy during implementing a certain algorithm. Such adaptation of the computing platform is an example of the implementation of the implicit learning method, the subject of which is the reconfiguration of the computational structure based on the principle of sufficient reason that caused heat dissipation when implementing a certain class of computational algorithms.

By its nature, such adaptation is not associated with the pure phenomenon of understanding the causes of the observed physical phenomenon, namely, the release of heat in the process of calculations, but thanks to the target orientation of the learning system, it makes possible to achieve an effect observed in so-called intelligent data processing systems based on the type of required solution (AIS—Analysis Information Systems) (Antonov et al., 2020a, 2020b).

In view of the above, it is quite appropriate to link the concept of "required solution," which is achieved through the use of computing resources of the data processing system, with the concept of "external" intellectual resources or computable exo-intellectual functions that can effectively complement natural human cognitive resources in the case that they have a pronounced operational character and are implemented within the framework of the context of specific functions of goal setting.

In the context of the problematic considered in the article, the introduction of the concept of "exo-intelligence" (Attig, 2011) allows to shift the emphasis from the ambiguously from the point of view of computer technologies concept of "artificial intelligence" to solutions related to the use of computing platforms endowed with the specific function of reflection, i.e., able to adapt their structure based on data obtained during operation.

This effect is achieved by "replenishing" the set of hardware-implemented BSCOs with new functionalities, but not only through the use of a more advanced electronic component base but also through the use of machine learning technologies. Ultimately, training heterogeneous computing platforms, similar to setting up artificial neural networks, allows you to reconfigure computational structures in the process of implementing a computational algorithm based on various performance or speed up criteria.

As a result, a new "space of opportunities" opens up for the developers of computer technologies to improve the developed computing systems by organizing a purposeful evolutionary process of their modernization both on-line and of-line regimes, combining the methods of the theory of algorithms, machine learning, mathematical modeling, nature-like processes within the proposed interdisciplinary approach (Attig, 2011), including evolution complex systems, which is an urgent scientific and technical problem.

2 The Problem of "Reverse" Translation of Algorithms

Consideration of computational processes from the point of view of the interaction of two fundamental entities—information and energy, or rather the interaction of the Turing machine and the Boltzmann thermodynamic machine, opens up new opportunities for increasing real productivity and specific energy-computational efficiency of both universal computer platforms and specialized computing systems. As noted above, when creating the concept of a universal Turing machine, the factors of the physical realizability of computational operations, as well as the fundamental provisions of mathematical theories associated with the axiom of choice and the existence of immeasurable sets, were not analyzed but were considered from the standpoint of the implementation of the theory of algorithms, including the problems of computability of functions, enumerability, and solvability of sets (Michael, 2008).

Given the fundamental nature of the "energy-time" relationship formalized by the Heisenberg inequality in Eq. (1):

$$\Delta E \times \Delta t \geq \hbar \quad (1)$$

Where $\hbar$ is Planck's constant, ΔE is the change in energy, Δt is the observation interval, and it is obvious that the acceleration of any, including the computational process, inevitably means an increase in the energy expended on this process.

The essence of the standard problem of the theory of algorithms, which originates in the works of Turing, consists in the construction of a finite state automaton, with the help of which, in principle, it is possible to implement a given algorithm or to solve the problem of computability specific function using a given algorithm. The inverse problem is to choose a hardware computer structure that not only effectively implements those parts of the algorithm that can be parallelized (below denoted as F), but can implemented speed up process with minimal power consumption.

A quantitative estimate of the possibility of accelerating computations when using multicore (N is the number of cores) microprocessor architectures were obtained in (Mark, 2008). Denoting (1-F) the fraction of the execution time of the algorithm that cannot be accelerated due to parallelization, therefore, is executed using only one core, the formula for accelerating computations due to the use of multicore processors can be written as (Mark, 2008):

$$S = 1/((1 - F)/1 + F/N) \tag{2}$$

As $N \to \infty$, the value of S tends to the value 1/(1-F). Thus, with a fixed structure of processor' cores, the possibility of accelerating an algorithm is determined only by its properties. This thesis is confirmed by the analysis of the degradation of the performance of the first ten supercomputers from the TOP500 list when the method for evaluating performance is changed from Linpack HPL to Linpack HPCG. According to J. Dongarra (2020), the performance measured on the basis of Linpack HPCG is a few percent of the performance measured on LinpackHPL2.0, a specific test that focused on existing universal multiprocessor computational structures with SIMD accelerators.

Therefore, an urgent task is to find ways to speed up the execution time of algorithms that are not associated with an increase in the number of parallel processor cores, but are based on the reconfiguration and machine learning capabilities in relation to:

- Computer architecture
- Memory organization systems
- Environment for switching processes

Taking into account modern achievements in the field of microelectronics production using technological processes of 7, 5, or even 3 nm (Intel FPGA, 2021; Xilinx FPGA, 2021), the engineering problem of creating computing systems with several millions of cores (TOP500 List, 2021) has been practically solved, but this does not remove the limitations of Eq. (2), but on the contrary, stimulates the search for innovative approaches to solving the problem of accelerating the implementation of algorithms while reducing energy consumption for computational processes.

Taking into account the so-called Pollack rule (Shekhar, 2011), according to which the performance of modern microprocessors increases with a change in their architecture in proportion to the square root of the increase in its complexity and the consumed electrical power increases in proportion to the complexity, we can conclude that the solution to this problem has a fundamental impact on the development of future computer technology.

In discussed this context, the complexity of a calculator is measured by the number of logic gates or the area of the silicon crystal used to manufacture microprocessor. In (Mark, 2008; Michael, 2008), a model was proposed for increasing the complexity of calculators by introducing a new abstraction—Base Core Equivalent (BCE), which is considered as a normalized unit of the computational performance of a multicore processor. So, if a microprocessor contains R parts of BCE, then its performance is estimated as some function denoted as Perf. As a result, the tasks of choosing the architecture of the computer, it does not have an unambiguous solution, but in any case, it comes down to ensuring the condition under which Perf> R.

For example (Mark, 2008; Michael, 2008), if the structure of a multicore microprocessor contains N elements BCE (see Fig. 1), and each core consists of R parts BCE, then the number of cores in the microprocessor is equal to N / R =

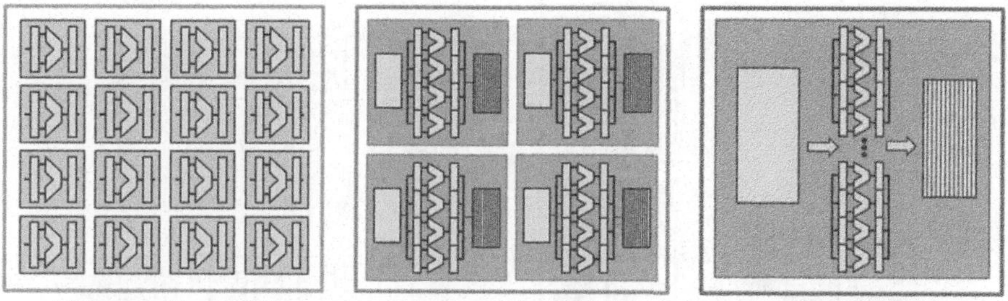

Fig. 1 Possible versions of the computer platform architectures. Source: Mark (2008) and Michael (2008)

M. Moreover, if the requirement of symmetry (homogeneity) of cores is preserved, then it is possible to form different versions of the computer platform architectures, in which the cores have n * BCE, where $n = 1, 2, 4$, and so on.

For $n > 2$, complex microprocessor cores can accelerate both the serial (1-F) and parallel (F) parts of the algorithm in accordance with the equations (Mark, 2008; Michael, 2008):

- Acceleration of the sequential segment of the algorithm—in Eq. (3)
- Acceleration of the parallel section of the algorithm—in Eq. (4)
- Acceleration of the algorithm as a whole—in Eq. (5)

$$S = (1 - F)/Perf(R) \tag{3}$$

$$S = F/(Perf(R) \times N/R) \tag{4}$$

$$S = 1/((1 - F)/Perf(R) + F/(Perf(R) \times N/R) \tag{5}$$

Where N / R = M is the number of cores in the microprocessor. Such architecture is ideal for computational algorithms with symmetric structures in which the proportion is F = 0.5 and R = sqrt (N). When F tends to 1, the performance of the microprocessor is maximum if R = 1. In other words, the analysis shows that if the algorithm allows full parallelization ($F \geq 1$), then the simpler cores can improve both speed up and performance of the computer platform. However, this reasoning does not consider the fact that parallelized operations may "poorly" correspond to the existing set of parallel operating kernels with a given set of arithmetic-logical operations (Antonov, Zaborovskij, & Kiselev, 2018).

Note that when modeling different class real objects, for example, biological systems, the factor of non-simplified complexity is of great importance; therefore it is impossible to construct algorithms with F close to 1 (Antonov, Kiselev, & Filippov, 2018).

As a result, the level of complexity of microprocessors C, which determines the real performance of the calculator, becomes a function of both software and hardware C = C (HW, SW). In other words, along with an increase in the number and

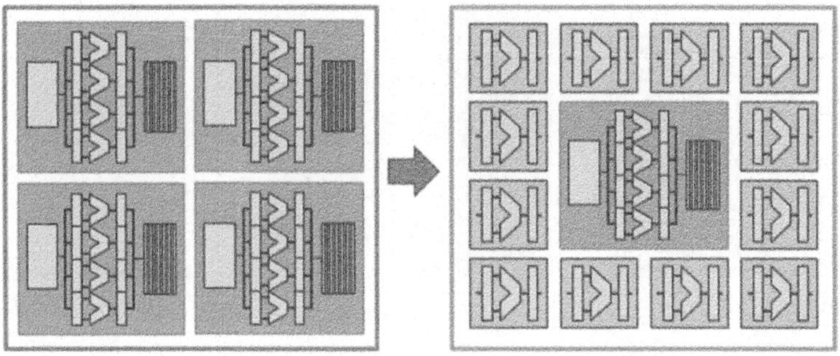

Fig. 2 Transition from a symmetric multicore computer to a heterogeneous multicore one while maintaining the number of used BCE. Source: Mark (2008) and Michael (2008)

heterogeneity of the architecture of cores, which is still the main direction of the development of modern computing technologies, hardware reconfiguration of the computer components that use BCE is required. Therefore, the development of technologies towards the formation of a reconfigurable asymmetric or inhomogeneous computational field becomes a priority, since it expands the space of possibilities increasing the real performance of hardware platforms for wide spectrum of application tasks.

In practice, with the traditional approach to design hardware components, the computing system includes MPP and SIMD microprocessors with different numbers of BCEs. In this case, if, for example, one core contains several BCE, and the other cores contain one BCE, then the equations will have the form of Eqs. (3), (4), and (5).

Thus, if computer with different classes of BCE is "correctly" balanced, then for a certain type of algorithms, it is possibly getting a great performance gain. Such a traditional approach provides higher performance due to the improved variability of the space of computing capabilities, but it complicates the process of dispatching, translating programs, control processes at the level of code execution and the operation of the operating system, giving rise to the so-called "races" and barrier restrictions (Antonov, Zaborovskij, & Kiselev, 2018).

Therefore, the logical development of the idea of heterogeneity of the computing platform is the transition to multicore structures, in which the combination of processors with different numbers of ALL processors in a computing structure occurs dynamically in accordance with a specific application (see Fig. 2) (Mark, 2008; Michael, 2008).

By changing the structure of the processor cores in accordance with the characteristics of the "external environment," i.e., According to the properties of the implemented algorithm, we act in the same way as the structure of mechanical links changes in the automatic transmission of a modern car. Considering the requirement to minimize power consumption limits the BCE amount used and increases the area of "dark silicon" in the microprocessor chip.

As a result (Mark, 2008; Michael, 2008), the acceleration of the algorithm execution can be expressed by Eq. (6).

$$S = 1/((1 - F)/Perf(R) + F/N) \tag{6}$$

Obviously, in practice, each parts of algorithm related to either the F or 1-F fractions of the execution time of the algorithm, which has specific structural features, namely, the serial part is not pure serial, and the parallel part is not completely parallel.

The problem of effective or pure scaling of performance requires building an accurate model that considers factors such as overloads, imbalances, etc., which is practically impossible without the use of ideas of additivity and adequate machine learning methods, in which the choice of parameters N, R and the estimate of F will be based on objective statistical data or digital data precisely glorified by statistics.

The above reasoning and estimates based on BCE components do not consider the fact that parallelized operations can "badly" fit on the existing cores architectures. For a specific algorithm (Antonov et al., 2020a, 2020b) of the problem being solved, the set of primitive operations used may be different: for example, for one problem, additions operation and nothing else are mainly used, and for the other, a lot of comparisons and multiplexing. Reducing such operations to elementary arithmetic-logical procedures implemented on a unified processor core is not effective for all classes of algorithms.

Therefore, in a computing system, it is necessary to have computing resources (cores) with reconfigurable hardware that consider peculiarities of the algorithm of the problem being solved and reconfigurable at the top level of the core internal structure. At this level, to increase the speed and performance of computing systems designed to solve computationally complex problems of different classes, it is relevant, in addition to the "classical" MPP decisions (architectures with a large number of complex BCE) and SIMD (architectures with a huge number of simple BCE) creating cores that are optimized for hardware to implement a specific algorithm (Mniszewski, 2021).

The basic possibilities of building distributed heterogeneous hardware reconfigurable computing platforms are based on the fact that entire classes of applied algorithms, characterized by a certain level of computational complexity, can be effectively implemented as a process of transforming the specific "input word" that define the algorithmic structure of executing programs into a hardware structure consisting of a finite number of heterogeneous BCE (HBCE). To do this, all application algorithms go through a preliminary classification stage based on machine learning methods, which allows, with a certain degree of probability, to determine for them "optimal" a computational structure that corresponds to selected criteria. (analog of the Turing machine), and then, based on the selected structure, make the appropriate reconfiguration of the computer platform that is used and make the necessary calculations (Dongarra, 2018).

Finding the best computational structure in accordance with the selected criteria, based on the analysis of previous computations using a finite set of HBCE components for one of the classes of computational algorithms, will immediately lead to an increase in computational efficiency for all other algorithms form this specific class. At the same time, it is obvious that the classical concepts of NP-completeness, computability of functions, enumerability, and decidability of sets turn out to be closely related to the problem of choosing a way to represent computational algorithms in terms of a finite set of operations implemented using HBCE (Blum, 1975).

Thus, to increase the speed and performance of computing systems used to solve various classes of computationally complex problems, it is necessary to develop a technology for adapting the computing platform to the peculiarities of the implemented algorithms, which can formally be considered as a solution to basic problems from theory of algorithms, that is similar to choosing the appropriate structure for the classical Turing machine.

3 Reconfigurable Heterogeneous Platform

As we have discussed, modern computer technologies are based on three fundamental principles of the theory of algorithms: computability of functions, enumerability, and decidability of sets (see Fig. 3).

The idea to archives the "computational superiority" of programmable finite automata is close related to the requirement of high energy-computational efficiency of operations without a decrease in the intensity of computations.

A similar principle of the implementation of the processes of functioning and self-reproduction is characteristic of cold-blooded living systems, which can be considered as distributed programmable controlled biological structures that calculate themselves (the phenomenon of computational self-similarity or fractality) based on genetic programs, the extensional carrier of which is DNA molecules containing finite sets of codes for the synthesis of protein structures. From the point of view of thermodynamics, in such living systems, the energy released in the process of bio "computing" is not only dissipated into the environment but is also used to reconfigure the functioning mechanisms used and change the microstates of the

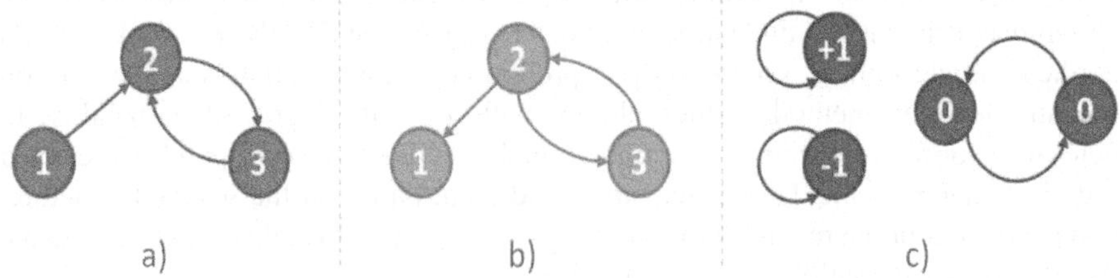

Fig. 3 Three type of physical system: (a) irreversible, (b) indeterminate, (c) discrete. (Source: authors' creation)

bio-computer itself. To objectify genetic information, such a bio-computer uses a gene expression mechanism that is structurally similar to a standard computational pipeline or systolic network-centric structure, which converts input data (endogenous or exogenous) into output protein structures that de facto implement computation. Protein molecules using genetic programs. Such a pipeline of operations, which sequentially performs the stages of "input-transformation-output" of data, is functionally similar to the processor architecture, which goes back to the Turing machine, but at the same time has a fundamentally higher energy efficiency calculations, since it not only dissipates the energy of the calculations themselves but also uses it to synthesize a new biomaterial that serves as the memory of a bio-computer.

The overwhelming complexity of the phenomenon of reality, which is not expressed in a finite number of concepts, has played a key role in the evolution of the theory of digital computing (ToDC). Today, ToDC occupies one of the key places in the structure of scientific knowledge, along with physics, biology, mathematics and economics, and also plays a central role in the technological revolution based on digital data processing under the control of a program that generates various classes of computational processes. For the development of the theory, it is important to be able to give an accurate answer to the questions: are there any fundamental flaws in the modern version of ToDC and what are their essence?

The real problems of both theoretical and applied plans are well known. Using the ideas of reductionism, modern ToDC cannot solve the fundamental problem, which is formulated as the problem of coincidence of complexity classes of algorithms, namely $P = NP$, in addition, the theory cannot explain the nature of algorithmically non-computable numbers, cognitive functions and undecidable sets and, of course, cannot gives a clear interpretation of the processes associated with intelligence and the phenomenon of reason.

From this point of view, the architecture of biological computers, which are in asymptotic thermal equilibrium with the environment, is a constructive analogy of the "oblique sail"—an innovative solution that changed the global logistics of the Ancient World, and made it possible to implement "information reversible routes of movement" due to the possibility of the zigzag ship sailing upwind.

Obviously, in this case, it was not possible to achieve complete physical reversibility of motion, but thanks to the equipping of ships with sails with fundamentally different physical characteristics and design, they became a clear example of the implementation of one of the fundamental laws of nature—the law of conservation of information, in the case under consideration, the preservation of information about a given direction of motion when changing the trajectory of movement. It is obvious that by endowing modern computers, which are functionally similar to the Turing machine, with new capabilities not only for transformation but also for storing information, which is just characteristic of evolutionary processes in a biological environment, we can count on a conceptual revolution in computer science and technology.

The essence of such a revolution will be, firstly, to reduce the level of non-constructive energy dissipation due to interaction with the environment and, secondly, to make the computational process partially reversible due to the

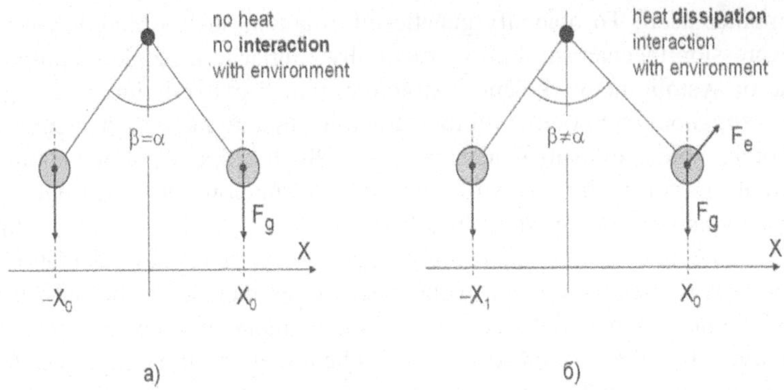

Fig. 4 Heat dissipation as results of interaction with environment. (Source: authors' creation)

accumulation of information that can be used to increase the efficiency of the computations themselves (see Fig. 4).

Further, it will be shown that the last property is achieved by imparting high adaptive functionality to computing structures, reflecting the consistency of processes at the software and hardware levels.

There is no doubt that in any process of technology innovation, the essence of which is to complement human capabilities, we need to understand the fundamental reason giving rise to all the problems listed above and must try to formulate accurately the essence of the exo-intellectual' paradigm of science.

In this context, the question of whether computer science belongs to the natural or mathematical sciences is currently not only of theoretical but also practical significance. In Avi Wigderson's book (Wigderson, 2019) we can read that "big bang" of pure Turing's approach nowadays has lost its constructive power because very basic tasks turn incomputable in the sense of this formal theoretical model.

4 Thermodynamics of Turing's Incompatibility

The basic conceptual question "Who is to blame, and what to do" with the problem of incompatibility—must be approached from the standpoint of searching for analogies in natural phenomena, and considering the principle of complementarity, first formulated by Niels Bohr.

Many natural processes can (and should) be understood both as physical and informational processes, including demands of similar computational representation (see Fig. 5).

Such factors that are asymptotically unstable can easily be significantly influenced by various factors and development scenarios, which lead to the formation of strange asymptotically evolutionary attractors (Amdahl, 1967; Wigderson, 2019).

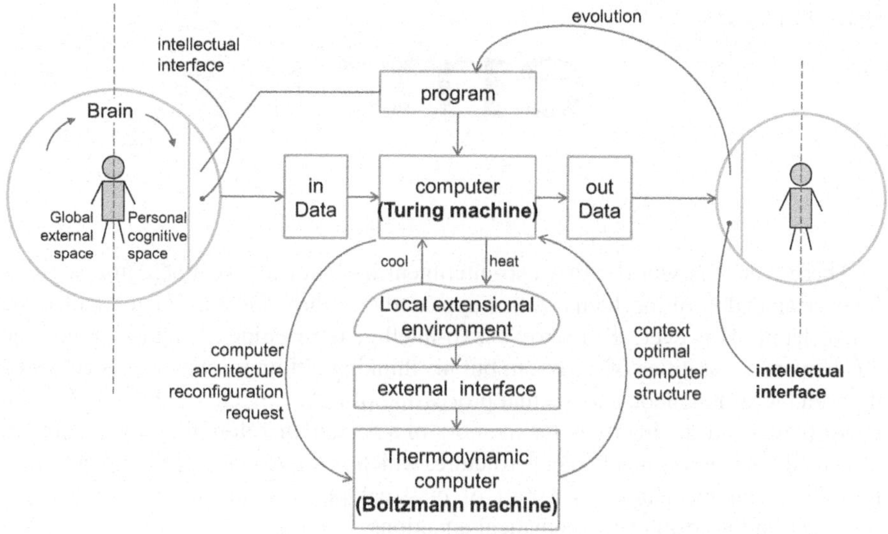

Fig. 5 Conceptual structure of proposal computer platform. (Source: authors' creation)

The key vector of the evolution of computing systems can be determined using the concept of the computational theory of mind (Le Fèvre, 2019), which is considered as a synthesis using the machine learning method of algorithms for choosing solutions from a set of possible solutions stored in the computer's memory.

Perhaps the problem lies in the very essence of the question posed, namely: in finding a solution in the form of a computational algorithm implemented with the help of a "machine," or is it all about the mechanical and deterministic nature of the "machine" itself?

First of all, we note that the understanding of "calculation" and the possibilities of its emulation using various machines has changed significantly (Amdahl, 1967; Wigderson, 2019). So almost until the middle of the nineteenth century, simple counting tasks were considered quite intellectual. Moreover, if a person was able to quickly and error-free calculate using well-known mathematical formulae, and, on this basis, manage, for example, some commercial activities, then his intellectual abilities were rated very highly.

However, thanks to the formalization of calculation algorithms, mathematical calculation problems were one of the first to be automated. In 1822 in England, C. Babbage created so-called difference machine, which allows automating the calculation process by approximating various mathematical functions by polynomials using a strictly ordered sequence of operations.

In 1832 in Russia N. S. Korsakov published a brochure "Outlining a New Method of Research Using Machines Comparing Ideas." In this brochure, many mechanical devices have been designed based on perforated tables to search for information and classify various information records (ideas) by a set of numerous features (details).

Fig. 6 Entropy as an intentional concept. Source: Xilinx FPGA (2021)

These were the world's first exo-intelligent mechanical machines, in a sense, a functional analog of mechanisms that appeared a century and a half later, called the exoskeleton. However, Korsakov's exo-intelligent machines "enhanced not the mechanical capabilities of a person, but his thinking abilities," which was achieved through the simultaneous contextual processing of large amounts of knowledge that are difficult to store directly in the memory of a person, therefore they were stored in a specially organized mechanical structure, which is the essence of the invention. It is known that mechanics is a part of classical physics, the laws of which are presented in the form of mathematical equations.

However, not all mathematical equations can reflect physical laws. For this, the equations must be not only deterministic but also reversible. This means, and this is principally important, that the laws of physics must be deterministic and reversible both in the past or in the future, both in one or other point of Earth.

Reversibility of physical laws essentially expresses the basic fundamental law mentioned above as the law of conservation of information. The concept of information is not directly applied to physics but often comes into play when describing the phenomenological laws, and intentional antonym of information (the entropy) is widely used.

Entropy or "transformation" (see Fig. 6) is considered as a function of the state space of a thermodynamic system, which characterizes the measure of irreversible loss of inhomogeneity or information about the states of the system. Entropy is qualitatively different from other thermodynamic quantities: such as pressure, volume, or internal energy because it is not an objective property of the system but a characteristic of what part of information about the system is available to its external observer.

Entropy is a characteristic of how much information the observer does not know about the system. The quantitative measure of entropy S is the number of symbols required to record the number of microstates of the considered physical system distinguished by the observer. Mathematically, this number is defined as the logarithm of the number of possible microstates Ω of the system (7).

$$S = \log \Omega \tag{7}$$

Therefore, the system has definite internal energy, impulse, charge, but it does not have a definite entropy: for example, the entropy of ten dice depends on whether you know only their total sum, or also the partial sums of the five dice.

Therefore, entropy in physics is, in fact, an analog of a program that calculates the state of a system in computer science. The informational essence of entropy has intentional nature that fundamentally distinguishes it from other characteristics, with which it is customary to deal in physics. The reason for this is that the logic and arithmetic underlying the theory of Turing' computation inevitably leads to the fact that the fundamental conclusions of first and second Gödel's theorem are fully relevant to the current version of computer science, clearly showing various aspects of the problems un-computability in formal terms of incompleteness and inconsistency that in practice mean the absence of a reversible equation of state, which is used to describe the relationship between all individual states of the studied physical object.

In fact, this is the crux of why the laws of physics are a formal record of the effect of so-called "glorified statistics." In other words, the more microstates correspond to a given macro-state, that is, the more particles are included in the system under study, the more accurately the system state equation describes this macro system. For gas, the characteristic values of the number of particles are equal to the Avogadro number, that is, of the order of 10^{23}. To find out all microstates of a system, we need to have a lot of "personal" information—to know the position and velocity of each particle. The amount of this information is, in fact, entropy.

But if the state space of a physical system can be divided into cycles, then the system acquires principal new properties. Such a system becomes the carrier of the new function—informational memory, i.e., the function of storing information about the state of the system, from which the dynamic process began.

In such a system, there is "something" that remains unchanged in an extensional sense, that is, unchanged in time and space. As a result, each cycle can be associated with a numerical value expressed in the format of an integer, and if this number is stored during the "movement" of a physical system, then such a system is not only discrete but also deterministic, that is, algorithmically predictable.

5 Discreteness of Cognitive Perception

The discreteness of the cognitive perception of reality, as well as entropy, is not the internal properties of the perceived objects themselves but is associated with the act of perceiving objects by an external "intellectual" observer, who uses the final concept thesaurus to describe reality

The non-isomorphism of discrete or digital descriptions is directly related to the fundamental problems of modern informatics, which are clearly manifested in the well-known Skolem's paradox, which declares "the admissibility of describing meaningful representations of continuous sets using the means of a formal language, which obviously contains a countable set of true expressions."

At the same time, the expressive means of modern programming languages are determined by a finite set of syntactically and semantically correct expressions, the power of which does not exceed the power of the class of predicate calculus formulas. It is obvious that the relativism of the meaningful description of objects and phenomena of physical reality is associated precisely with the homomorphic nature of the possible forms of its intellectual perception.

Consequently, the human mind, if modeled as a kind of "cognitive machine," has a potentially countable set of states. The ultimate accuracy of the brain's resolving power is determined by the homomorphic nature of the process of mapping "being into thinking," which is realized in acts of cognition. The nature of mind violates the presumption of the continuity of physical reality, and in connection with this, phenomena of quantum mechanics can be regarded as a special case associated with the scale of processes not directly perceived by the senses.

Obviously, the discreteness structure of the cognitive perception of reality makes it possible to increase the "accuracy" of the description of the results of observation of objects and processes, and to use for this not only rational or natural numbers, but also to name the perceived facts and phenomena using the "epsilon-network" of concepts and ontology relationships. One of the broadest ways to informally define computation is the famous Church-Turing thesis: Computing is the process of evolution of an environment through a series of "simple, localized" steps.

This definition seems to cover almost any natural process that we know, so it sounds strange, especially since in the physical world, we do not see the "authors" of the Turing machine tape! The most basic idea (from which the word "computation" originally originated) is the idea of evolution as a process of changing the sequence of physical states of some machines (adding machine, calculator, processors, or even human brain) under the control of a pre-formed local program or directly via the specific goals of a person.

Formally, the representation of computations as a sequence of operations performed under the control of a program written by a person now is being extended to many other areas where the effects associated with the phenomenon of intelligence are manifested.

The environment referred to in the formal definition of computation can be associated with various physical objects and associated information transformation processes, including bits in the computer, atoms in matter, neurons of the brain, proteins in the cell, etc.

6 Algorithmic Efficiency

Algorithmic efficiency (Haidar, 2018) has many contexts, including accuracy and the presence of errors, speed of calculation, required resources, and the trade-off between performance and power consumption.

A separate aspect requiring in-depth study is the efficiency of algorithms obtained as a result of machine learning of various types of artificial neural networks. Experience shows that the search for the most accurate implementations for such algorithms under the same conditions and for some training datasets may require total retraining.

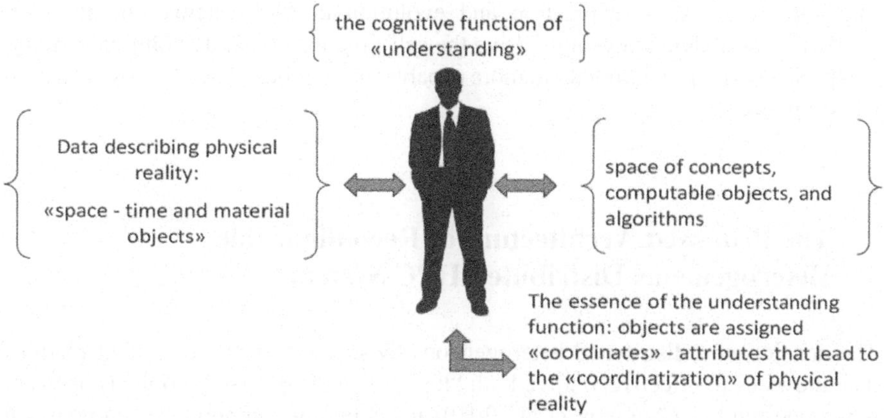

Fig. 7 Cognitive space with law of "craving for knowledge". (Source: authors' creation)

History of science shows that some of the greatest innovations have arisen from ignoring realistic constraints and intuitive biases about what is possible in principle. Examples of the success of such approach are non-deterministic machines, random evidence, counting without the algorithm, persuasion without knowledge, anonymous ownership, proof of the existence of justice, etc. In the space of human cognitive functions, special "laws of attraction" operate.

An attempt to make various model assumptions and then, with their help, calculate not yet realized, but potentially possible states—this is the essence of the law of "craving for knowledge," which by its nature, of course, differs from I. Newton's law of universal gravitation and other laws of physics. Based on the principle of causality, but, like the latter, it manifests itself objectively; therefore its influence on the surrounding reality cannot be ignored (see Fig. 7).

Currently, the greatest practical successes in solving intellectual problems have been achieved using methods that, in principle, are not inherent in humans but are based on "brute computing power" or, in other words, on the ability to quickly sort possible solutions, for example, as required for a successful gameplay chess.

Concretize the task of building exo-intelligent platforms—systems of "weak intelligence" that do not perform any goal-setting function (Amdahl, 1967; Wigderson, 2019), we will rely on data aggregation and classification methods based on similarity criteria for objects or processes based on functional or structural associations, using the search for solutions based on heterogeneous symbiosis of biological and artificial intelligence resources.

The concept of thermodynamic processes that transform information is fundamental, and the scope of this concept goes far beyond the scope of modern digital computer technology.

To make computers function more efficiently (Harris, 2021) we should care not only about software but also about energy source and its ability to efficiently and with high speed change the processor states—i.e., should care about thermodynamic aspects of calculation. It is clear that in nature, thermodynamics plays fundamental role—drives the self-organization and evolution of bio systems, so, no doubt similarly thermodynamics might drive the self-organization and evolution of future computing systems, making them more capable, more robust, and less costly to build and program.

7 The Proposed Architecture of Reconfigurable Heterogeneous Distributed HPC System

The creation of a distributed heterogeneous hyper-convergent computing platform that allows us to effectively solve both "forward" and "reverse" problems opens up new opportunities (Antonov et al., 2019) for applying computing technologies in various fields of science and technology (see Fig. 8) (Antonov et al., 2016).

The infrastructure of the investigated hyper-convergent platform consists of three levels:

- Predictive analytics and "explanation" of the resulting solutions, the energy-computational efficiency of the level corresponds to 2–4 GFlops/W.
- Data aggregation of modeling results and creating datasets for machine learning systems, energy-computational efficiency 5–10 GFlops/W.
- Reconfigurable accelerators of algorithms and computational pipe between heterogeneous processors and data arrays of application tasks, energy-computational efficiency 10–20 GFlops/W.

Proposed organization of the hyper-convergent platform allows to maintain different software computing models such as procedure «call-on mention /pass-by-reference» and the procedure « call by value/transfer by data context» when the arguments of a procedure are evaluated before they are passed to the procedure. The such functional and algorithmic flexibility, which is also complemented by the capabilities of the hardware reconfiguration of edge node (see Fig. 9) (Antonov et al., 2019), allows to apply this hyper-convergent platform to solves all listed above "direct" and "inverse" tasks.

Modern DRH HPC consists of multiprocessor units (MPUs) (Antonov et al., 2019), Single Instruction Multiple Data (SIMD) accelerators, commonly known as General Purpose Graphics Processing Units (GPGPU), and Reconfigurable Accelerators (RA), based on Field Programmable Gate Arrays (FPGAs) (Intel FPGA, 2021; Xilinx FPGA, 2021). FPGA (Intel FPGA, 2021; Xilinx FPGA, 2021) is an Integrated Circuit (IC) that can change its internal structure in accordance with the particular task. A modern FPGA consists of programmable logic cells (LCELL), which can perform any functions of logic or memory, and a hierarchy of programmable matrices, which can connect nearly all LCELL in FPGA together to implement complex logic and memory functions. The modern FPGAs contain not only LCELL and the programmable matrices but also digital signal processing units (DSP), integrated memory units (BRAM), high-throughput memory units (HBM),

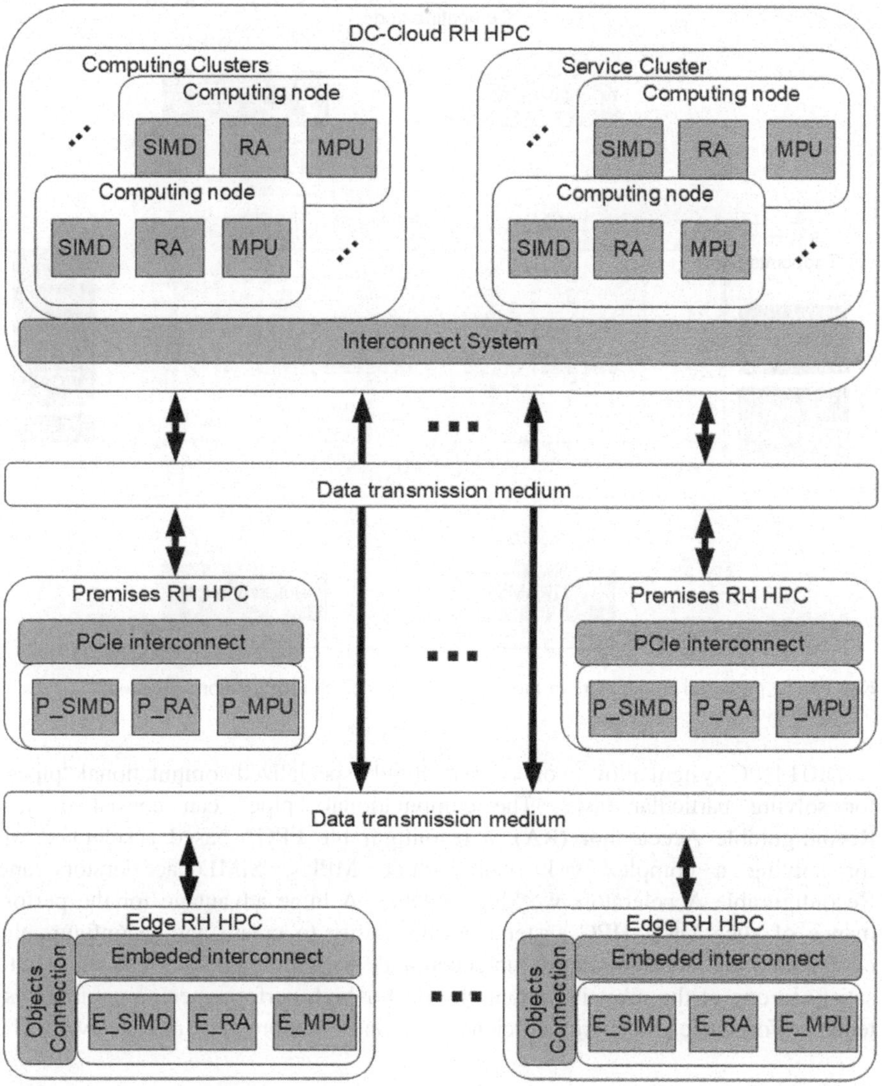

Fig. 8 The proposed architecture of reconfigurable heterogeneous distributed HPC system. (Source: authors' creation)

hardware-implemented controllers for external DDR4 memory and multigigabits transceivers for external PCIe interfaces and 10–100G Ethernet ports. State-of-art FPGAs can be configured "on the fly;" it means that ones can be configured during the normal operation of the device. Some modern FPGAs support partial configuration and reconfiguration via PCIe and Ethernet. Partial reconfiguration of the FPGA means that a part of the FPGA can be reconfigured while the rest of the FPGA continues to solve the current task (Antonov et al., 2020a, 2020b).

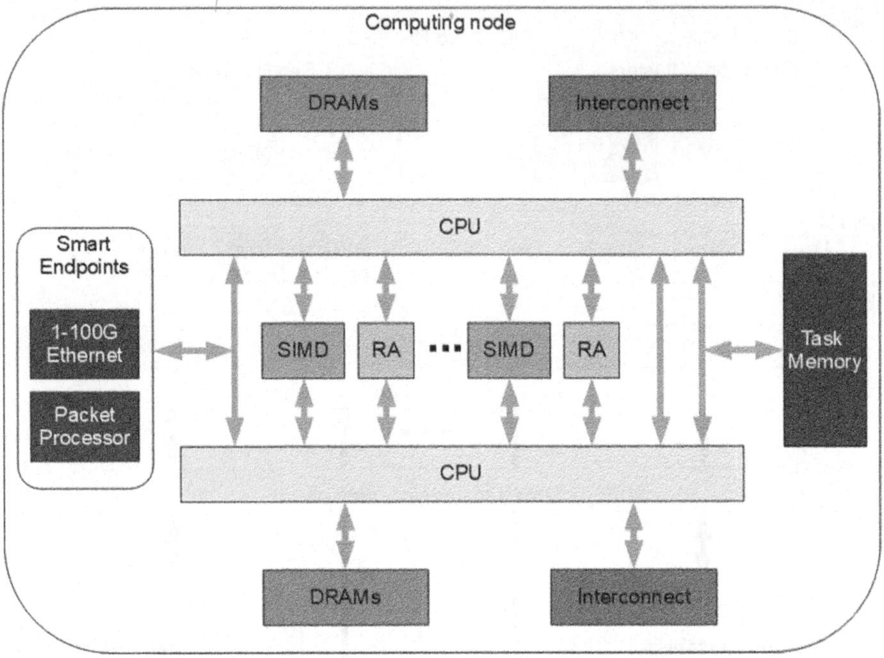

Fig. 9 The proposed architecture of the Computing Node. (Source: authors' creation)

DRH HPC system allows you to create highly specialized computational "pipes" for solving particular tasks. The computational "pipe" can consist of just Reconfigurable Accelerator (RA), a reconfigurable FPGA-based accelerator, or, for solving a complex task, can include MPUs, SIMD accelerators and Reconfigurable Accelerators working together. A huge advantage for the performance of such DRH HPC systems is the ability to create and reconfigure the computational "pipes" on the fly, in accordance with the particular task, and so, to satisfy to one of the most important criteria for high-performance computing systems: performance and energy efficiency (Antonov, Zaborovsky, & Kiselev, 2021).

8 Discussion

Currently, living systems rely on energy-efficient, universal, self-healing, and complex computational capabilities that dramatically transcend current industrial technologies. Spontaneously finding energy-efficient configurations enables biosystem to thrive in complex, resource-constrained environments.

As we well know, in nature, all matter evolves toward low energy configurations in accord with the laws of thermodynamics. For near equilibrium systems, these ideas are well-known and have been used extensively in the theory of computational efficiency and in machine learning techniques.

Now we need to apply thermodynamic approach to create complex, non-equilibrium, but reconfigurable and self-organizing computing systems that will use both artificial and nature's based source of power.

Therefore, the discussed solution can achieve high levels of efficacy by use of "machine learning" like methods to find the optimal configuration of the computer hardware running the software, that can decrease energy consumption and corresponding energy dissipation.

9 Conclusions

To overcome the shortcomings of the Turing machine, it will probably be necessary to provide an order of magnitude greater energy-computational efficiency and developed self-organization capabilities of the internal structure of a computer through its purposeful reconfiguration, taking into account the features of the computational algorithms being implemented.

For this, various neuromorphic structures capable of learning from representative datasets can be used, as well as computational tools for predictive modeling of high performance. For the effective use of such an approach, deep interdisciplinary research is needed that covers both fundamental and applied aspects of computer sciences, physics, direct digital modeling, big data mathematics, artificial intelligence and machine learning.

Acknowledgments The research was funded as a part of the state assignment for basic research (code of the research is 0784-2020-0026).

References

Amdahl, G. (1967). Validity of the single processor approach to achieving large scale computing capabilities. *AFIPS Press, Reston, 30*, 483–485.

Antonov, A., Besedin, D., & Filippov, A. (2020a) Research of the efficiency of high-level synthesis tool for FPGA based hardware implementation of some basic algorithms for the Big Data Analysis and management tasks. In: Conference of Open Innovation Association, FRUCT, *26*, 23–29. https://doi.org/10.23919/FRUCT48808.2020.9087355

Antonov, A., Besedin, D., & Filippov, A. (2020b). Research of hardware implementations efficiency of sorting algorithms created by using Xilinx's High-Level Synthesis Tool. In *Communications in computer and information science* (Vol. 1331, pp. 449–460). Springer. https://doi.org/10.1007/978-3-030-64616-5_39

Antonov, A., Kiselev, I., & Filippov, A. (2018). Development of a hardware reconfigurable computer with support for the OpenCL standard. *Communications in Computer and Information Science, 11*(14), 108–118. https://doi.org/10.18721/JCSTCS.11408

Antonov, A., Mamoutova, O., Fedotov, A., & Filippov, A. (2016). Next generation FPGA-based platform for network security. In: 18th Conference of Open Innovations Association and Seminar on Information Security and Protection of Information Technology (FReOI). https://doi.org/10.1109/FRUCT-ISPIT.2016.7561501

Antonov, A., Zaborovskij, V., & Kalyaev, I. (2019). The architecture of a reconfigurable heterogeneous distributed supercomputer system for solving the problems of intelligent data processing in the era of digital transformation of the economy. *Cybersecurity Issues, 33*(5), 2–11. https://doi.org/10.21681/2311-3456-2019-5-02-11

Antonov, A., Zaborovskij, V., & Kiselev, I. (2018). Specialized reconfigurable computers in network-centric supercomputer systems. *High Availability Systems, 14*(3), 57–62. https://doi.org/10.18127/j20729472-201803-09

Antonov, A., Zaborovsky, V., & Kiselev, I. (2021). Developing a new generation of reconfigurable heterogeneous distributed high performance computing system, In: Proceedings of International Scientific Conference on Telecommunications, Computing and Control. Smart Innovation, Systems and Technologies, Springer, 220. DOI: https://doi.org/10.1088/1742-6596/1864/1/012104

Antonov, A., Zaborovsky, V., & Polyanskiy, V. (2021). Neural computations in control problems: Aspects of computability and spatial-time characterization of cognitive functions. *Journal of Physics: Conference Series, 1864*(1). https://doi.org/10.1088/1742-6596/1864/1/012104

Attig, N. (2011). Trends in supercomputing: The European path to exascale. *Computer Physics Communications, 182*(9), 2041–2046.

Blum, M. (1975). A machine-independent theory of the complexity of recursive functions. *Lecture Notes in Computer Science Book Series, 32*, 13–29.

Dongarra, J. (2018). Big data and extreme-scale computing: Pathways to convergence-toward a shaping strategy for a future software and data ecosystem for scientific inquiry. *The International Journal of High Performance Computing Applications, 32*(4), 435–479. https://doi.org/10.1177/1094342018778123

Dongarra, J. (2019). Race to exascale. *Computing in Science and Engineering, 21*(1), 4–5. https://doi.org/10.1109/MCSE.2018.2882574

Dongarra, J. (2020). HPL—A portable implementation of the high-performance linpack benchmark for distributed-memory computers. Retrived July 09, 2021, from https://www.researchgate.net/publication/244449955_HPL_a_Portable_Implementation_of_the_Higherformance_Linpack_Benchmark_for_Distributed-Memory_Computers

Haidar, A. (2018). Investigating power capping toward energy-efficient scientific applications. In: *Concurrency and Computation Practice and Experience*, 1–14. https://doi.org/10.1002/cpe.4485

Harris, A. (2021) Exascale models of stellar explosions: Quintessential multi-physics simulation. *The International Journal of High Performance Computing Applications*. https://doi.org/10.1177/10943420211027937

Horst, S. (2021). The computational theory of mind in the stanford encyclopedia of philosophy. Retrieved July 09, 2021, from https://plato.stanford.edu/entries/computational-mind/

Intel FPGA. (2021). Retrieved July 09, 2021, from https://www.intel.com/content/www/us/en/products/programmable.html.

Le Fèvre, V. (2019). Comparing the performance of rigid, moldable and grid-shaped applications on failure-prone HPC Platforms. *Parallel Computing, 85*, 1–12.

Mark, D.. (2008). Retrieved July 09, 2021, from https://www.cs.washinton.edu/mssi/2008/talks/hill_msr_uw_0808.pdf

Michael, R. (2008). Amdahl's law in the multicore era. *IEEE Computer, 41*(7), 33–38. https://doi.org/10.1109/MC.2008.209

Mniszewski, S. (2021). Enabling particle applications for exascale computing platforms. *The International Journal of High Performance Computing Applications*. https://doi.org/10.1177/10943420211022829

Pais, A. (1991). Held C the meaning of complementarity in physics, philosophy, and polity. *Studies in History and Philosophy of Science, 25*, 871–893.

Shekhar, B. (2011). The future of microprocessors. *Communications of the ACM, 54*(5), 67. https://doi.org/10.1145/1941487.1941507

TOP500 List. (2021). Retrived July 09, 2021, from https://www.top500.org/lists/top500/2021/06/

Usman, A. (2018). Performance and power efficient massive parallel computational model for HPC heterogeneous exascale systems. *IEEE Access, 6*, 23095–23107. https://doi.org/10.1109/ACCESS.2018.2823299

Wigderson, A. (2019). *Mathematics and computation*. Princeton University Press.

Xilinx FPGA. (2021). Retrieved from July 09, 2021, from https://www.xilinx.com/products/silicon-deices/fpga/virtex-utrascale.html

Critical Factors and Challenges of Healthcare Digital Transformation

Igor Ilin, Victoria M. Iliashenko, Alissa Dubgorn, and Manfred Esser

Abstract The focus of countries is currently aimed at ensuring high-quality medical care and optimizing the cost of its provision. The last decades were characterized by rapid progress in the introduction of new technologies, many of which are capable of significantly improve the prognosis regarding serious illnesses. Healthcare organizations are seriously considering how to evaluate the effectiveness of the introduction of new technologies and how to correctly correlate it with the cost treatment and optimize costs within the health care system. This article analyzes modern trends in the field of healthcare, such as value-based medicine, personalized, and value-oriented. Within this framework, the authors make an overview of the current state of digitalization of healthcare not only in the Russian Federation but also in the world arena. The key factors in the development of digital healthcare are discussed, as well as the risks in the implementation of digital solutions.

Keywords Healthcare · Digital technologies · Value-based medicine

1 Introduction

At the present stage of the development of society, the main goal in the field of public health is not just an increase in life expectancy but an extension of a high-quality and healthy life. The problem of preserving and strengthening the health of the population has been declared one of the priority directions of the socio-economic policy of Russia. That is why the most important strategic direction of the socio-economic development of Russia as a whole is the preservation and augmentation of human capital, which cannot be imagined without improving the health care

I. Ilin · V. M. Iliashenko (✉) · A. Dubgorn
Peter the Great St. Petersburg Polytechnic University, Saint-Petersburg, Russia

M. Esser
Get IT, Grevenbroich, Germany

A. Rudskoi et al. (eds.), *Digital Transformation and the World Economy*, Studies on Entrepreneurship, Structural Change and Industrial Dynamics,
https://doi.org/10.1007/978-3-030-89832-8_11

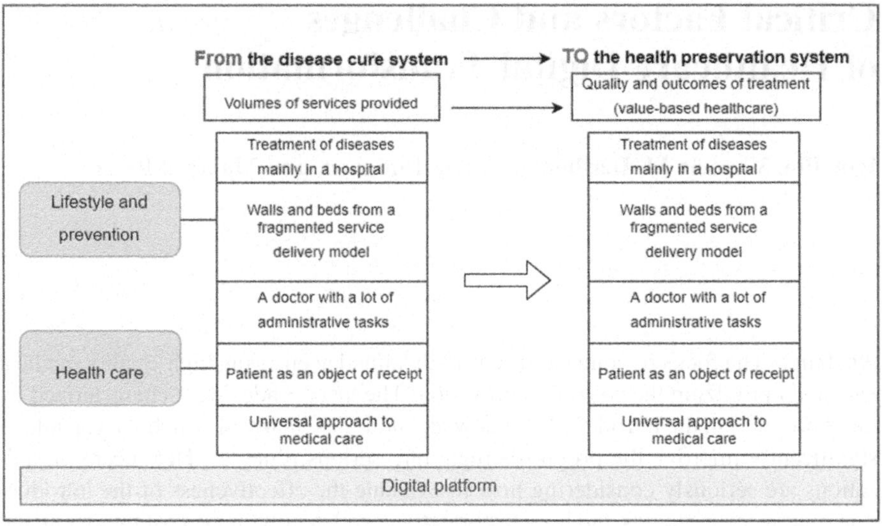

Fig. 1 Scheme of the transition to a new trajectory of health values (source: authors' creation)

system—pinions (Maydanova & Ilin, 2019). According to the definition of the World Health Organization (WHO), health is a collection of all organizations, institutions, and resources, the main goal of which is to improve health.

Creating a truly modern a health system that would correspond to the highest international standards implies an improvement in both the quality and accessibility of medical care, which in the context of tense financial situation, large area, limited resources and changing demographic situation requires new technological solutions (Wong, 2015). Most of the developed countries of the world, like Russia, see a way out only in the further technologization of all processes of providing medical help. In modern conditions of the dominance of information technology (IT), target the state of the industry is called "digital medicine" and "digital health."

The structure and level of morbidity are the most important components of a comprehensive, integrated assessment of the health of the population. Its study is necessary to substantiate management decisions at the federal, regional, and municipal levels of healthcare management. Only on its basis is it possible to correctly plan, predict the development of a network of healthcare institutions, its needs for various types of resources, including information technology (Ilin et al., 2019) (Fig. 1).

The main prerequisites for the development of digital health are (Karpov et al., 2019):

- Scientific and technological progress—advances in the development of science and technology in medicine, molecular biology, computer science, and an increase in computing power. New effective methods and tools diagnosis and treatment.

- Global informatization and mobility—people are no longer limited by geographic barriers in communication; they are actively using the Internet, mobile devices, social networks, and communication apps at a convenient time.
- Patient-centered—modern a person leads a healthy lifestyle, but how the patient makes decisions on voluntary health monitoring, actively participates in the collection of data, familiarization with information resources, selects the attending physician and treatment strategies.
- Data centricity—an abundance of data on the health status of citizens, on the basis of which analytical tools are created for decisión-making.

A number of factors can be identified that affect the speedy transfer of medicine to a digital format—these are huge distances, a highly educated population, a large number of small settlements where primary health care is provided by Feldsher-midwife stations or with the involvement of households.

Below in the article, the authors describe in detail the key trends in health care development, development factors and the main risks that medical institutions face.

2 Modern Trends in Healthcare Development

Technologies of the future, special attention of people to their health, scientific research and discoveries—all this sets trends in the development of the industry. Among them, there are several main directions in which the health care of the future will move (10 technologies, etc.). One way or another, each of them is aimed at improving the lives of patients and facilitating the work of the doctor (Fig. 2).

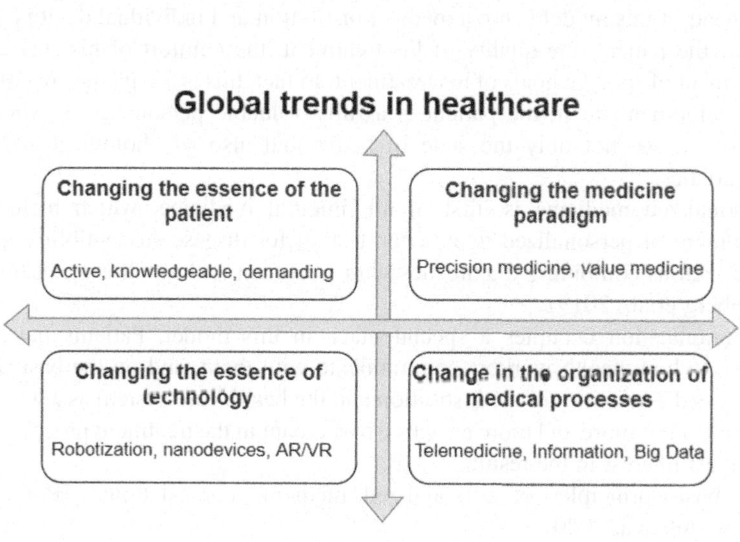

Fig. 2 Global trends in healthcare (source: authors' creation)

2.1 *Digitalization*

Digital technologies are laying the foundation for increasing the efficiency of health systems, expanding the ability to track health indicators, and improving the quality and safety of treatment through the use of artificial intelligence and personalized medicine (Mitchell & Kan, 2018).

The market for digital technologies in healthcare is growing by a quarter every year. According to Global Market Insight, its volume will reach $116 billion by 2024. The rapid growth rates are due to active support from the states, because digitalization can help to reduce health care costs in general significantly.

Today in medicine, developments related to artificial intelligence are most in demand. AI is actively used in diagnostics, drawing up a personal treatment plan and selecting the optimal formula for drugs (Iliashenko et al., 2019).

The Internet of Medical Things (IoMT) is also in demand—various devices with the function of exchanging data over a global network. They are mainly used for patient monitoring. According to experts, by 2020, about 30 billion IoMT devices will be used in the world (Dilawar et al., 2020).

Telemedicine also belongs to digitalization. Despite the fact that it is no longer something innovative, this trend is not slowing down. There are still many areas in the world where medical care remains difficult to access. Video and audio chats with doctors are still the most popular telemedicine technology.

2.2 *Patient Centricity*

At the head of this model is not a medical institution and individual doctors, but the needs of the patient, the quality of his treatment, the comfort of his stay and the achievement of specific goals of his treatment. In fact, this is a separate area of health care development. In it, the patient is a fully valuable personality in whom it is important to see not only the state of health but also psychological and social characteristics.

Personalized medicine is, first of all, integral medicine, which includes the development of personalized treatments, testing for disease susceptibility, prevention, as well as combining diagnostics with treatment and monitoring of treatment (Vogenberg et al., 2019).

Communication occupies a special place in this model. Patients pay special attention to how health workers communicate with them, and on the basis of this, they assess the activities of the institution and the health care system as a whole. The patient becomes more and more an active participant in the treatment process, having the greatest interest in the result.

The basic principles of personalized medicine (Translational 7P medicine) include (Ishikawa, 2020):

- Ability to "predict" the disease (predictiveness).
- Taking specific measures to prevent the disease (prevention).
- Individual treatment of each (personalization).
- Training of new personnel for health care through transdisciplinary medical education (providing).
- The possibility of direct participation of the patient himself in the process of prevention and treatment (participation).
- The ability to conduct interdisciplinary research on the distant horizon (proactive).
- The possibility of forming the evolution of the patient's contact with medicine not only in the hospital but also outside it (point of patient care).

2.3 *Datacentricity*

The active digitalization of medicine has led to the availability of huge data on patients, specific cases of diseases and treatment histories. Thus, it is predicted that by 2025 the volume of medical data will be 1 ze-tabyte (trillion gigabytes). The presence of such a large amount of data provides a good basis for the analysis and output of statistics. Big Data will make it possible to make informed decisions both on the choice of the most effective methods of diagnostics and treatment of a particular patient and for the preparation of medical forecasts and the method of organizing care in general (Povorina & Kosinova, 2020).

Tech giants Microsoft, Amazon, Google, and Salesforce are trying to cement their place in the trillion-dollar market. Improving the use of electronic health records is considered a priority, as research has shown that doctors spend more time taking medical records than working with patients. Cloud service Google Cloud already generates Google $8 billion in revenue per year. Clients of Google Cloud include the private medical and research center Mayo Clinic, pharmaceutical company McKesson and insurance company Kaiser Permanente.

2.4 *Values-Oriented Healthcare*

This concept was originally proposed by the American economist Harvard Business School professor Michael Porter (Musina et al., 2020). The model is based on the focus on the values of patients, their expectations from the health care system. Further allocation of resources is carried out in accordance with the results obtained by the institutions of the health care system with the use of drugs or technologies. The model is based on the focus on the values of patients, their expectations from the health care system. Further allocation of resources is carried out in accordance with the results obtained by health care institutions using drugs or technologies.

The difference between classical health care systems is that in the traditional system, more attention is paid to planning, control and payment of processes and volumes of medical care. The value-based model determines the amount of payment for medical services, based on the results of treatment, the quality of life of patients and the level of satisfaction of their needs.

Value-Based Healthcare is based on six pillars and is about improving patient outcomes while optimizing costs for the healthcare system (Achieving value-based health):

1. Organization of integrated medical care for each nosology.
2. Monitoring outcomes and costs at the individual level.
3. Development of batch payments for the treatment cycle.
4. Interdisciplinary system of medical care.
5. Expansion of geographical coverage.
6. Development of an IT platform to support the health care delivery system and record results.

As part of a value-based approach to healthcare, practices such as:

1. Providing a "second opinion" and supporting informed decision-making by the patient.
2. Diagnostics and prevention of conditions preceding the disease.
3. The use of information technology for the accumulation of data about the patient and further monitoring of the state of health.
4. The use of telemedicine as an auxiliary tool to support the patient's health.
5. Measurement of satisfaction and analysis of patient needs.

In those countries where a value-based health model is already being implemented, studies have been carried out which have shown that the use of this approach allows (Shlyakhto & Conradi, 2019):

1. Reduce the number of planned and emergency hospitalizations to 20%.
2. Reduce the costs of the health care system by 6–15%.
3. Improve the quality of life of patients.

If we talk about Russia, the transition to value-based health care will require significant reorganization and restructuring of the functioning system. However, in my opinion, this model is the best way to improve the quality of medical care.

Speaking about the factors of health care development, one can single out:

- Increase in life expectancy
- Prolongation of a quality and healthy life

For the high-quality use of modern solutions in the field of health care, it is necessary to focus on three main points:

- High-quality data collection.
- Deep analytics of the received data.
- Integration of information systems and received data into a single digital circuit.

Effective digitalization of the healthcare system is built on the basis of a platform that unites all participants in the system into a single circuit. The cornerstone of the platform is the creation and development of digital twins (patient, doctor, medical organization). In addition, the creation of a single digital circuit will increase the efficiency of management, the accuracy of statistics and the quality of medical care—the data will make it possible to analyze in detail the incidence on a national scale (Shlyakhto et al., 2020).

For its creation in the period from 2019 to 2024, 177.7 billion rubles were allocated in the federal budget of the Russian Federation. The digital contour is, first of all, the regulation of business processes, a tool for effective interaction between participants in the healthcare system.

3 Digital Transformation of Healthcare: Global Experience, Key Factors, Difficulties

The widespread introduction of digital technologies, in turn, solves several important problems at once that have held back the growth of the market:

- Information about new goods and services, new technologies in the field of healthcare is easier and faster to reach the consumer.
- Information about the patient, his medical history becomes more accessible to doctors. This simplifies the diagnosis, reduces the risk of errors, speeds up the exchange of information between medical institutions.
- Mobile digital technologies simplify health monitoring, make complex wearable devices more accessible, such as, for example, heart monitors.
- The use of digital technologies makes it possible to develop new drugs more efficiently, faster and cheaper.
- Blockchain technologies reduce the risks of counterfeiting medical and biologically active drugs (Moosavi et al., 2017).

Medical organizations are already converting information into digital format, business processes are being automated, and centralized systems are being created in all subjects. The use of information technologies is aimed, among other things, at improving the quality of medical care provided through the latest diagnostic and treatment methods, systems for interpreting the results of medical research. All this should lead to a reduction in the number of medical errors, a decrease in the time spent waiting for medical assistance, and an increase in the effectiveness of treatment.

3.1 World Experience

Strategic geographic location, combined with a modern IT infrastructure and a favorable climate for innovation, creates all the necessary conditions for the accelerated development of digital health in Southeast Asia. Therefore, in this part of the article, we will present the world experience from these countries.

South Korea Experience

Using the example of South Korea, one can see a clear plan for the development of digital vision in the health sector.

South Korea's health care system is regulated by the Ministry of Health and Welfare (MoHW) and funded by the Compulsory Health Insurance System (NHIS), which covers 97% of the population. There are about 70,000 medical institutions in Korea, of which almost half are located in Seoul and the Gyeonggi province surrounding the capital, which explains the predominance of the national health industry in Seoul.

To combat rising costs, the government is implementing various measures aimed at developing the digital health industry. These include increased investment in the development of new technologies and improved regulatory policies for digital health products and services (Digital Health South Korea Market Intelligence Report).

The digital health ecosystem is made up of government agencies, regulators, industry associations, healthcare centers, large corporations, blockchain-based healthcare providers, and a range of startups. Key players in digital health include leading clinics such as the National University Clinic and Asan Medical Center, large conglomerates such as Samsung and LG Electronics, telecom providers (SK Telecom and KT), system integrators (LG CNS, SK CNC) as well as startups (H3Systems, Lunit and Insung) (Fig. 3).

Korea's well-developed ICT infrastructure serves as the foundation for digital healthcare, with the adoption rate of electronic health records (EMR) systems in Korea reaching 93.6% in 2017 in hospitals. Wide coverage is associated with universal digitization of patient data, digital storage of clinical images, electronic databases of hospital administrations and increased use of remote sensing technologies.

South Korea leads the world in terms of smartphone ownership (94% of adults own smartphones and use the Internet). This high penetration rate of smartphones makes it possible to integrate the use of wearable devices quickly.

Korea's largest consumer electronics giants—Samsung Electronics and LG Electronics—are investing heavily in medical applications and wearable devices such as the S Health app and smartwatches. In addition, SK Telecom and Seoul National University Hospital have formed a joint venture Health Connect, which develops mobile solutions. For hospital management and diabetes management in Korea, also intended for the market China. Products in the mobile consumer health market

Fig. 3 South Korea's digital healthcare ecosystem (source: IntraLink Ltd, 2021)

include wearable devices such as sweat rate sensors in the form of watches, patches for non-invasive blood glucose monitoring and painless drug delivery, biosensor smart contact lenses capable of measuring glucose levels in diabetic patients. Insulin delivery systems These include functions such as drug dosage control, glucose monitoring and emergency signaling.

Singapore Experience

The strategic geographic location, combined with a modern IT infrastructure and a favorable climate for innovation, creates the necessary conditions in Singapore for the accelerated development of digital health in this country in the Asia-Pacific region.

The country's health care system is designed to provide everyone with timely, cost-effective and unimpeded access to various levels of health care. The Singapore government controls and finances the bulk of the healthcare system; more than 80% of the hospital fund in Singapore is concentrated in government clinics, government subsidies shape patient and provider decisions and affect pricing (Digital health ecosystem in Singapore).

Singapore's health financing structure is structured around the "three Ms:" Medisave, Medishield and Medifund (Fig. 4).

Medisave—is a mandatory health savings account; each employee contributes from 8% to 10.5% of their monthly salary (depending on age group) to a personal

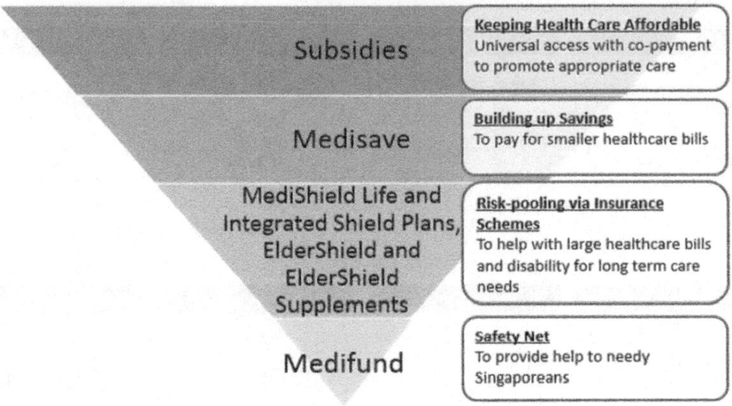

Fig. 4 The structure of the public health insurance system in Singapore (Source: https://ec.europa.eu/health/sites/default/files/ehealth/docs/ev_20180515_co23_en.pdf)

Medisave account. Patients can only use their Medisave accounts to buy pre-approved drugs, and the government subsidizes many medical bills directly. Medishield—is a nationwide emergency insurance program with higher deductibles. Medifund, $3 billion fund, helps citizens who cannot afford medical care through Medishield and Medisave tools.

The National Electronic Health Record (NEHR) is the backbone of digital healthcare in Singapore and is used by over 14,000 doctors in 280 healthcare facilities.

The main features of NEHR include (Fig. 5):

- A system for the exchange of patient data throughout the national health network.
- Management of the patient's medical record, collection of clinically significant information based on the results of contacts with medical workers throughout life.
- Ensuring secure access to the patient's medical record by authorized clinicians and healthcare professionals.
- Ensuring greater coordination and informed decision-making, supporting more accurate diagnosis, better treatment and comprehensive patient-centered care.

Singapore's policy to expand the use of mHealth wearable digital devices focuses on the following main objectives:

- Health promotion and disease prevention—related programs are based on SMS notifications.
- Diagnostics—used for ophthalmological examinations, as well as in the field of dermatology and stroke.
- Treatment—providing patients with recommendations for rehabilitation.
- Monitoring—allows you to monitor chronic diseases.
- Support of medical services—registration for an appointment for full-time visits to specialists.

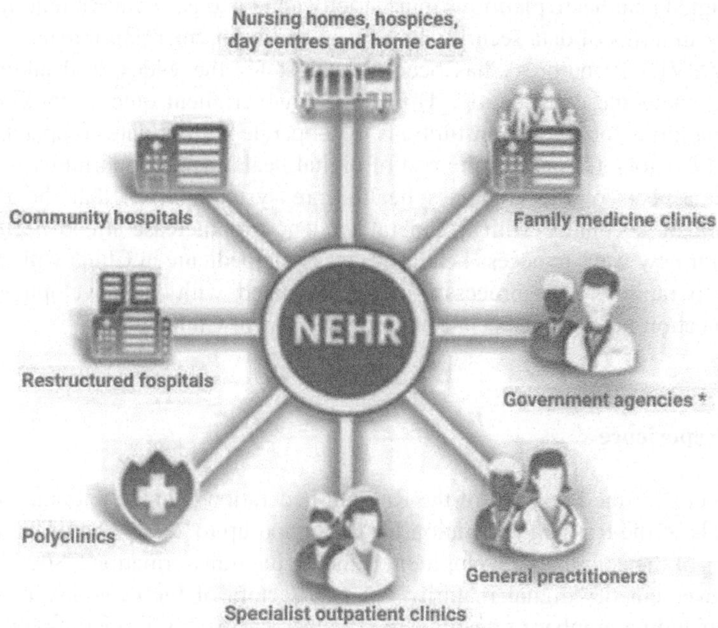

Fig. 5 NEHR System (2021)

China Experience

The concept of telemedicine is relatively new in China, although the first applications of these technologies in the country began in the 1980s. As in many countries, the outbreak of COVID-19 has changed approaches to digitalizing healthcare, especially in the area of telemedicine. China currently has over 1000 telemedicine technology companies, and the growth is expected to continue exponentially. The PRC government and digital health service providers are united by a common goal—to accelerate the development of telemedicine technologies in the country (Li et al., 2020).

Despite the fact that the size of the Chinese healthcare market is the second largest in the world after the USA, the country's healthcare system is faced with many problems, including complex relations between doctors and patients, lack of access to services in rural areas, high costs, and poor quality of medical services, slow and inefficient hospital operations.

As in many other countries, telemedicine in China faces challenges such as current government regulatory policies that need to be improved and potential cybersecurity threats. In Ki-tai, doctors cannot establish an initial diagnosis or prescribe treatment using a digital platform; during a session, the patient receives only consultations. But the regulatory enactments in China have been improving lately. Digital healthcare platforms must strictly adhere to government requirements, especially in terms of data security, to prevent and limit emerging threats.

The COVID-19 outbreak has been a catalyst for the widespread adoption of online telemedicine consultation. The Chinese government quickly took steps to create conditions for medical institutions to cooperate with private companies (Ping An Good Doctor). China sees the rise of digital health as an opportunity to fix the imperfect aspects of the country's health care system. Given that the growing population of a country with a general tendency to increase life expectancy is looking for new ways to access health services, telemedicine in China will continue to develop rapidly. This process is also associated with the development of a communication network, especially in remote areas of China.

Russia Experience

In the Decree of the President of the Russian Federation "On the national development goals of the Russian Federation for the period up to 2030" one of the priority directions of the country's development is the digital transformation associated with the achievement of "digital maturity" of key sectors of the economy and social sphere, including number of health care. The task has been set to increase the share of mass socially significant services available in the electronic form to 95% (Izmailova et al., 2021).

The national priority project "Healthcare" defines the digitalization of the healthcare system of the Russian Federation as one of the key tasks, which is being implemented within the framework of the federal project "Creation of a single digital health care circuit based on the Unified State Health Information System."

Within the framework of this federal project, it is necessary to solve the tasks of transforming the country's healthcare system through automated information support, as well as monitoring and analyzing the use of healthcare resources and providing medical care to citizens.

The main patient-oriented service that provides a wide range of services to citizens is the My Health super service (Healthcare in Russia). Currently, it is possible for citizens:

- Making an appointment with a doctor and for undergoing medical examination and professional examination.
- Attachment to a medical organization; filing an application for the choice of an insurance medical organization.
- Obtaining information about the provided medical services and their cost.

The "road map" of the service also provides for citizens' access to medical documents in electronic form. Available in 2020:

- Medical certificate of admission to driving a vehicle.
- Referral for hospitalization, rehabilitation treatment, examination, consultation.

- Medical record of a patient receiving medical care on an outpatient basis.
- Medical professional advisory opinion.

The super service "My Health" will have electronic prescriptions, which will become a key element of the federal register of preferential drug provision, which allows you to keep track of, analyze, plan, and provide for the needs of the population in drugs.

Also, projects of the Ministry of Health of Russia in the field of digital health include:

- Introduction of a system of mandatory labeling of medicinal products from July 1, 2020.
- The launch of the federal register of preferential drug provision from January 1, 2021.
- Development of a network of national medical research centers (NMRC) and the introduction of innovative medical technologies, which includes the introduction of specialized vertically integrated medical information systems for individual profiles of medical care: oncology, cardiology, etc.; development of telemedicine technologies.

3.2 *Key Factors in the Health Care Development*

If we talk about the impact on the health indicators of mankind, there are four main factors of influence:

- Lifestyle and prevention
- Medical assistance (quality, availability)
- Socio-economic factors
- Environment

The main trends in the digitalization of healthcare are:

- Improvement of the regulatory framework.
- Setting the task of using digitalization for strategic management of the industry.
- Coming into the sphere of the country's leading IT companies.
- Increasing the importance of information security issues in health care.
- The formation of tasks for the intellectualization of management and the treatment process from public policy, the functioning of an institution to diagnosis and treatment.

3.3 *The Challenges of Digital Healthcare Transformation*

The research of the main trends in the development of digitalization of healthcare at the global and local levels showed that global technological progress provides medicine with various hardware and software tools that facilitate the work of specialists and reduce the cost of providing medical care. However, despite serious positive transformations in the field of digitalization of healthcare, for the full implementation of this practice throughout the Russian Federation, it is necessary to overcome a number of obstacles:

- Lack of financial resources
- Lack of personnel in specialties, ensuring the transformation of digitalization of medicine
- Underdeveloped digital health infrastructure
- Threats to information security
- Low level of development of intelligence of expert medical systems

Thus, the digitalization of healthcare is considered by the highest state power in Russia as one of the priorities for its development, which, however, requires additional and careful management work to make specific decisions. Nevertheless, positive trends and innovations are obvious, which will move from the category of experimental innovations and will be introduced into the healthcare sector for its normal functioning during the period of digital transformation of attributes.

4 Conclusion

Healthcare today is undergoing an incredible digital transformation that is changing virtually every aspect of the industry. It is obvious that in the coming years, this sector will constantly develop, including through the emergence and implementation of new technologies. In this regard, cooperation between major market players and startups is very important. And here, not only the financial component plays a role, but also the mentoring of industry experts who help bring innovation to life.

The digital transformation strategy of Russian healthcare is aimed, first of all, at creating conditions for increasing the efficiency of activities in the provision of medical services through the introduction of digital technologies. Optimization of the development of digital transformation is carried out by ensuring equal access to the Internet and cellular communications of the population of the country, reengineering of public services and services for receiving medical services, taking into account the possibilities of digital technologies, development, and implementation of industry platforms. Changes at the national level, creating a single space for the exchange of medical data of patients at all stages of service provision, modernizing the unified state information system in the field of health care (hereinafter referred to as the Unified State Health Information System) to create the possibility of quick access to primary health care, increasing high-speed information exchange in medical organizations.

Within the framework of this article, the authors made an overview of the current state of digitalization of healthcare not only in the Russian Federation but also in the world arena. The key factors in the development of digital healthcare were given, the risks in the implementation of digital solutions were analyzed.

In the future, it is planned to implement the concept of a single digital circuit for a large geographically distributed medical organization.

Acknowledgments The reported study was funded by RFBR according to the research project № 19-010-00579.

References

10 Technologies that Will Drive the Future of Healthcare. Retrieved July 15, 2021, from http://interestingengineering.com/10-technologies-that-will-drive-the-future-of-healthcare

Achieving value-based health: Six approaches to patient-centered care. Retrieved July 15, 2021, from https://www.ibm.com/industries/healthcare/resources/value-based-health-steps/

Digital health ecosystem in Singapore. Retrieved July 15, 2021, from https://globaluniversityventuring.com/digital-health-ecosystem-in-singapore/

Digital Health South Korea Market Intelligence Report. Retrieved July 15, 2021, from www.intralinkgroup.com/getmedia/3153c79b-463d-47c7-84e6-56848c98aab7/Intralink-Report_Life-Sciences_June

Dilawar, N., Rizwan, M., Akram, S., & Ahamd, F. (2020). Blockchain: Securing Internet of Medical Things (IoMT). *International Journal of Advanced Computer Science and Applications, 10*(1).

Healthcare in Russia: The Russian healthcare system explained. Retrieved July 15, 2021, from https://www.expatica.com/ru/healthcare/healthcare-basics/healthcare-in-russia-104030/

Iliashenko, O., Bikkulova, Z., & Dubgorn, A. (2019). Opportunities and challenges of artificial intelligence in healthcare. E3S Web of Conferences, 110, 02028.

Ilin, I., Levina, A., Lepekhin, A., & Kalyazina, S. (2019). Business requirements to the IT architecture: A case of a healthcare organization. *Advances in Intelligent Systems and Computing, 983*, 287–294.

Ishikawa, T. (2020). Personalized medicine basic principles. *PanVascular Medicine*, 1–22.

Izmailova, M. A., Veselovsky, M. Y., & Trifinov, V. A. (2021). *Digitalization of economy and socio-economic development of Russia: Points of connection*, In Conference: International Scientific and Practical Conference "Russia 2020—A new reality: Economy and society" (ISPCR 2020).

Karpov, O. E., Subbotin S.A., Shishkanov D.V., & Zamyatin M.N. (2019). *Digital public health. Necessity and background.* Pirogov National Medical & Surgical Center, Moscow, Russia.

Li, I., et al. (2020). Quality of primary health care in China: Challenges and recommendations. *The Lancet, 395*(10239), 1802–1812. https://doi.org/10.1016/S0140-6736(20)30122

Maydanova, S., & Ilin, I. (2019). Strategic approach to global company digital transformation. In: Proceedings of the 33rd International Business Information Management Association Conference, IBIMA 2019: Education Excellence and Innovation Management through Vision 2020, pp. 8818–8833.

Mitchell, M., & Kan, L. (2018). *Digital technology and the future of health systems*. Health Systems & Reform. https://doi.org/10.1080/23288604.2019.1583040

Moosavi, S. R., et al. (2017). SEA: A secure and efficient authentication and authorization architecture for IoT-based healthcare using smart gateways. *Procedia Computer Science, 52*, 452–459.

Musina, N. Z., Omelyanovskiy, V. V., & Gostischev, R. V. (2020). Concept of value-based healthcare. FARMAKOEKONOMIKA. *Modern Pharmacoeconomics and Pharmacoepidemiology, 13* (4).

Ping An Good Doctor launches commercial operation of One-minute Clinics in China | MobiHealthNews. Retrieved July 15, 2021, from https://www.mobihealthnews.com/news/apac/ping-good-doctor-launches-commercial-operation-one-minute-clinics-china

Povorina, A. V., & Kosinova, N. N. (2020). Digitalization of healthcare: Domestic and foreign experience, development trends. *Advances in Economics, Business and Management Research, 156*.

Shlyakhto, E. V., & Conradi, A. O. (2019). *Value based medicine—New paradigm in healthcare.*

Shlyakhto, E. V., et al. (2020). *Health organization management: The Smart Hospital concept.*

Vogenberg, F., Barash, C., & Pursel, M. (2019). Personalized medicine: Part 1: Evolution and development into Theranostics. *PubMed, P&T, 35*(10), 560–576.

Wong, P. (2015). *Challenges and successes in implementing international standards: Achieving convergence to IFRSS and ISAAS.* Cambridge University Press.

Digital Transformation Maturity Model

Igor Ilin, Alexandra Borremans, Anastasia Levina, and Manfred Esser

Abstract Currently, digitalization has become a key engine for the development of all industries. More and more enterprises are focusing on the digitalization of their processes and the introduction of digital services. However, the transition from business to digital is quite complex and requires a gradual transition. This chapter raises questions of the maturity of various enterprises and their processes, as well as criteria and attributes for assessing maturity. In addition, a comparative analysis of some of the existing maturity models is carried out. As a result of the study, a five-level model for assessing the maturity of digital enterprises and transformation in them is presented, which was developed on the basis of modern maturity models, such as CMMI, OPM3, and others. Moreover, the levels of maturity and the criteria for their achievement, as well as the stages of transition between them, are described.

Keywords Maturity model · Digital transformation · Digitalization · Digital maturity · Company assessment

1 Introduction

Nowadays, the question of enterprises' digital maturity is quite relevant in the modern developing world, where digitalization, business transformation, and the introduction of the latest IT technologies have come to the fore. The tendency of the information community to qualitatively change the management of enterprises determines the development of the economy, an increase in labor efficiency and an improvement in the quality of life. Companies need to understand how to conduct

I. Ilin · A. Borremans · A. Levina (✉)
Graduate School of Business Engineering, Peter the Great Saint-Petersburg Polytechnic University, St. Petersburg, Russia

M. Esser
Get IT, Grevenbroich, Germany

A. Rudskoi et al. (eds.), *Digital Transformation and the World Economy*, Studies on Entrepreneurship, Structural Change and Industrial Dynamics,
https://doi.org/10.1007/978-3-030-89832-8_12

business in a changing environment, what strategies and management methods to use in order to maintain their competitiveness in the future.

All companies are at different stages of their development and have different business processes, so there is no single algorithm for transformation. It is necessary to conduct a comprehensive analysis of the use of information technology in the activities of the company, considering both internal processes and interaction with the environment, customers, competitors, and partners.

In order to clearly understand which processes and models need transformation, at what stage of development the company is now, they use such a concept as "digital maturity."

2 Methods

To achieve the goals of this chapter, information from open sources was analyzed on modern approaches to assessing the maturity of enterprises, their main levels. Moreover, the existing approaches to the assessment of processes, IT, business, and IT harmonization were analyzed.

According to experts, digital maturity is a cumulative assessment of the level of development of companies in several important areas of digital transformation, such as digitization of business processes, digital infrastructure, data-driven management, the use of customer orientation principles and product value management, R&D and creation of new products, digital culture, and digital partnership (Colli et al., 2019).

In other words, the digital maturity of an enterprise is the level of its readiness to properly respond to digital innovations in the company's processes.

The maturity of a company can be thought of as milestones that also have some variation but have common features.

Having determined the level of maturity of the company in the field of digital transformation, it is possible already at the first stage to form a list of changes in the organization to adapt it to a changing world, both in the external and in the internal environments. Achieving the desired level is possible only with a clear description of the further strategy for achieving the required state.

Let us introduce a definition of the concept of a maturity model. According to the ISO standard, the maturity model is a model that reflects the elements necessary for efficient processes and describes the path of a gradual improvement from immature processes to regulated, mature processes with higher quality and efficiency. In contrast, the maturity of an organization's project management refers to the organization's ability to select projects and manage them in the most efficient way to support the achievement of its strategic objectives (Al-Qutaish & Abran, 2011).

Various models for assessing maturity exists:

- SW CMM
- Integrated model CMMI
- ISO 15504 standard

- Model of maturity COBIT 4.1 (COBIT Process Assessment Model, PAM)
- SPICE (Software Process Improvement and Capability determination) model
- PMMM (Project Management Maturity Model)
- OPM3 model (PMI community)
- etc.

Let us take a closer look at some of them to get a general picture of the existing methodologies for determining the maturity of companies.

2.1 Capability Maturity Model

The most popular model is CMM (Capability Maturity Model for Software), which describes the maturity of software development processes in enterprises, developed by the Software Engineering Institute (USA). The success of the idea lies in the ease of understanding, the practicality of applying the model, and effective advancement from one level to another with significant changes in product quality for the better. This model is focused on optimizing the price–performance ratio (Paulk, 2009).

2.2 Capability Maturity Model Integration

In the process of development, the model was refined and received the name CMMI (Capability Maturity Model Integration), which differs in some details, but retains the basic principles of CMM, discreteness of maturity gradations, focus on the project business (Team, 2002). Maturity levels according to the CMMI model are as follows: 1—initial, 2—controlled, 3—definite, 4—quantitatively controlled, and 5—optimized. In Table 1, comparison of SW CMM and CMMI is presented.

The integration of the models resulted in a five-tier methodology for determining the maturity of enterprises:

- Level 1—Initial. The key concept is Heroism. It is characterized by unpredictable, poorly controlled processes that are reactive in nature. The success of the project is determined by the heroism of the staff and the qualifications of individual employees. Projects are often out of budget, results do not meet expectations, and are of poor quality.

Table 1 SW CMM and CMMI comparison

№.	SW CMM	CMMI
1	Elementary	Elementary
2	Repeatable	Managed
3	Definite	Definite
4	Managed	Quantitatively managed
5	Optimizable	Optimizable

- Level 2—Managed. Project and requirements management. All processes in the company are planned, they are constantly monitored and controlled. Stakeholders are committed in advance and are aware of the state of the product being developed at any given time. The generated requirements are almost completely consistent with the results of the project and have the proper quality in accordance with the standards and goals of the company.
- Level 3—Defined. Process engineering. Drawing up a unified system of approaches of the organization to the standard processes in the company. Each project is considered as a set of general processes, described earlier in the provisions, which are finalized and improved depending on their tasks. The processes and procedures for their adaptation have a formal rigorous form. Based on the standards, senior management sets the objectives of the processes and monitors their achievement.
- Level 4—Quantitatively Managed. Process and product quality. At this level, the company determines the quantitative characteristics of the quality and performance of processes. Methods of statistical analysis and data processing are applied. Indicators that deviate from the norm are being investigated to prevent such occurrences in the future. Data analytics allows you to predict the execution of processes not only qualitatively, but also quantitatively. The results obtained are stored in databases and are used by the management to make decisions on process management.
- Level 5—Optimizing. Continuous process improvement. The company is trying to improve the processes taking place during the project. This is due to the constant comparison of old quantitative indicators with new ones. Employees can monitor the results and independently optimize their activities (Henriques, 2018).

2.3 COBIT 4.1

The COBIT 4.1 maturity model initially turned out to be difficult to implement in practice and did not provide a definite understanding of the state of the company. So, the processes could have signs of different levels, not even going in a row, which also happened with the attributes, making it difficult to assess the level at which the company is located. This led to the loss of a holistic view of her digital maturity (Brand & Boonen, 2007).

2.4 ISO / IEC 15504

The model was improved and became based on the international standard ISO / IEC 15504 "Information technology—process assessment." International Standard defines process evaluation as a complete process optimization program or as part

Table 2 ISO / IEC 15504 levels

Level	Process attributes	Rating score
Level 0	Process initiation	–
Level 1	Process implementation	Mainly or completely
Level 2	– Process implementation – Implementation management – Work product management	– Completely – Mainly or completely – Mainly or completely
Level 3	– Process implementation – Implementation management – Work product management – Process definition – Process deployment	– Completely – Completely – Completely – Mainly or completely – Mainly or completely
Level 4	– Process implementation – Implementation management – Work product management – Process definition – Process deployment – Process measurement – Process control	– Completely – Completely – Completely – Completely – Completely – Mainly or completely – Mainly or completely
Level 5	– Process implementation – Implementation management – Work product management – Process definition – Process deployment – Process measurement – Process control – Process innovation – Process optimization	– Completely – Completely – Completely – Completely – Completely – Completely – Completely – Mainly or completely – Mainly or completely

of the process capability. Optimizing processes means continually increasing performance and applying sustainable practices across an organization. Determination of process capabilities according to the standard—correct representation of potential capabilities from ongoing processes (Mesquida et al., 2012, p. 15504).

This standard also presupposes five levels of digital maturity of the company, which directly depends on the maturity of the processes taking place inside (Table 2).

These levels are the following:

- Level 0. Incomplete process. When processes are underway, but have not yet reached it. There is no single basis for systematic approaches to standard processes.
- Level 1. Implemented process. Achievement of the processes of the final stage of their purpose without the use of special management methods.
- Level 2. Guided process. The processes carried out are planned in advance, then subsequently regulated. The processes are monitored, the compliance of the developed product or service with the assigned goals is checked.
- Level 3. Established process. A base of basic processes is being formed, which are standardized and have common control algorithms. The described processes

are used at all stages of the project, but are individually modified in the course of implementation for the purpose of the product being developed.
- Level 4. Predictable process. The results of the processes at this stage are predicted and known in advance. Achievement of certain results is easily controlled and monitored.
- Level 5. Optimization process. Predictable processes are constantly being improved to achieve the set business goals (El Emam & Birk, 2000, p. 15504).

The levels are arranged in such a way that it is impossible to skip or slip through one of them, the transition through the levels is carried out in order. If the company decides to skip several levels, then the simultaneous implementation of several optimization tools can lead to unpredictable consequences, jeopardizing the entire project activities of the company. Each level of maturity forms the basis for the rational and efficient implementation of processes at the following levels. However, organizations can use and benefit from the implementation of processes that are associated with higher levels of maturity than those achieved. All maturity changes do not have to be consistent.

The levels are determined by the achievement of the process attributes.

N—Not achieved—0–15% achievement.
H—Partially achieved—15–50% achievement.
B—Mainly achieved—50–85% achievement.
P—Fully achieved—85–100% achievement.

2.5 SPICE

Basic concepts of the SPICE maturity model (ISO / IEC 15504 standard) are:

- Practice—An activity that introduces contribution to the objectives of the process to increase its capabilities.
- Process—A set of interrelated or interacting activities, transforming inputs into outputs.
- Process assessment attribute—A measurable characteristic of the process capability (Mitasiunas & Novickis, 2011).

Unlike CMMI, the SPICE maturity model is implemented in only one version—continuous representation. Therefore, SPICE defines only the concept of "level of opportunity," which corresponds to the scale of assessing the possibility separately the processes taken, and, as a consequence, does not allow make an assessment of the organization's software development process as a whole. Model maturity SPICE describes 6 levels of capability. To reach a particular maturity level, certain process attributes need to be realized in order to meet the desired level requirements. For all processes, the standard defines 9 different attributes.

SPICE Model Capability Level List:

Table 3 Comparison of SPICE and CMM

SPICE	CMM
Two-dimensional structure	Sequential, one-dimensional structure
Allows flexibility in developing an improvement strategy	Contains a predefined development path
Opportunity levels for every process	One maturity level for all process
Results need to be simplified	Results are easy to understand
Results are very detailed	Simplified results

- Level 0—Process not running
- Level 1—Process in progress
  - Measurement of process performance
- Level 2—Guided process
  - 2.1 Performance management
  - 2.2 Product Creation Management
- Level 3—Established process
  - 3.1 Documenting the process
  - 3.2 Tracking process resources
- Level 4—Predictable process
  - 4.1 Process measurement
  - 4.2 Process control
- Level 5—Optimization Process
  - 5.1 Process change
  - 5.2 Continuous improvement

Despite the fact that the SPICE standard has absorbed the best from a number of other standards, it has not become a simple amalgamation of them. In order to show how SPICE differs from its predecessors, it is advisable to compare SPICE and other well-known standards (Laksono et al., 2019) (Table 3).

Maturity methodologies of process approaches are constantly changing and new models such as OPM3 (Project Management Institute, PMI) model and BPMM appear.

2.6 Project Management Maturity Model

The Kerzner Project Management Maturity Model (PMMM) is a qualitative assessment of the levels of project management maturity and consists of 5 levels (Kerzner, 2019).

The model assumes that many levels are required and detectable, but the order of transition from one level to another will remain unchanged.

Maturity model levels are the following:

- Level 1—Terminology. At this level, the organization realizes the importance of project management and the need to deeply master the basic knowledge of project management and study the terminology that accompanies it.
- Level 2—General processes. The organization recognizes the importance of defining and developing common processes so that the success of one project can be replicated by others.
- Level 3—Unified methodology. The organization recognizes the importance of synergies that arise from integrating project management with other methodologies (quality management, process management, etc.).
- Level 4—Benchmarking. There is a realization that it is necessary to improve corporate processes if the corporation wants to maintain its superiority over competitors.
- Level 5—Continuous improvement. At this level, the company evaluates the information obtained in the course of benchmarking, and must decide whether this information will be used in the expansion (development) of a unified methodology (Faifr, 2020).

2.7 *Organizational Project Management Maturity Model*

OPM3 (Organizational Project Management Maturity Model) is an organizational project management maturity model. A standard for assessing the maturity of project management organizations, published in 2003 by the American Project Management Institute (PMI). The standard's goal is to identify problems in the project management process and define a strategy for other employees to carry out operations (Farrokh & Mansur, 2013).

OPM3 standard consists of three main elements:

- Knowledge of what is project management in an organization, how to determine the level of maturity of project management, and what are the best practices in PM.
- Evaluation (assessment) of the current level of maturity of project management.
- Means for improving project management processes to achieve a higher level of maturity.

OPM3 includes:

- Body of knowledge—A book describing the basic concepts and structure of the standard, the content of the model itself and the procedure for its use.
- The best practices base is a database and tools presented in electronic form. The base is structured into three domains (project portfolio, program, and project) and four levels of project formalization (processes are standardized, measurable,

controlled, and optimized). In addition, the base of best practices includes the so-called OE (Organizational Enablers), which are necessary for the organization to maintain the processes and organizational structure of project management (Bento et al., 2019, p. 3).

2.8 BPMM

The BPMM standard provides details on how to use its maturity model in practice. Including the description of 30 groups of processes, the creation and management of which will allow the organization to go from the first level to the fifth. Each group of processes is assigned a certain level of process maturity (starting with the second) and the area of application of efforts (thread). Thus, it is possible to track how each group of processes evolves as the level of process maturity increases (Kneuper, 2018).

All approaches have their own characteristics and different criteria, so they need a detailed analysis before applying.

3 Results

In order to clearly understand at what level the company is located, special attributes of maturity are applied. Using a general approach to assessing the health of companies, usually from 5 to 8 elements are identified. Key ones are presented below:

1. Buyers.

Provide an experience where customers see your organization as a digital partner and use their preferred communication channels to manage their future offline.

2. Strategy.

It focuses on how companies change or act to increase their competitive advantage through digital initiatives; is integrated into the overall business strategy.

3. Technology.

It supports the success of the digital strategy, helping to create, process, store, protect, and share data to meet customer needs at low cost and overhead.

4. Operations.

Execution and development of processes and activities using digital technologies for strategic management and increasing the efficiency and effectiveness of the company.

5. Culture.

Define and develop an organizational culture with leadership and talent processes to support the development of the digital maturity curve.

The state of each element allows you to give a complete picture of the state of the company as a whole (Maydanova & Ilin, 2019).

Not all companies have full knowledge of the digital spectrum, so such a comprehensive assessment provides an understanding of possible growth concepts, the introduction of new technologies, and methods for improving customer service. Knowing where the company is located, as well as its capabilities and needs, help determine a successful strategy (Ilin et al., 2020).

This model corresponds to a certain scale of attributes, with the help of which the state of maturity of the company is assessed.

Despite the high variety of methodologies and the development of new models, they are all built in such a way that it is impossible to miss any level of maturity, the transition through the levels is carried out in sequence. If the company decides to skip several levels, then the simultaneous implementation of several optimization tools can lead to unpredictable consequences, jeopardizing the entire project activities of the company. Each maturity level is the basis for the rational and effective implementation of processes at subsequent levels.

If we consider the Russian market, then for complete digitalization Russian companies do not have the maturity of current business processes and qualified specialists (Zaychenko et al., 2018).

The introduction of new technologies can lead to significant changes in work processes, an increase in the qualifications of employees, the development of previously unused skills that require constant optimization and understanding of all the nuances and complexities of unforeseen technological problems. Assessment of the maturity of the process helps to understand how the processes are manageable, controlled, optimized. Each company in the process of its growth goes through certain stages, characterized by different cultural, management, and strategic characteristics.

There is a strong link between the transition from process maturity to digital. A company's readiness for technological transformation is determined by an assessment of the level of compliance with fundamental processes and their management, methods of using the accumulated information. Determining the level of maturity of the management system, one can characterize the stage of the company's readiness for digital transformation, identify the company's potential for development, choose the direction of modernization and growth.

It can be noted that a company, a company that works effectively and efficiently, achieves a stable state in the global market and has a high index of readiness for digital transformation (Borremans et al., 2018). The management of such companies is able to identify weaknesses that need improvements and innovations through IT technologies, organize monitoring of changes in the environment, increase satisfaction of the needs and expectations of stakeholders, and structure goals.

Based on the methodologies described earlier, a model of digital maturity of companies was formed, which, by analogy with the process, also includes 5 levels (Table 4).

Based on the previously described methodologies, a model of digital maturity of companies was formed, which, by analogy with the process, also includes 5 levels (Fig. 1):

- Level 0. Basic infrastructure. Technologies that do not give business effects by themselves, but are necessary for the introduction of advanced technologies.
- Level 1. Computerization. The process is automated by any IT system. Entering data into the system is carried out manually.
- Level 2. Connectivity. Operational data of the process enter the system automatically, without human intervention. Adjacent systems are integrated. The control action is carried out remotely.
- Level 3. Transparency. Key process indicators are visualized and tracked in real time.
- Level 4. Predictiveness. Predictive systems have been introduced to predict the future state.
- Level 5. Adaptability. Systems have been introduced that have a corrective effect on equipment either independently or within a corporate system to maximize efficiency.

To achieve the highest level or move from one to the other, two approaches were identified.

The first of them is the replication of existing developments and technologies. It is assumed that the company is using basic digital tools that give positive results, or there are best practices for future implementation with a high level of versatility that can be applied to most standardized enterprise processes.

This approach requires the transformation of the processes in individual production sections of the enterprise. It should be remembered that they can have different levels of maturity at the same time. Thus, there is a transformation based on the replication of digital tools that have been introduced and need to be improved, or have been considered by the management as planned implementations with a certain result for the enterprise.

A second approach to the improvement and implementation of IT technologies in enterprises is proposed, which takes as a basis a detailed analysis of processes down to operational activities. New modern technologies are taken as the basis for optimization. Thus, the output is a detailed program for the digital transformation of the main problematic processes to improve the efficiency of the enterprise.

It should be noted that both approaches are practically applicable and are chosen by the company depending on its transformation objectives and the level of digital maturity. One more feature can be noted—this is the application of the described approaches to digital transformation at the same time, analyzing both the instrumental basis of the company and the internal business processes.

Moreover, when assessing the digital maturity of an enterprise, it is important to consider and develop the following attributes:

Table 4 Digital maturity of a company

Maturity level	Processes	Technologies	Employees
Level 5	– Development of processes for autonomous decision making by systems. – Development of processes for regular forecasting and planning of future production.	– Integration with external data of suppliers and buyers. – Using artificial intelligence systems.	– Developing a culture of continuous improvement and innovation. – Implementation of responsible persons for the corresponding direction of predictive analytics and adaptability.
Level 4	– Development of audit processes for historical and current data and the use of the information obtained for optimization. – Introduction of procedures for regular optimization initiatives.	– Real-time implementation of activity analysis systems that automatically perform analytics, generate warnings, and recommendations. – Implementation of digital twins for prototyping and optimization testing.	– Organization of cross-functional sessions and data exchange sessions to work on urgent problems and optimization methods based on new data. – Attracting additional data analysts.
Level 3	– Formalization of data flow management processes. – Creation of processes for active exchange of knowledge and data between all project participants. – Creation of a cross-functional data exchange network.	– Improving data accuracy, reducing the amount of useless information. – Implementation of data mining systems. – Integration of systems for data exchange.	– Training employees to work with system data, various devices, and interfaces. – Development of "Digital" skills. – Development of a culture of knowledge management.
Level 2	– Formalization of the implementation of the "digital factory." – Processes for attracting external actors to ensure connectivity.	– Elaboration of directions of integration of existing systems and technologies with future elements of the "digital factory." – Formation of a single information space and data streams, connection of systems.	– Involvement of employees in the development of a target vision. – Separation of roles and areas of responsibility, attraction of employees with competencies in business, IT, and production.
Level 1	– Elimination of paper forms and media, execution of processes through system interfaces. – Data transfer automation.	– Implementation of basic production and enterprise management systems. – Integration of systems for automatic data transfer.	– Employees trained to work with systems in their area of responsibility.

(continued)

Table 4 (continued)

Maturity level	Processes	Technologies	Employees
Level 0	– There is no direct influence on the processes.	– Creation of infrastructure for subsequent implementations of industrial Wi-Fi, local networks.	– Employees do not need additional digital competencies.

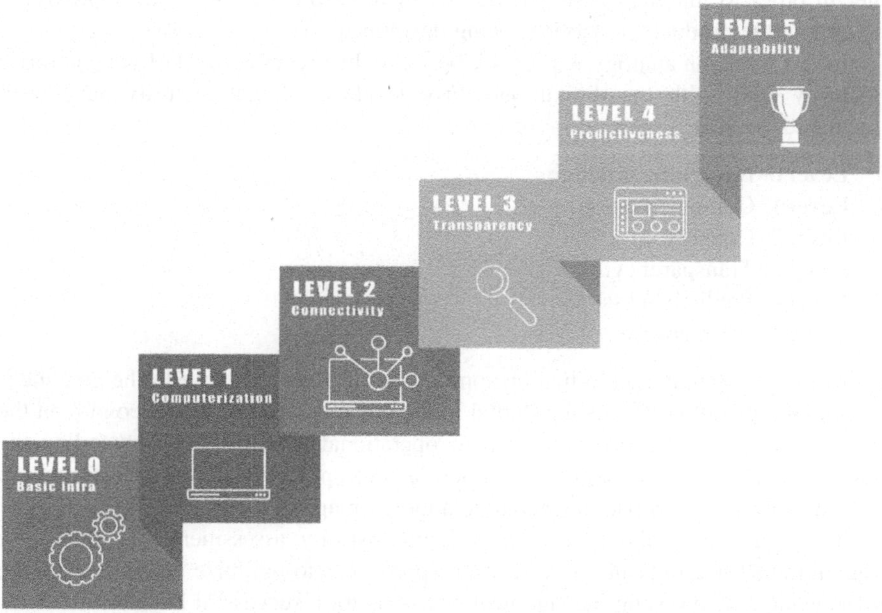

Fig. 1 Levels of digital maturity (Source: authors' creation)

- Digital culture—An organizational culture that supports continuous improvement and innovation processes.
- Human Resources—Employees with the skills needed to be successful in a digital environment.
- Processes—Optimized business processes, as well as their constant analysis and monitoring, as well as the application of process management practices.
- Digital products—Digital solutions for business.
- Models—Constantly updated models, valid and included in the activity processes.
- Data—Data available in real time with the required level of security, complete and high-quality for making management decisions.
- Infrastructure and Tools—Modern and digital infrastructure to enable cross-device connectivity and integration (Dubgorn et al., 2019).

4 Conclusion and Discussion

The basis for the rapid transformation of a business is specific and understandable goals, adjusted to changes, and strengthening of positions among competitors, improving the quality of customer service.

This research examined several models for assessing the maturity of an enterprise. The challenge for every organization is to move from a lower tier to a higher tier in order to maintain competitiveness, increase productivity, and improve the quality of the products or services being developed.

In this work, an analogy was drawn between the process model of the enterprise maturity level with the digital one. Five levels of digital maturity have been identified, such as:

- Level 0. Basic infrastructure.
- Level 1. Computerization.
- Level 2. Connectivity.
- Level 3. Transparency.
- Level 4. Predictiveness.
- Level 5. Adaptability.

Moreover, digital transformation approaches have been reviewed. The first one is based on replication of existing digital tools on the enterprise. The second—on the detailed analysis of processes down to operational activities. Understanding the current level of digital maturity is important for planning digital transformation activities for an enterprise to migrate to a target image.

Thus, knowledge about the level of digital maturity, assessment of readiness for digital transformation, the use of certain approaches to optimize activities help the management in choosing management decisions for a successful business.

Acknowledgments The reported study was funded by RSCF according to the research project № 19-18-00452.

References

Al-Qutaish, R. E., & Abran, A. (2011). A maturity model of software product quality. *Journal of Research and Practice in Information Technology, 43*(4), 307–327.

Bento, I., Gomes, J., & Romão, M. (2019). The relationship between OPM3 and Project Performance: A multiple case study. *The Journal of Modern Project Management, 6*(3), 47–57.

Borremans, A., Zaychenko, I., & Iliashenko, O. (2018). Digital economy. IT strategy of the company development. In I. Ilin & O. Kalinina (Eds.), *MATEC Web of Conferences*, 170, (p. 01034). https://doi.org/10.1051/matecconf/201817001034

Brand, K., & Boonen, H. (2007). *IT governance based on CobiT® 4.1-A management guide*. Van Haren.

Colli, M., et al. (2019). A maturity assessment approach for conceiving context-specific roadmaps in the Industry 4.0 era. *Annual Reviews in Control, 48*, 165–177.

Dubgorn, A. S., et al. (2019). Analysis of digital business transformation tools. In *Proceedings of the 33rd International Business Information Management Association Conference. IBIMA 2019: Education Excellence and Innovation Management through Vision 2020* (pp. 9677–9682). Granada.

El Emam, K., & Birk, A. (2000). Validating the ISO/IEC 15504 measure of software requirements analysis process capability. *IEEE transactions on Software Engineering, 26*(6), 541–566.

Faifr, A. (2020). Use of project management maturity models as a evaluation framework for Project Risk Maturity Assessment. In *DOKBAT 2020-16th International Bata Conference for Ph. D. Students and Young Researchers*. Tomas Bata University in Zlín, Faculty of Management and Economics.

Farrokh, J., & Mansur, A. K. (2013). Project management maturity models and organizational project management maturity model (OPM3®): A critical morphological evaluation. *Project Management, 2*(7), 23–33.

Henriques, V. (2018). *Assessing the association between agile maturity model levels and perceived project success*. Master's Thesis. University of Cape Town.

Ilin, I. V., Iliashenko, O. Y., & Levina, A. I. (2020). "Application of service-oriented approach to business process reengineering". In Proceedings of the 28th International Business Information Management Association Conference-Vision'.

Kerzner, H. (2019). *Using the project management maturity model: Strategic planning for project management*. John Wiley & Sons.

Kneuper, R. (2018). Software process assessment and improvement. In *Software Processes and Life Cycle Models* (pp. 211–260). Springer.

Laksono, M. A., Budiardjo, E. K., & Ferdinansyah, A. (2019). Assessment of test maturity model: A comparative study for process improvement. In *Proceedings of the 2nd International Conference on Software Engineering and Information Management*, pp. 110–118.

Maydanova, S., & Ilin, I. V. (2019). Strategic approach to global company digital transformation. In *Proceedings of the 33rd International Business Information Management Association Conference. IBIMA 2019: Education Excellence and Innovation Management through Vision 2020* (pp. 8818–8833). Granada.

Mesquida, A. L., et al. (2012). IT Service Management Process Improvement based on ISO/IEC 15504: A systematic review. *Information and Software Technology, 54*(3), 239–247.

Mitasiunas, A., & Novickis, L. (2011). Enterprise SPICE based education capability maturity model. In *International Conference on Business Informatics Research* (pp. 102–116). Springer.

Paulk, M. C. (2009). A history of the capability maturity model for software. *ASQ Software Quality Professional, 12*(1), 5–19.

Team, C. P. (2002). Capability maturity model® integration (CMMI SM), version 1.1. In *CMMI for systems engineering, software engineering, integrated product and process development, and supplier sourcing (CMMI-SE/SW/IPPD/SS, V1. 1)*, 2.

Zaychenko, I. M., Ilin, I. V., & Lyovina, A. I. (2018). Enterprise architecture as a means of digital transformation of mining enterprises in the Arctic.

The manufacturer's authorised representative in the EU is Springer Nature Customer Service Centre GmbH, Europaplatz 3, 69115 Heidelberg, Germany. If you have any concerns regarding our products, please contact ProductSafety@springernature.com

Printed and bound by CPI Group (UK) Ltd, Croydon, CR0 4YY
28/09/2026
02224088-0011